OT 31:
Operator Theory: Advances and Applications
Vol. 31

Birkhäuser Verlag
Basel · Boston · Berlin

Efim M. Polishchuk

Continual Means and Boundary Value Problems in Function Spaces

1988

Birkhäuser Verlag
Basel · Boston · Berlin

Author's address:
Prof. Efim M. Polishchuk
ul. Wosstanija 53, kw. 39
191123 Leningrad
USSR

English text revised by:
Dr. Bernd Luderer
Technische Universität
Sektion Mathematik
Karl-Marx-Stadt, GDR

Library of Congress Cataloging in Publication Data

Polishchuk, Efim Mikhailovich.
Continual means and boundary value problems in function spaces.
(Operator theory, advances and applications ; vol. 31)
Bibliography: p.
Includes index.
1. Integration, Functional. 2. Function spaces.
3. Boundary value problems. I. Luderer, Bernd. II. Title. III. Series: Operator theory, advances and applications ; v. 31.
QA312.P65 1988 515.4'3 88-16719

CIP-Titelaufnahme der Deutschen Bibliothek

Poliščuk, Efim M.
Continual means and boundary value problems in function spaces / Efim M. Polishchuk. [Engl. text rev. by: Bernd Luderer]. – Basel ; Boston ; Berlin : Birkhäuser, 1988
(Operator theory ; Vol. 31)
ISBN 3–7643–2217–9 (Basel …) Pb.
ISBN 0–8176–2217–9 (Boston) Pb.
NE: GT

Licensed edition for the distribution in all non-socialist countries by Birkhäuser Verlag, Basel 1988
Printed in GDR
ISBN 3-7643-2217-9
ISBN 0-8176-2217-9

CB-SAK
SCIMON

FOREWORD

The fates of important mathematical ideas are varied. Sometimes they are instantly appreciated by the specialists and constitute the foundation of the development of theories or methods. It also happens, however, that even ideas uttered by distinguished mathematicians are surrounded with respectful indifference for a long time, and every effort of interpreters and successors has to be made in order to gain for them the merit deserved. It is the second case that is encountered in the present book, the author of which, the Leningrad mathematician E.M. Polishchuk, reconstructs and develops one of the directions in functional analysis that originated from Hadamard and Gâteaux and was newly thought over and taken as the basis of a prospective theory by Paul Lévy.

Paul Lévy, Member of the French Academy of Sciences, whose centenary of his birthday was celebrated in 1986, was one of the most original mathematicians of the second half of the 20th century. He could not complain about a lack of attention to his ideas and results. Together with A.N. Kolmogorov, A.Ya. Khinchin and William Feller, he is indeed one of the acknowledged founders of the theory of random processes. In the probability theory and, to a lesser degree, in functional analysis his work is well-known for its conceptualization and scope of the problems posed. His expressive style, rich in ideas rather than technically polished, which sometimes led to a lack of clarity at first, will be remembered by all who read his papers and books about probability theory and functional analysis.

I would like to note that even the gap between these two disciplines, which began to be bridged systematically only in the fifties, had an influence on the general theory of random processes. Measure theory in functional spaces had to become the foundation of the theory of random processes as was intended by P. Lévy, N. Wiener and A.N. Kolmogorov. Later on, such unification actually occurred; however, even today there exist theories in functional analysis connected with probability concepts that are remote from this general direction. One of them, presented in the book of E.M. Polishchuk, is the development of Lévy's ideas on the mean value of a functional over a domain in a function space and its applications to boundary value problems with an elliptic functional operator, "Lévy's Laplacian". P. Lévy explained his concepts in his books on functional analysis published in 1922 and 1951.

It is common knowledge that Lévy's Laplacian as well as the harmonic functionals and averaging processes associated with it are objects of a different nature in comparison with those studied by Lévy and his colleagues in their papers on the theory of random processes. Maybe this is the reason why they are not very popular even today.

E.M. Polishchuk, a mathematician and historian of mathematics, author of many papers about analysis as well as the scientific biographies of mathematicians "Vito Volterra", "Émile Borel", "Sophus Lie" and others published by the Academy of Sciences of the USSR, is the initiator of the renaissance and further development of the theory of continual means in the direction indicated by P. Lévy.

The peculiar feature of the averaging procedure of a functional in the sense of Lévy-Polishchuk consists in the fact that it, in principle, fails to fit in the scheme of usual integration with respect to measure, although it is related to it. In order to avoid associations possibly arising from terms and notations of the same name, the reader should have in mind this circumstance. By comparison, the theory developed by E.M. Polishchuk is closer to the theory of generalized functions of infinitely many variables and to ergodic concepts. This is not unusual - we know that the Feynman integral, which became now one of the most important instruments of mathematical methods in theoretical physics, also fails to fit in the common scheme of integration even with respect to complex and unbounded measure. Summarizing, the difference between these and those theories of averaging consists in the choice of normalization in passing to an infinite number of arguments. This difference happens to appear also in physics: one may normalize the total energy, but one can also normalize the energy for one particle. The second method occurred to me when I became acquainted with the approach of P. Lévy advanced in the book of E.M. Polishchuk.

The specifications and far-reaching generalizations of the theory of continual means as well as the connections and possible applications of the theory to diffusion processes, normed rings, control systems governed by differential equations involving functional parameters, statistical mechanics and other branches of pure and applied mathematics discovered by E.M. Polishchuk and explained in the present book will be of interest to mathematicians engaged in various fields and, it is to be hoped, will encourage young scientists to further develop this direction of functional analysis, the foundations of which were laid by Paul Lévy.

Prof. A.M. Vershik

Vice-president of the
Leningrad Mathematical Society

CONTENTS

INTRODUCTION

Ihr naht euch wieder, schwankende Gestalten,
Die früh sich einst dem trüben Blick gezeigt.

(Goethe. Faust. Zueignung)

The present book is concerned with the theory of integration in infinite-dimensional spaces, i.e. continual means, and their applications to boundary value problems for function domains. To begin with, the questions considered below can be described as follows. We consider the classes $\{F\}$ of functionals $F[x(t)]$ whose arguments are functions $x(t)$ defined on the interval $q = a < t < b$ or vector functions $x(t) = (x_1(t),\ldots,x_s(t))$. It is supposed that $x(t)$ and $x_k(t)$, $k=1,\ldots,s$, respectively, belong to some space $A(q)$ (A is the space of measurable functions bounded on q , the space of continuous functions, the space of functions summable to the p-th power, $p \geq 1$, etc.). In the space $A(q)$ we select sets D referred to as the function domains and define continual means over these domains. We establish their properties and effective formulae for their calculation.

On the set D , we define the elliptic functional operator L . Then we pose the boundary value problems

a) $LH = 0, \quad x \in D; \quad H\big|_{D'} = F, \quad F \in \{F\}$,

b) $LF = \Phi, \quad x \in D; \quad \Phi \in \{F\}, \quad F\big|_{D'} = 0$

(where D' is the boundary of D) as well as some other analogous problems.

By virtue of the specific character of the operator L and the fact that all considerations are located in infinite-dimensional spaces, our approach to these problems differs quite significantly from that in the classical treatment, although there are also many connections.

The theory of continual means presented in the book will be used as a basic research device for the problems under consideration. This theory goes back to earlier work by R. GÂTEAUX [1],[2] and P. LÉVY [1],[2] and was almost forgotten for a long time.

It was reconsidered only recently from a new point of view and further developed in different directions. In addition, interrelations between this theory and a number of other branches of classical analysis (equations of mathematical physics, trigonometric series and integrals, analytical functions of several variables), functional analysis (B-algebras, measures in linear spaces, semigroups) and applied theories (statistical mechanics, control systems governed by ordinary differential equations) were discovered. Some of these relations will be discussed under various aspects when we study the problems formulated above. It should be noted that the utilization of continual means allows all solutions to be presented in an explicit form admitting, when required, algorithmic calculations.

The structure of the book is as follows (see also the introductory remarks to any chapter and section):

In Chapter 1, after a preliminary discussion of the nonlinear functional classes considered below (Volterra, Picard, Gâteaux functionals) we shall introduce the definition of function domains D and consider two principal types - uniform and normal domains. The definition of the mean value of a functional over the domain D is given and explicit formulae for its calculation are deduced. Furthermore, the procedure of functional averaging is shown to result in a Dirac measure concentrated at a certain point, which is a generalized function. The subsequent investigations of this fact yield the notion of the centre of a function domain and the class of weak harmonic functionals. The latter leads, in a natural way, to a Dirichlet problem in a function space.

Several definitions of the functional Laplace operator (weak, strong, and others) are given at the end of the chapter. Their properties are essentially different from the Laplacian in a space of a finite number of dimensions. We do not consider the interrelations of these definitions in detail, since the corresponding boundary value problems are studied in the book separately and by different methods.

Chapter 2 deals with the weak Dirichlet problem for a normal domain with boundary values from the Gâteaux class. Under analogous assumptions, we also consider the Poisson equation and the solution of an exterior Dirichlet problem in a function space.

Furthermore, we indicate a generalization of these results based on the utilization of the integral over a regular (orthogonal) measure in a linear space. The notion of this integral is explained in the text. Besides, we shall study the semigroup of continual means and compare the formulae obtained for boundary value problems with the probability solutions of classical elliptic differential equations.

In Chapter 3 a completely different approach to functional boundary value problems is proposed. We shall consider strong problems with boundary values from the Gâteaux class and obtain solutions following the analogy with parabolic equations in the finite-dimensional space. The established analogy is shown to extend fairly widely and, in a certain sense, to be of a dual character.

In the same chapter we examine boundary value problems for uniform domains, which appeared in the literature not very long ago. They occupy an intermediate position between problems for normal domains (related, however, not to parabolic but to elliptic equations in E_m) and the classical equations of mathematical physics. In the limit case, when the curves under consideration degenerate into points, the Dirichlet problem for uniform domains reduces to the classical Dirichlet problem.

The relations to the theory of control systems are also discussed in this chapter. We show that the functional Dirichlet problem with boundary values from the Volterra and Picard classes can be interpreted as a transformation of a given control system into a "harmonic system" having new important properties.

In Chapter 4 it is shown that we succeed in extending some of the previous results to boundary value problems with a general elliptic functional operator. For this purpose we use the theory of diffusion processes and the notion of a compact extension of a given function domain.

The explanation is self-contained. The present book is the first to deal with the theory of continual means and their applications. Earlier, this material was to be found only in various papers of the author.

Notations

All spaces in question are supposed to be real. The m-dimensional Euclidean space of points (vectors) $\xi = (\xi_1,\dots,\xi_m)$ will be denoted by E_m . The norm in E_m is denoted by $|\xi|$: $|\xi| = \sqrt{\xi_1^2+\dots+\xi_m^2}$. By $Q_m(a,b)$ we designate the cube $Q_m = \{t=(t_1,\dots,t_m) \mid a < t_i < b,$ $i=1,\dots,m\}$. The closure of the set E of a topological space will be denoted by $\bar{E}$, while E' is the boundary of E . The symbols τ_m and σ_m , respectively, are used to denote the unit ball $|\xi| < 1$ and the sphere $|\xi| = 1$ in E_m . Furthermore, $A_s(a,b)$ denotes one of the following function spaces: $C_s[a,b]$ - the space of vectors $x=(x_1(t),\dots x_s(t))$ with co-ordinates being continuous on $[a,b]$, $M_s(a,b)$ - the space of vectors the co-ordinates of which are bounded measurable functions on (a,b) , the space $L_s^p(a,b)$ of vectors x with co-ordinates summable on (a,b) to the p-th power, $p \geq 1$.

The Hilbert norm $\left(\int_a^b \sum_1^s x_k^2(t)dt \right)^{1/2}$ of a vector x will be denoted by $\|x\|$. The sphere $\|x-a\| = R$ with centre at the point a and radius R will be designated by $\Omega_{a,R}$.

Functionals on A_s will be denoted, unless specifically stated, by capital letters with the arguments enclosed in square brackets, i.e. $F = F[x(t)]$, ...If it is desirable to emphasize that the argument on which x depends varies on the interval (a,b) , we write $F[x]_a^b$.

Continuity of $F[x]$ over the set $\mathfrak{a} \subset A_s$ means that if $x_o, x_n \in \mathfrak{a}$, we have $\lim_n F[x_n] = F[x_o]$ when $x_n \longrightarrow x_o$ in the topology of the space A_s (uniformly if $A_s = C_s$ and so on).

If $s=1$, the function space A_s will be denoted by A , thus L^2 means L_1^2 etc. If the functional F depends also upon a scalar parameter τ , we write $F = F[x|\tau]$.

If B_1 and B_2 are two Banach spaces and Ψ acts from B_1 into B_2 and is a strongly continuous operator, we write $\Psi \in \{B_1 \longrightarrow B_2\}$.

Some other notations will be indicated in the text. We shall often use abbreviated notations parallely to the complete ones. Formulae and theorems are numbered separately in each section.

CHAPTER 1. FUNCTIONAL CLASSES AND FUNCTION DOMAINS. MEAN VALUES. HARMONICITY AND THE LAPLACE OPERATOR IN FUNCTION SPACES

1. Functional classes

We begin by describing (for the time being formally) the functional classes which will be considered later.

Let there be given the differential equation

$$\frac{dy}{dx} = f(t,y,x_1(t),\dots,x_s(t)) \tag{1}$$

with respect to the function y and containing the parameters $x = (x_1,\dots,x_s)$, which depend on the same argument t as y ("control parameters"). We vary x in some subset $\mathfrak{A} \subset A_s(a,b)$ and suppose that, for each $x \in \mathfrak{A}$, (1) has, on the interval $(a<t<b)=q$ (or almost everywhere on q), the unique solution $y(t)$ satisfying the initial condition $y(t_0)=y_0$. Varying x, this solution is a functional

$$Y = Y[x|t], \quad x \in \mathfrak{A}, \quad a<t<b,$$

which is said to be a Volterra functional.

Another functional class under consideration can be described as follows. We consider a function g_m of 2m variables $\xi = (\xi_1,\dots,\xi_m)$, $t=(t_1,\dots,t_m)$; $\xi \in E_m$; $t \in Q_m$; $g_m = g_m(\xi;t)$ and form the integral

$$F_m[x] = \int_{Q_m}\!\!\cdots\!\int g(x(t_1),\dots,x(t_m);t_1,\dots,t_m)dt_1\dots dt_m, \quad x \in A(a,b). \tag{2}$$

We shall call (2) a Gâteaux functional and g_m its generating function. We suppose that $g(\xi;t)$ is symmetric with respect to the pairs (ξ_i,t_i) and that the Carathéodory conditions hold: for almost all $t \in Q_m$, the function g_m is continuous with respect to ξ and, for all ξ, it is measurable with respect to t. Other conditions imposed on g_m will be indicated later.

The functional defined by the uniformly convergent series

$$F = \sum_1^\infty F_m[x]$$

will also be called a Gâteaux functional. In particular, if $g_m = k_m(t_1,\dots,t_m)\xi_1^{p_1}\dots\xi_m^{p_m}$ and p_i are natural numbers, we obtain the E. Schmidt-Lichtenstein series occurring in the theory of nonlinear in-

tegral equations. The particular case

$$F = k_0 + \int_a^b k_1(t)x(t)dt + \int_a^b\int_a^b k_2(t_1,t_2)x(t_1)x(t_2)dt_1dt_2 + \dots$$

was introduced by Volterra at the end of the last century. The Volterra series play an important role in the modern theory of nonlinear control systems.

The generality of the classes Y and F is evident. They involve very different functionals from pure and applied analysis. We shall consider the classes Y and F separately. But our considerations can be extended towards their unification, for instance, in the functional

$$\Phi = \int_a^b f(x(t), Y[x|t], t)dt , \tag{3}$$

which is referred to as the Picard functional.

Let us return to the Gâteaux functional (2). It can also be considered over the set of vector functions $x=(x_1(t),\dots,x_s(t))$. We denote (2) with x being a vector from A_s by

$$F_m = \int_{Q_m} g_m(X(t),t)dt^m . \tag{4}$$

Clearly, not only the sum but also the product of two Gâteaux functionals is a functional of the same type: From

$$F' = \int_{Q_{m'}} g'(X'(t),t)dt^{m'}, \quad F'' = \int_{Q_{m''}} g''(X''(t),t)dt^{m''}$$

we obtain

$$F'F'' = \int_{Q_{m'+m''}} g'(X'(t'),t')g''(X''(t''),t'')dt^{m'}dt^{m''} .$$

If V is a subset of A_s , then the set of Gâteaux functionals defined and bounded on V generates a ring $R(A_s,V)$ with the usual product operation. On $R(A_s,V)$ we can introduce the norm $\|F\| = \sup_V |F|$. The closure $\bar{R}(A_s,V)$ of $R(A_s,V)$ with respect to this norm is called the Gâteaux ring.

We shall also consider Gâteaux functionals of the kind $\int_E g(X(t),t)dt^m$ where E is a measurable subset of Q_m . Some of our constructions remain valid for "Gâteaux-Stieltjes functionals"

$$F[x] = \int_E g(X(t),t)d\varphi(t_1,\dots,t_m) .$$

2. Function domains

By the term "function domain" we shall understand a set of functions in the space $A_s(a,b)$ defined with the aid of certain analytic relations, or a set open in the topology of A_s.

All the domains considered are supposed to be bounded, i.e. lying within some sphere of A_s, and having boundaries which are also called function domains. We distinguish two basic classes of domains: uniform and normal domains.

2.1. Uniform domains

Let Σ_t, $t \in q=(a,b)$ be a family of manifolds in E_s (domains, surfaces, curves, ...) of dimension $\nu \leq s$. The set of all vector functions $x \in A_s(a,b)$ such that, for $t \in q$, the range of vectors $x(t)$ coincides with Σ_t will be called a uniform function domain and denoted by $G = G(\Sigma_t, A_s(a,b))$.

If $A_s = C_s[q]$, we demand that this holds for all $t \in q$, while for the spaces M_s, L_s^p this is assumed to be valid almost everywhere on q.

If Σ_t' is the boundary of Σ_t, we shall say that $G' = G(\Sigma_t', A_s(q))$ is the boundary of $G(\Sigma_t, A_s(q))$.

Remark. From the topological point of view, G' is, generally speaking, the skeleton of the domain G.

Examples. 1) Σ_t - the interval $u(t) < \xi < v(t)$; u and v - fixed functions; G - the functional beam $u(t) < x(t) < v(t)$;

2) Σ_t - the balls $\xi^2 + \eta^2 + \zeta^2 < R^2(t)$, $t \in q$; G: $x^2(t)+y^2(t)+z^2(t) < R^2(t)$; Σ_t': $\xi^2+\eta^2+\zeta^2 = R^2(t)$; G': $x^2(t)+y^2(t)+z^2(t) = R^2(t)$.

2.2. Normal domains

A set of functions is called a normal domain in $L^2(q)$ if it is an open set of $L^2(q)$ in the Hilbert topology. The boundary D' of a normal domain D is also called a normal domain.

Example. D: $\int_a^b k^2(t)x^2(t)dt < 1$, $k \in M_s(q)$; D': $\int_a^b k^2(t)x^2(t)dt = 1$.

A wide class of domains D can be represented constructively as $U[x] < 0$, where U is a functional from the Gâteaux ring continuous on $L^2(q)$.

The boundary of D, i.e. D', can be described by the equation $U[x] = 0$ ("a surface in the space L^2").

In the same way we define a normal domain D as a subset of other spaces A_s. However, in this case the topology in A_s is the Hilbert topology induced on A_s.

3. Continual means

3.1. The mean over a uniform domain

Let $G = G(\Sigma_t, C_s[\bar{q}])$ be a uniform function domain in the space $C_s[q]$. We subdivide the interval $\bar{q} = [a,b]$ as follows: $a=t_o < t_1 < \ldots < t_n = b$. Set

$$x_k(t_i) = \xi_{ik}; \quad i=1,\ldots,n; \; k=1,\ldots,s; \quad \zeta_i = (\xi_{i1},\ldots,\xi_{is}) \in \Sigma_{t_i}.$$

Let $\hat{x}_k(t)$ be a continuous function on $\bar{q}$ linear on the intervals (t_{i-1}, t_i) and satisfying the conditions $\hat{x}_k(t) = x_k(t)$ if $t = t_i$. The value of $F[x]$ on the set of functions $\hat{x}_n = (\hat{x}_1,\ldots,\hat{x}_s)$ is denoted by $f_n = f_n(\zeta_1,\ldots,\zeta_n; t_1,\ldots,t_n)$. Assume that, for any t, Σ_t has a positive Lebesgue measure $\mu(t)$. Let $\bar{f}_n$ be the average value of f_n over the set $\Sigma_{t_1} \times \ldots \times \Sigma_{t_n}$ (where $t_1,\ldots,t_n$ are fixed and "x" is the sign of the direct product). If, for $n \longrightarrow \infty$ and $\max\limits_i (t_i - t_{i-1}) \longrightarrow 0$, there exists the limit $\lim\limits_n \bar{f}_n$, then it is called the <u>mean value</u> $\underset{G}{M}F$ of F over the domain G.

<u>Theorem 3.1.1</u>. Suppose that $\mu(t)$ is continuous on $[a,b]$, and let the generating function $g(\zeta_1,\ldots,\zeta_m; t_1,\ldots,t_m) = g(\Xi, t)$ of the Gâteaux functional (2) from Section 1 be continuous with respect to $\zeta_1,\ldots,\zeta_m; t_1,\ldots,t_m$ on the set $\bar{\Sigma}_{t_1}(\zeta_1) \times \ldots \times \bar{\Sigma}_{t_m}(\zeta_m)$. Then the mean value of this functional over the domain G exists and is of the form

$$\underset{G}{M}F = \int_{Q_m} \frac{dt_1 \ldots dt_m}{\mu(t_1)\ldots\mu(t_m)} \int_{\Sigma_{t_1}} \ldots \int_{\Sigma_{t_m}} g(\zeta_1,\ldots,\zeta_m; t_1,\ldots,t_m)\, dv_{t_1} \ldots dv_{t_m}, \quad (1)$$

where dv_{t_i} is the differential of the measure of the set $\Sigma_{t_i}(\zeta_i)$.

Proof. The restriction $f_n = F[\hat{x}_n(t)]$ of the functional F to the set of functions $\hat{x}_n(t)$ can be written in the form

$$f_n = \sum_{i_1,\dots,i_m=1}^{n} \lambda_{ni_1\dots i_m}\, g(\zeta_{i_1},\dots,\zeta_{i_m};\tau_{i_1},\dots,\tau_{i_m}),$$

where τ_{i_k} are fixed numbers not depending on $\hat{x}_n$ and lying in the intervals (t_{i-1},t_i), and λ are the cubature coefficients.

Averaging f_n over the set $\Sigma_{t_1}(\zeta_1)\times\dots\times\Sigma_{t_n}(\zeta_n)$ and denoting the mean value by the bar, we have

$$\overline{f}_n = \overline{F[\hat{x}_n(t)]} = \sum_{i_1,\dots,i_m=1}^{n} \lambda_{ni_1\dots i_m} \frac{\int_{\Sigma_{t_1}}\dots\int_{\Sigma_{t_n}} g(\zeta_{i_1},\dots,\zeta_{i_m};\tau_{i_1},\dots,\tau_{i_m})\,dv_{t_1}\dots dv_{t_n}}{\mu(t_1)\dots\mu(t_n)}$$

or

$$\overline{f}_n = \sum_{i_1,\dots,i_m=1}^{n} \lambda_{ni_1\dots i_m} \frac{\int_{\Sigma_{t_{i_1}}}\dots\int_{\Sigma_{t_{i_m}}} g(\zeta_{i_1},\dots,\zeta_{i_m};\tau_{i_1},\dots,\tau_{i_m})\,dv_{t_{i_1}}\dots dv_{t_{i_m}}}{\mu(t_{i_1})\dots\mu(t_{i_m})}.$$

Passing to the limit $n \longrightarrow \infty$ $(t_i - t_{i-1} \longrightarrow 0)$, we obtain

$$\underset{G}{M}F = \int\dots\int_{Q_m} \frac{dt_1\dots dt_m}{\mu(t_1)\dots\mu(t_m)} \int_{\Sigma_{t_1}}\dots\int_{\Sigma_{t_m}} g(\zeta_1,\dots,\zeta_m;t_1,\dots,t_m)\,dv_{t_1}\dots dv_{t_m},$$

which was to be proved.

Note that the mean value $\underset{G}{M}F$ does not depend on the way of subdividing the interval (a,b) into intervals (t_{i-1},t_i), on the way of choosing the points τ_{i_k} and the coefficients λ. We would come to the same formula, approximating x not by $\hat{x}$ (i.e. by piecewise linear) but by step or other functions.

In particular, the formula obtained allows us to calculate the mean value of F over the ball $\sum_1^s (x_k(t)-a_k(t))^2 < r^2(t)$ or over the sphere $|x-a|=r$.

In the simplest case, if $s=1$ and G is the function beam $u(t) < x(t)$

$< v(t)$, we have

$$MF = \int\limits_{Q_m}\cdots\int \frac{dt_1\ldots dt_m}{\prod_{i=1}^{m}\left(v(t_i)-u(t_i)\right)} \int\limits_{u(t_1)}^{v(t_1)}\cdots\int\limits_{u(t_m)}^{v(t_m)} g(\xi_1,\ldots,\xi_m;t_1,\ldots,t_m)d\xi_1\ldots d\xi_m \; . \qquad (2)$$

3.2. The mean value $\mathfrak{M}_{a,R}F$ over the Hilbert sphere and its main properties

3.2.1. Let $\Omega_{a,R}$ be the sphere $\|x-a\|=R$. By Δ_i we denote the intervals $(a+\frac{i-1}{n}(b-a),\ a+\frac{i(b-a)}{n})$, $i=1,\ldots,n$. Let

$$\xi_{ki} = R\left[\frac{n}{b-a}\int\limits_{\Delta_i} x_k^2(t)dt\right]^{1/2} ,$$

and let x_{n^k} be step functions having the constant values ξ_{ki} on each interval Δ_i . Moreover, let

$$\Omega_n:\qquad \sum_{s=1}^{k}\sum_{i=1}^{n}(\xi_{ki}-a_{ki})^2 = \frac{nR^2}{b-a}$$

be the restriction of $\Omega_{a,R}$ to the set of such step functions, and let $f_n=f_n(\zeta_1,\ldots,\zeta_n)$ be the value of F on Ω_n . Evaluate the mean value of f_n over Ω_n :

$$\overline{f}_n = \frac{\int\limits_{\Omega_n} f_n d\Omega_n}{|\Omega_n|} \; .$$

By definition,

$$\mathfrak{M}_{a,R}F = \lim_n \overline{f}_n$$

if this limit exists.

Remark. In the following we shall often define $\mathfrak{M}_{a,R}F$ via the equation $\mathfrak{M}F[a+Ry] = \Phi$, where $\mathfrak{M} = \mathfrak{M}_{\|y\|=1}$ is the mean of Φ over the unit sphere $\|y\|=1$. Henceforth, we suppose that in the present subsection we have $s=1$ and $A_s(a,b)=L^2(a,b)$.

Examples. 1) Let $F=\varphi(U)$, $U = \int\limits_a^b k(t)x^2(t)dt$, $k\in M(a,b)$, and let

$\varphi(\xi)$ be continuous for all ξ . Then $\mathfrak{M}F = \varphi(\int_a^b k(t)dt)$.

2) $F = \varphi(\Phi)$, $\Phi = \int_a^b k(t)x(t)dt$. Then $\mathfrak{M}F = \varphi(\int_a^b k(t)dt)$.

<u>3.2.2</u>. The following property of the operation $\mathfrak{M}_{a,R}F$ will play an important role in later considerations. Let $f(\xi_1,\dots,\xi_n)$ be the value of the functional F on the sphere Ω_n , $|\Omega_n|$ the area of this sphere, and M some constant. We shall use $\mu_n(\delta)$ to denote the measure of the set of those points of the sphere Ω_n for which $|f_n-M| > \delta > 0$. If, for arbitrary $\delta > 0$, we have

$$\lim_n \frac{\mu_n(\delta)}{|\Omega_n|} = 0 ,$$

then we shall say that the equation $F[x] = M$ holds almost everywhere on the sphere $\Omega_{a,R}$.

<u>P. Lévy's theorem (LEVY [1], p. 243)</u>. If the mean $\mathfrak{M}_{a,R}F$ exists and the functional F is uniformly continuous (continuity being taken with respect to the norm topology in L^2 , i.e. the Hilbert topology) on the sphere $\Omega_{a,R}$, then the equation $F[x] = \mathfrak{M}_{a,R}F$ holds almost everywhere on this sphere.

The requirement of uniform continuity is not a necessary condition for the theorem but it was needed for the geometrical method of the proof presented in LEVY [1].

<u>3.2.3</u>. The theorem just mentioned can be physically interpreted as follows. Let there be given a dynamical system specified by the Hamiltonian $H(p,q)$ with variables $p=(p_1,\dots,p_n)$ and $q=(q_1,\dots,q_n)$. Moreover, let a surface Σ_E of constant energy be given defined by the equation

$$\Sigma_E\colon\ H(p,q) = E . \tag{1}$$

In addition, let $A=A(p,q)$ be a given function of the variables p and q (the "phase function"). The expression

$$\bar{A} = \frac{1}{\omega(E)} \int_{\Sigma_E} A(p,q) \frac{d\Sigma_E}{|\mathrm{grad}\, H|} ,$$

where $\omega = \int_{\Sigma_E} \frac{d\Sigma_E}{|\mathrm{grad}\, H|}$ and $d\Sigma_E$ is an element of the surface

Σ_E , is known in statistical mechanics as the microcanonical mean of the function $A(p,q)$. Let $\mu(\delta)$ be the measure of the set of points of the surface (1) for which

$$|A(p,q) - \bar{A}| > n\delta \ . \tag{2}$$

It can be shown (see KHINCHIN [1]) that, under natural assumptions concerning the surface Σ_E and the function $A(p,q)$, we have the estimate

$$\frac{\mu(\delta)}{\omega(E)} = O\left(\frac{1}{n\cdot\delta^2}\right) . \tag{3}$$

In statistical mechanics the function $A(p,q)$ and its mean $\bar{A}$ are quantities of order n and, moreover, the number $n\delta^2$ is reckoned to be very large if δ is small. In view of (2), the substitution of $A(p,q)$ by $\bar{A}$ yields a relative error of order $1/n$, and the estimate (3) shows that the equation $A=\bar{A}$ is "reasonable for practical purposes".

This is known as the "representation principle of microcanonical means of statistical mechanics". Some of the lemmas used below are based on the functional analogue of this "representation principle".

3.2.4. Let us return to the consideration of the mean $\mathfrak{M}_{a,R}F$, which we also represent in an abbreviated form as $\bar{F}$. First of all, we state the following obvious facts:

(i) If two bounded functionals F_1 and F_2 satisfy the equation $F_1=F_2$ almost everywhere, then clearly $\bar{F}_1=\bar{F}_2$. Moreover, if the mean exists for one of the functionals, then the mean for the other exists, too.

(ii) If the equation $F=\bar{F}_n$ is satisfied almost everywhere, then the sequence f_n defined in 3.2.2 converges to $\bar{F}$ in probability. From this we get the following proposition analogous to Slutskii's theorem on stochastic limits (see CRAMER [1], p. 255). If $\bar{F}_i$, $i=1,\dots,m$, exist and $F_i=\bar{F}_i$ a.e., then for any rational function $r(F_1,\dots,F_m)$ such that $r(F_1,\dots,F_m)$ is finite, the equation

$$r(F_1,\dots,F_m) = r(\bar{F}_1,\dots,\bar{F}_m)$$

holds almost everywhere, from which, in particular, we obtain

$$\mathfrak{M}_{a,R}(F_1\cdots F_m) = \mathfrak{M}_{a,R}F_1 \cdots \mathfrak{M}_{a,R}F_m \ . \tag{4}$$

Relation (4) together with the evident additivity of the operation $\mathfrak{M}_{a,R}$ expresses the ring property of the symbol $\mathfrak{M}_{a,R}$.

(iii) For convenience of presentation we formulate another proposition.

Lemma 3.2.1. Let $\Phi[x]$ be a functional bounded on the sphere $\Omega_{a,R}$ and having the form $\Phi = F[x,U[x]]$. Moreover, let $\overline{U}$ and $F[x,\overline{U}]$ exist and U be uniformly continuous on the sphere $\Omega_{a,R}$. Then

$$\overline{F[x,U[x]]} = \overline{F[x,\overline{U}]} . \tag{5}$$

In fact, by Lévy's theorem, we have $U=\overline{U}$ a.e. But then $F[x,U[x]] = F[x,\overline{U}]$ almost everywhere. In view of (i), this implies equation (5).

3.3. The spherical mean of a Gâteaux functional

Let in the space $L_s^2(q)$ the Gâteaux functional

$$F = \int_{Q_m} g(x(t_1),\ldots,x(t_m);t_1,\ldots,t_m)dt^m = \int_{Q_m} g(X(t),t)dt^m \tag{1}$$

be given. If its generating function

$$g(\Xi,t) = g(\zeta_1,\ldots,\zeta_m;t_1,\ldots,t_m) , \quad \zeta_i=(\xi_{i1},\ldots,\xi_{is}),\ i=1,\ldots,m,$$

satisfies the condition

$$|g(\Xi,t)| \leq U(t) + B|\zeta_1|^2\ldots|\zeta_m|^2 , \tag{2}$$

where $U>0$, $U\in L(Q_m)$, $B=\text{const}>0$, then the mean value $\mathfrak{M}_{a,R}F$ exists and satisfies the equation

$$\mathfrak{M}_{a,R}F = \left(\frac{s\sqrt{b-a}}{R\sqrt{2\pi}}\right)^{ms} \int_{Q_m} dt^m \int_{E^{ms}} g(a_1(t_1)+R\xi_{11},\ldots,a_s(t_1)+R\xi_{s1},$$

$$\ldots,a_1(t_m)+R\xi_{1m},\ldots,a_s(t_m)+R\xi_{sm};t_1,\ldots,t_m)\exp\left(-\frac{s(b-a)(|\zeta_1|^2+\ldots+|\zeta_m|^2)}{2R^2}\right)d\Xi \tag{3}$$

with $d\Xi = d\xi_{11}\ldots d\xi_{sm}$.

We would like to note that (2), together with the Carathéodory condition, which is assumed to be satisfied throughout the book, is a necessary and sufficient condition for the continuity of (1) in the whole space L_s^2 .

In particular, if $s=1$, $q=(0,1)$, then (3) provides the Gâteaux formula (LEVY [2], III,18). The general formula (3) can be proved in different ways and is a consequence of the following proposition.

Borel's lemma. Let Ω_N be the sphere $\sum_1^N \xi_i^2 = NR^2$ in E_N, and let $M=(\xi_1,\dots,\xi_N)$ be a random point on it (randomly in the sense of the uniform distribution on this sphere). Then, for $N \longrightarrow \infty$, all its co-ordinates are asymptotically normal with parameters (0,R) and, for an arbitrary choice of $i_1,\dots,i_p$ and fixed p, $\xi_{i_1},\dots \xi_{i_p}$ are asymptotically independent.

This implies that, if $N \longrightarrow \infty$, the co-ordinates of the points lying on the sphere $\sum_1^N |\zeta_i|^2 = \frac{Ns}{b-a}$ are asymptotically normal with parameters $(0, \frac{R}{\sqrt{s(b-a)}})$ and asymptotically independent. Taking into account this fact and arguing as in Theorem 3.1.1, we obtain (3).

In the same way formula (3) may be established for other spaces. For its validity in the space $C_s[q]$ it is sufficient that

$$|g(\Xi,t)| \exp\left(-\frac{s(b-a)(|\zeta_1|^2+\dots+|\zeta_m|^2}{2R^2}\right)$$

be summable over the set $E_{ms} \times Q_{ms}$.

The comparison of equation (3) and the definition of averages of statistical mechanics shows that in our considerations (3) plays the role of the canonical mean $\langle f \rangle$, and $\mathfrak{M}_{a,R}F$ is an analogue to the microcanonical mean $\bar{f}$. For the most important phase functions f in statistical mechanics, the estimate

$$|\bar{f} - \langle f \rangle| = O(1/N)$$

holds, where N is the dimension of the phase space. Of course, in our case both averages coincide.

3.4. Functionals as random variables

Comparing formulae (1) from 3.1 and (3) from 3.3, we see that they are built up along the same lines. Denoting the left parts by MF, we can write these formulae in the form

$$MF = \int_{Q_m}\!\!\dots\!\int dt_1\dots dt_m \, Eg(\theta_{t_1},\dots,\theta_{t_m}; t_1,\dots,t_m), \qquad (1)$$

where θ_{t_i} are vectors independent of each other, and E is the symbol of mathematical expectation. Furthermore, for the case (1) from

3.1, θ_{t_i} are uniformly distributed over the domain Σ_{t_i} and, for formula (3) of 3.3, θ_{t_i} have a normal distribution law with independent components, the centre $a_1(t_i),\dots,a_s(t_i)$ and the dispersion vector $(\frac{R^2}{s(b-a)},\dots,\frac{R^2}{s(b-a)})$.

In both cases we have additivity

$$M(C_1F_1+C_2F_2) = C_1MF_1 + C_2MF_2$$

and multiplicativity

$$M(F_1F_2) = MF_1MF_2 . \tag{2}$$

If $F_n \rightrightarrows F$ over the considered domain and if MF_n exists for any n, there exists also MF and we have

$$MF = \lim_n MF_n .$$

Thus, passing to the limit, we can calculate MF for all F from the Gâteaux ring.

Setting $F_1 \equiv F_2$ in (2), we get $MF^2 = (MF)^2$, which can also be written as $DF=0$, where D is the dispersion symbol.

This shows that the functional F, considered as a random value, is equal to its mean value almost everywhere (cf. Lévy's theorem from 3.2).

Let us continue the discussion of the fact just mentioned.

3.5. The Dirac measure in a function space. The centre of a function domain. Harmonicity

3.5.1. Let $\mathfrak{F}$ be some set of functionals defined on a uniform or normal domain D, and let MF be the mean value of $F \in \mathfrak{F}$ over D. If, for each $F \in \mathfrak{F}$, we have $MF = F[x_0]$, where x_0 does not depend on F, then x_0 is said to be a point of measure concentration in D. In this case, either $x_0 \in D$ or x_0 belongs to some extension of D (x_0 is a generalized function, i.e. $x_0 \in [D]$, where $[\cdot]$ means a compact extension of D).

Later on we shall see that the existence of points of measure concentration is a characteristic property of the considered averaging procedure.

We return to formula (1) of 3.4 and rewrite it in the form

$$\underset{D}{MF} = \int\dots\int_{Q_m} dt^m \int\dots\int g(\xi_1,\dots,\xi_m;t_1,\dots,t_m)p(\xi_1;t_1)\dots p(\xi_m;t_m)d\xi^m. \tag{1}$$

The term $p(\xi,t)$ is called the law of distribution (distribution density) of the domain D with respect to which the average is produced. If p does not depend on t, i.e. $p=p(\xi)$, then D is said to be a domain of the first kind. In the opposite case, i.e. if $p(\xi,t)$ is a family of densities with parameter t, D is referred to as a domain of the second kind. Thus, the beam $u < \xi < v$ and the sphere $\|x-a\| = R$ are domains of the first kind if u, v and R are constants.

Formulae (1) from 3.1 and (3) from 3.3 are particular cases of the general formula of functional averaging of the form (1). The function domains may have different laws of distribution, and a general theorem on the existence of this law can be formulated.

In the sequel, in addition to the uniform and normal distribution laws, we shall consider some other particular laws of distribution. Hence, we shall start from the general formula (1),assuming it as the mean value of the Gâteaux functional (1) from 3.3 over the domain D with the distribution density $p(\xi,t)$. We suppose $p(\xi,t)$ to be a continuous function of its arguments. The integral (1) exists, for instance, if g is a bounded function.

Note that the same formulae are valid if we replace the cube Q_m by any of its measurable subsets E, for example, by

$$E: \quad a \leq t_1 < \ldots < t_m \leq b \, . \tag{2}$$

Thus, the general formula of a functional mean is of the form

$$MF = \int_E dt^m \int g(\Xi,t) \prod_i p(\xi_i,t_i) d\xi^{ms} \, . \tag{3}$$

3.5.2. First of all, we consider a simple case. Let Q_m: $0 < t_i < 1$, $s=1$, $g=g(\xi)$, $|g(\xi)| < C=\text{const}$, $A_s=C[0,1]$,

$$F = \int_{Q_m} g(x(t))dt^m \, . \tag{4}$$

As a consequence of equation (1), we have

$$MF = \int_{Q_m} g(w(t))dt^m = F[w] \, , \tag{5}$$

where w is the function inverse to the monotonic function $\varphi(\xi) = \int_{-\infty}^{\xi} p(\xi)d\xi$. Since w is one and the same for all F of the considered kind, then w may be called a point of measure concentration in the domain D.

If x and y are two equimeasurable functions, i.e. if

$$|E\{x(t)<\eta\}| = |E\{y(t)<\eta\}|$$

for any η (where E is the symbol of the set in curly brackets and $|\cdot|$ its measure), we have $F[x] = F[y]$.

Naturally, the mean (5) does not change if we replace, in (5), w by any equimeasurable function $\tilde{w}$. Now we construct $\tilde{w}$ as follows. Let $0 \leqslant t_1 < t_2 < \ldots < t_n \leqslant 1$ be some subdivision of the interval $0 \leqslant t \leqslant 1$ and $\lim\limits_n \max\limits_i (t_i - t_{i-1}) = 0$. On $(0,1)$ we define a continuous or piece-wise-continuous function $\gamma_n(t)$, assigning to it on the intervals $(t_{i-1}, t_i) = \Delta_i$ one of the values

$$\gamma_n = \frac{t - t_{i-1}}{t_i - t_{i-1}} \quad \text{or} \quad \gamma_n = \frac{t_{i-1} - t}{t_i - t_{i-1}} \quad . \tag{6}$$

If γ_n is required to be continuous on $(0,1)$, then this can be done by choosing the corresponding value γ_n in (6). The values of γ_n at the ends of Δ_i , however, are not important for us.

It is easy to see that the functions $x(t)$ and $x(\gamma_n(t))$ are equi-measurable on $(0,1)$. Therefore, equation (5) may be written in the form

$$\underset{D}{M}F = F[w(\gamma_n)] \quad ,$$

and $w(\gamma_n)$ is also a point of measure concentration.

For functions of more general classes and domains of the second kind, points of measure concentration in the sense mentioned above fail to exist, but the equation

$$\underset{D}{M}F = \lim_n F[w(\gamma_n)] \tag{7}$$

may be valid.

The sequence $w(\gamma_n)$ has no limit if $n \to \infty$, but it determines a certain generalized function Θ_∞ . Completing the definition of F by continuity at the point Θ_∞ , we can write (7) as

$$\underset{D}{M}F = F[\Theta_\infty] \quad . \tag{8}$$

We see that the averaging in (8) is constructed by the Dirac measure concentrated at the point Θ_∞ .

The previous considerations remain valid if we replace $(0,1)$ by an arbitrary finite interval $q=(a,b)$ and define $\gamma_n(t)$ in the same way as in (6).

Before proceeding, let us consider one particular case.

Let $\mathcal{g}$ be a domain in E_m bounded by planes perpendicular to the co-ordinate axes, let F be the functional (4) and $\varphi(\xi)$ the distribution function of the domain D . Then equation (5) does not hold in general, but there exists an n_o such that, for $N \geqslant n_o$,

$$\underset{D}{M}F = F[w(\gamma_N)] \quad . \tag{9}$$

Let us prove this statement for $m=2$. For other m the argument is similar. Let $F = \int_{\mathcal{g}} g(x(t),x(\tau))dtd\tau$, where $\mathcal{g}$ is a figure bounded by intervals parallel to the axes (t,τ) . Projecting the ends of these intervals onto the axes t and τ , we obtain on them the subdivisions

$$-\infty < t_1 < t_2 < \ldots < t_k < \infty \ ; \quad -\infty < \tau_1 < \tau_2 < \ldots < \tau_s < \infty \ . \tag{10}$$

Numbering these $k+s$ numbers in increasing order, we get a certain subdivision

$$-\infty < \rho_1 < \rho_2 < \ldots < \rho_r < \infty \ ; \quad r \leqslant k+s \ . \tag{11}$$

For the function γ_r constructed according to this subdivision, equation (9) holds. Indeed, the inequalities (10) subdivide the domain $\mathcal{g}$ into disjoint rectangles:

$$\mathcal{g} = \bigcup_{i=1}^{n} \mathcal{g}_i ; \quad \mathcal{g}_i : \ \rho_{i1} \leqslant t < \rho_{i2}, \ \ \rho_{i1}' \leqslant \tau < \rho_{i2}'$$

(here ρ are the numbers occurring in (11)).

Hence, in view of (11) and since

$$\underset{D}{M}F = |\mathcal{g}| \int_0^1 \int_0^1 g(w(t_1),w(t_2))dt_1dt_2 \ ,$$

we can write

$$\underset{D}{M}F = \sum_1^r |\mathcal{g}_i| \int_0^1 \int_0^1 g(w(t_1),w(t_2))dt_1dt_2$$

$$= \sum_i \iint_{\mathcal{g}_i} g\left(w\left(\frac{t-\rho_{i1}}{\rho_{i2}-\rho_{i1}}\right), w\left(\frac{\tau-\rho_{i1}'}{\rho'_{i2}-\rho'_{i1}}\right)\right)dtd\tau$$

$$= \sum_i \iint_{\mathcal{g}_i} g(w(\gamma_r(t),w(\gamma_r(\tau)))dtd\tau = F[w(\gamma_r)] \ .$$

If we add some new points to the partition (11), then the function $w(\gamma_n)$, $n > r$, constructed according to this new subdivision will also be a point of measure concentration. This proves our assertion.

3.5.3. It is convenient to define here generalized functions by means of equivalent sequences. For this purpose, we recall the following definitions (see MIKUSINSKI and SICORSKI [1], pp. 11-16).

Definition 3.5.1. The sequence $h_n(t)$ of functions piecewise-continuous on $[A,B]$ is said to be fundamental, if there exists a sequence $H_n(t)$ and an integer $k \geqslant 0$ such that, at the points of continuity of h_n, we have $\frac{d^k H_n}{dt^k} = h_n$ and $H_n(t)$ converges almost uniformly on $[A,B]$ ("almost uniformly" means uniformly on any interval $[\alpha,\beta] \subset [A,B]$).

Definition 3.5.2. Two sequences of functions $h_n(t)$ and $\psi_n(t)$ are called equivalent on (A,B) if there exist two sequences $H_n(t)$ and $\Phi_n(t)$ as well as an integer $k \geqslant 0$ such that $H_n - \Phi_n \longrightarrow 0$ almost everywhere on $[A,B]$ for $n \longrightarrow \infty$, where $H_n^{(k)} = h_n(t)$ and $\Phi_n^{(k)} = \psi_n(t)$. Equivalence of sequences will be denoted by the sign $\sim$.

Definition 3.5.3. Any class of equivalent fundamental sequences will be called a generalized function.

The generalized functions to be considered later have the following properties: h_n diverges everywhere on (A,B), $h_n \sim \psi$, ψ does not depend on n.

Lemma 3.5.1. Let $w(\alpha,t)$ be a function continuous on the set $0 < \alpha < 1$, $A \leqslant t \leqslant B$ and such that $|w(\alpha,t)| < l(\alpha)$, $l(\alpha) \in L(0,1)$. Let γ_n be a function constructed according to the subdivision of the interval (A,B). Then

$$\lim_n \int_A^u w(\gamma_n(t),t)dt = \int_A^u \left\{ \int_0^1 w(\alpha,t)d\alpha \right\} dt$$

uniformly on the interval $[A,B]$.

Proof. It is not hard to see that the integral $\int_0^1 w(\alpha,t)d\alpha$ is a continuous function on $[A,B]$. Let the subdivision

$$\sigma_n: \quad A \leqslant u_0 < u_1 < \ldots < u_m = u \leqslant u_{m+1} < \ldots < u_n \leqslant B$$

be given. From the definition of the function γ_n we have

$$\int_A^u w(\gamma_n(t),t)dt = \sum_{k=1}^m \Delta u_k \int_0^1 w(\alpha,\alpha\Delta u_k + u_{k-1})d\alpha .$$

Now we intend to estimate the expression

$$I_n = \left| \int_A^u \left(\int_0^1 w(\alpha,u)d\alpha \right) du - \sum_{k=1}^m \Delta u_k \int_0^1 w(\alpha,\alpha\Delta u_k + u_{k-1})d\alpha \right. .$$

We have

$$I_n \leqslant \left| \int_A^u \int_\eta^{1-\eta} w(\alpha,u)du - \sum_{k=1}^{m} \Delta u_k \int_\eta^{1-\eta} w(\alpha,\alpha\Delta u_k+u_{k-1})d\alpha \right|$$

$$+ \left| \int_A^u \left(\int_0^\eta + \int_{1-\eta}^1 \right) \left[w(\alpha,u)-w(\alpha,\alpha\Delta u_k+u_{k-1}) \right] d\alpha\, du \right| .$$

For any $\varepsilon > 0$ one can choose an $\eta > 0$ such that $\int_0^\eta l(\alpha)d\alpha < \varepsilon$ and $\int_{1-\eta}^1 l(\alpha)d\alpha < \varepsilon$. Then

$$I_n < \left| \int_A^u \int_\eta^{1-\eta} w(\alpha,u)du - \sum_{k=1}^{m} \Delta u_k \int_\eta^{1-\eta} w(\alpha,\alpha\Delta u_k+u_{k-1})d\alpha \right| +4(u-A)\varepsilon .$$

Since the function $w(\alpha,t)$ is uniformly continuous on the rectangle $[\eta,1-\eta] \times [A,B]$ and $u_{k-1} < \alpha\Delta u_k+u_{k-1} < u_k$, we can assume that, starting from some n,

$$\left| w(\alpha,\alpha\Delta u_k+u_{k-1})-w(\alpha,\tau_k) \right| < \varepsilon ,$$

where $\tau_k \in [u_{k-1},u_k]$ and the numbers τ_k do not depend on α. Then

$$|I_n| \leqslant \left| \int_A^u \left(\int_\eta^{1-\eta} w(\alpha,u)d\alpha \right) du - \sum_{k=1}^{m} \Delta u_k \int_\eta^{1-\eta} w(\alpha,\tau_k)d\alpha \right| + 5(u-A)\varepsilon$$

$$\leqslant 5(B-A)\varepsilon + \sum_{i=1}^{n} \Delta u_i\, \omega_i ,$$

where ω_i are the oscillations of the function $\int_0^1 w(\alpha,u)d\alpha$ on the intervals (u_{i-1},u_i). Due to the continuity of this function and the fact that η is an arbitrary number, the proof is complete, since the right-hand side does not depend on u.

Lemma 3.5.2. Let $\varphi = \varphi(\xi,t)$, $-\infty < \xi < \infty$, $A \leqslant t \leqslant B$ be the distribution function of the domain D, and let $w(\alpha,t)$, $0 < \alpha < 1$ be its inverse function for each t. If $w(\alpha,t)$ satisfies the conditions of Lemma 3.5.1, then the sequence $w(\gamma_n(t),t) = \theta_n$ defines a generalized function and

$$\theta_n \sim \int \xi \varphi(d\xi,t) = \int \xi\, p(\xi,t)d\xi .$$

Proof. Owing to Lemma 3.5.1, the sequence $\psi_n = \int_A^t \theta_n dt$ converges uniformly on $[A,B]$. Hence $\theta_n = \psi_n'$ with the possible exception of those points where θ_n is discontinuous. Taking into account the continuity of $\int_0^1 w(\alpha,t)d\alpha$ and the equality $\int_0^1 w(\alpha,t)d\alpha = \int \xi \varphi(d\xi,t)$, we obtain the assertion of the lemma.

In the following, we shall use the notation

$$\int_0^1 w(\alpha,t)dt = \Theta(t) ,$$

where the function $\Theta(t)$ is called the centre of the domain D . Thus, for domains of the first kind, we get

$$\Theta_n \sim c = \text{const} .$$

As an illustration we consider the beam $u(t) < x(t) < v(t)$, where u, x and v are continuous functions on $[A,B]$. In this case,

$$w(\alpha,t) = u(t) + \alpha(v(t)-u(t)) ,$$

$$\Theta_n \sim \int_0^1 w(\alpha,t)d\alpha = \frac{u(t)+v(t)}{2} ,$$

$$\Theta_n = u(t) + \gamma_n(t)(v(t)-u(t)) .$$

In particular, if $u \equiv 0$ and $v \equiv 1$, we have

$$\gamma_n(t) \sim \tfrac{1}{2} .$$

All this is represented in Fig. 1.

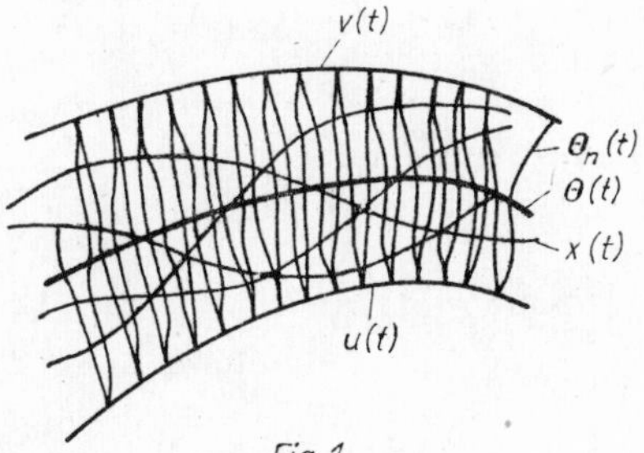

Fig.1

Fig. 1
Function beam $u(t) < x(t) < v(t)$ (bold lines - u(t), v(t) and the centre $\Theta(t)$; thin lines - x(t) ; toothed line - $\Theta_n(t)$).

Furthermore, let the ellipsoid

$$\int_A^B \frac{(x(t)-a(t))^2}{\sigma^2(t)} dt = 1$$

be given. The corresponding distribution law is normal with parameters a and σ , $\sigma > 0$. In this case the conditions of the lemma are valid and we obtain

$$\Theta_n \sim \int_0^1 w(\alpha,t)d\alpha = a(t) .$$

Let $\mathcal{G}$ be some bounded domain in the space E_m having a finite positive measure.

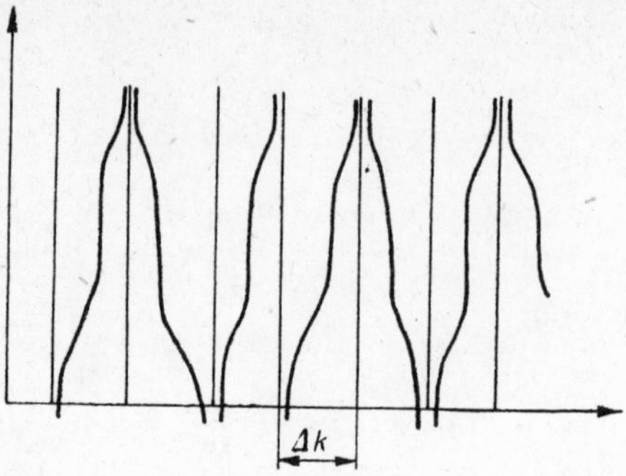

Fig.2

Fig. 2
A normal domain cannot be visualized. It is only possible to plot the functions θ_n. If w does not depend on t (domain of the first kind), then the operator $\Gamma w = w(\gamma_n, t)$ "prints" in the intervals Δ_k the graph of $w(\alpha)$ or its reflections.

<u>Lemma 3.5.3</u>. Suppose that $h(\alpha_1, \ldots, \alpha_m; t_1, \ldots, t_m)$ is continuous on the set $\alpha \in Q_m$, $t \in \mathcal{G}$ and, moreover, $|h(\alpha, t)| \leq l(\alpha) \in L(Q_m)$. Then

$$\lim_n \int_{\mathcal{G}} h(\gamma_n(t_1), \ldots, \gamma_n(t_m); t_1, \ldots, t_m)\, dt_1 \ldots dt_m = \int_{\mathcal{G}} dt \int_{Q_m} h(\alpha, t)\, d\alpha .$$

<u>Proof</u>. According to the conditions of the lemma, there exists a sequence of domains $\mathcal{G}_\nu$ such that, for each ν, the boundary of $\mathcal{G}_\nu$ consists of planes parallel to the co-ordinate planes (step domains) and $\lim_\nu |\mathcal{G}_\nu| = \mathcal{G}$. In addition, we may assume that all $\mathcal{G}_\nu \subset \mathcal{G}$. Obviously

$$I_n = \left| \int_{\mathcal{G}} h(\gamma_n(t), t)\, dt - \int_{Q_m} \int_{\mathcal{G}} h(\alpha, t)\, dt\, d\alpha \right|$$

$$\leq \left| \int_{\mathcal{G}} h(\gamma_n, t)\, dt - \int_{\mathcal{G}_\nu} h(\gamma_n, t)\, dt \right| + \left| \int_{\mathcal{G}_\nu} h(\gamma_n, t)\, dt - \int_{\mathcal{G}_\nu} \int_{Q_m} h(\alpha, t)\, d\alpha\, dt \right|$$

$$+ \left| \int_{\mathcal{G}_\nu} \int_{Q_m} h(\alpha, t)\, dt\, d\alpha - \int_{\mathcal{G}} \int_{Q_m} h(\alpha, t)\, dt\, d\alpha \right| = A_1 + A_2 + A_3 . \qquad (12)$$

We fix $\varepsilon > 0$ and estimate A_1, A_2 and A_3 separately. Since

$$|A_3| < |\mathcal{G} - \mathcal{G}_\nu| \int_{Q_m} l(\alpha)\, d\alpha ,$$

starting from some ν, one has

$$A_3 < \varepsilon K , \qquad (13)$$

where $K = \int_{Q_m} l(\alpha)\, d\alpha$. Furthermore, it is not hard to see that

$$A_1 \leq \int_{\mathcal{G} \setminus \mathcal{G}_\nu} l(\gamma_n(t), t)\, dt .$$

Let Σ be a step domain covering $\mathcal{G}\setminus\mathcal{G}_\nu$ and such that $|\Sigma|<\varepsilon$. Then

$$A_1 < \int_\Sigma l(\gamma_n(t),t)dt .$$

The right-hand side of this inequality can be written as $|\Sigma|\int_{Q_m} l(\gamma_N)dt$, where N is some integer (see the end of 3.5.2). In view of the relation

$$\int_{Q_m} l(\gamma_N(t))dt = \int_{Q_m} l(\alpha)d\alpha ,$$

we obtain

$$A_1 < K|\Sigma| \leqslant \varepsilon K . \tag{14}$$

In order to estimate A_2, we note that since $\mathcal{G}_\nu$ is a step domain, we have

$$\int_{\mathcal{G}_\nu} h(\gamma_n,t)dt = \sum_{i_1=1}^{N}\cdots\sum_{i_m=N_1(i_1,\dots,i_{m-1})}^{i_m=N_2(i_1,\dots,i_{m-1})} \int_{\Delta_{i_1}}\cdots\int_{\Delta_{i_m}} h(\gamma_n(t_1),\dots$$

$$\dots,\gamma_n(t_m);t_1,\dots,t_m)dt_1\dots dt_m .$$

This can also be written as

$$\int_{\mathcal{G}_\nu} h(\gamma_n,t)dt = \sum_{i_1}\cdots\sum_{i_m} \Delta t_{i_1}\dots\Delta t_{i_m}\int\cdots\int_{Q_m} h(\alpha_1,\dots,\alpha_m;$$

$$\alpha_1+\Delta t_{i_1},\dots,\alpha_m\Delta t_{i_m}+t_{i_{m-1}})d\alpha_1\dots d\alpha_m .$$

Taking into account the last equation, we can argue as in the proof of Lemma 3.5.1 (which can be extended to any integer m) and choose an n_o such that, for $n>n_o$,

$$A_2 = \left|\int_{\mathcal{G}_\nu} h(\gamma_n,t)dt - \int_{\mathcal{G}_\nu} d\alpha\int_0^1 h(\alpha,t)dt\right| < \varepsilon . \tag{15}$$

From (13)-(15) it follows that

$$|I_n| < (2K+1)\varepsilon ,$$

which concludes the proof.

<u>Theorem 3.5.1</u>. Let the following conditions be fulfilled:

(i) D is a domain as in Lemma 3.5.2;

(ii) the mean value of the functional

$$F = \int_{\mathcal{G}} g(x(t),t)dt \tag{16}$$

exists and is of the form (1), where only Q_m has to be replaced by $\mathcal{G}$;

(iii) $|g(w(\alpha,t),t)| \leq l(\alpha) \in L(Q_m)$.

Then

$$\underset{D}{M}F = F[\theta_\infty] .$$

Proof. From (16) and the relation

$$\int g(w(\alpha,t),t)d\alpha = \int g(\xi,t)\,\varphi(d\xi,t) \tag{17}$$

and due to Lemma 3.5.3, we obtain

$$\underset{D}{M}F = \lim_n F\left[w(\gamma_n(t),t)\right] = F\left[\theta_\infty\right] , \tag{18}$$

which was to be proved.

It is necessary to note that if $\theta_n \sim \varphi_n$, then $\lim_n F[\theta_n]$ and $\lim_n F[\psi_n]$ (even when these limits exist) can have different values. In particular, $\theta_n \sim \theta$ does not necessarily imply $\lim_n F[\theta_n] = F[\theta]$.

3.5.4. It is natural to ask the question: For what types of functionals does the equality

$$\underset{D}{M}F = F[\theta] \tag{19}$$

hold?

Let us make this question more precise. Let $\varphi = \varphi(\xi, a_1(t),\dots,a_\nu(t))$ be the distribution function of the domain D containing the parameters $a_1,\dots,a_\nu$. Suppose that each vector $a=(a_1,\dots,a_\nu)$ corresponds to some domain D_a. Let V be a manifold in a function space which can be considered as the union of D_a, $a \in \mathcal{A}$, i.e. $V = \bigcup_{\mathcal{A}} D_a$ (for example, an open set in L^2 considered as the union of all balls included).

We shall say that F is a functional of class $\mathcal{H}$ on the set V or a harmonic functional, if, for every $D_a \in V$, the relation

$$\underset{D_a}{M}F = F[\theta_a]$$

is valid and θ_a can be considered as an ordinary function, i.e. a point of D_a.

If, for instance, D_a is the ellipsoid $\left\| \frac{x-a}{6} \right\| = 1$, in particular, the sphere, then (19) means $\underset{D_a}{M}F = F[a]$.

If D is the beam $a_1 < x < a_2$, (19) means that $\underset{D_a}{M}F = F\left[\frac{a_1+a_2}{2}\right]$ and we see that F is also a harmonic functional, but in a somewhat different sense. In general, we can say that condition (19) defines a class of functionals harmonic with respect to a given type of domains and the corresponding laws of distribution. The class $\mathcal{H}$ is closed. In fact, if $F_n \rightrightarrows F$ on D with $F_n \in \mathcal{H}$, then also $F \in \mathcal{H}$. Above we supposed that our function space A_s is $C[q]$, however, all what was said may be transferred to other spaces A. The centre is again defined as $\theta(t) = \int \varphi(d\xi, t)$, however, for $A=M(q)$ and $A=L_p(q)$, respectively, φ and θ are assumed to be defined only for almost all t on q.

The generalization of the notion of a centre in case of the space A_s, $s > 1$, is immediate. Let D be a normal or uniform function domain having the distribution density $p(\xi_1, \ldots, \xi_s; t)$. The vector $(\theta_1(t), \ldots, \theta_s(t))$ with $\theta_k(t) = \int \xi_k p(\xi_1, \ldots, \xi_s; t) d\xi^s$ will be called the centre of D provided that these integrals exist. For a normal ellipsoid $\left\| \frac{x-a}{\sigma} \right\| = 1$ as well as for a uniform ellipsoid $\left| \frac{x-a}{\sigma} \right| = 1$, we obtain $\theta = (a_1(t), \ldots, a_s(t))$. For the beam $a_k(t) < x_k < b_k(t)$, we have $\theta(t) = \left(\frac{a_1(t)+b_1(t)}{2}, \ldots, \frac{a_s(t)+b_s(t)}{2} \right)$.

The notions of a centre and of harmonicity lead, in a natural way, to boundary value problems which we shall consider in the following chapters. These problems are also related to the Laplace operator in a function space. Although the problems under consideration differ quite significantly from the corresponding classical boundary value problems, the statements are analogous. For example, the Dirichlet problem reads as follows: Let the function domain D be given. Then we seek for a functional $H[x]$ harmonic in D and having given values on the boundary D' of D. In addition, the domain can be normal or uniform, harmonicity may be understood in different senses, and different spaces can be examined.

In order to classify the variety of arising particular cases, we introduce some definitions.

4. The functional Laplace operator

4.1. Definitions and properties

Let the functional $F[x]$ be given over the space $A_s(q)$, and let

$$\delta F = \left. \frac{dF[x+\varepsilon\eta]}{d\varepsilon} \right|_{\varepsilon=0}, \quad \delta^2 F = \left. \frac{d^2F[x+\varepsilon\eta]}{d\varepsilon^2} \right|_{\varepsilon=0}$$

be its two first variations. We suppose that they exist and are of the form

$$\delta F = \sum_1^s \int_a^b A_{ok}[x|t]\,\eta_k(t)dt\ , \qquad (1)$$

$$\delta^2 F = \sum_1^s \int_a^b A_{1k}[x|t]\,\eta_k^{\,2}(t)dt + 2\sum_{k,l=1} \int_a^b\int_a^b A_{2kl}[x|t_1,t_2]\,\eta_k(t_1)$$

$$\eta_l(t_2)dt_1dt_2 + 2\sum_{k\neq l}\int_a^b A_{1kl}[x|t]\,\eta_k(t)\,\eta_l(t)dt\ . \qquad (2)$$

Here

$$A_{ok} = \frac{\delta F}{\delta x_k(t)}\ ,\quad A_{1k} = \frac{\delta^2 F}{\delta x_k^{\,2}(t)}\ ,\quad A_{2kl} = \frac{\delta^2 F}{\delta x_k(t_1)\,\delta x_l(t_2)}\ ,$$

$$A_{1kl} = \frac{\delta^2 F}{\delta x_k(t)\,\delta x_l(t)}$$

are the first and second variational derivatives of F with respect to x_k at the values of its arguments $t;\ t_1,\ t_2$. The existence of δF and $\delta^2 F$ imposes some evident restrictions on A_{ok}, A_{1k}, A_{1kl}, and A_{2kl}. Moreover, $A_{1k}(t)$ is supposed to be a summable function over q.

We define the <u>strong functional Laplace operator</u> by the equation

$$\Delta F = \sum_{k=1}^s \int_a^b A_{1k}[x|t]\ dt\ . \qquad (*)$$

If, for $x\in E\subset A_s(q)$, one has $\Delta F=0$, then F is said to be a <u>strongly harmonic functional</u> on E.

4.1.1. Let D be a normal function domain in $A_s(q)$ and $\|e\| = 1$ the Hilbert sphere in A_s (i.e. the intersection of A_s with the sphere $\|y\| = 1$, $y\in L_s^{\,2}(q)$).

Let the mean $\mathfrak{M}F[x+\lambda e]$, $\mathfrak{M} = \mathfrak{M}_{\|e\|=1}$ exist for $x\in D$ and λ sufficiently small. If the limit

$$\Delta_o F = 2\lim_{\lambda\to 0}\frac{\mathfrak{M}F[x+\lambda e] - F[x]}{\lambda^2}$$

exists, then it is called the <u>weak functional Laplace operator</u> of F at the point x. The functional F is said to be <u>weakly harmonic</u> in D if, for $x\in D$, one has

$$\mathfrak{M}F[x+\lambda e] = F[x]\quad .$$

Clearly, in this case $\Delta_o F=0$.

Let G be a uniform functional domain in $A_s(q)$ and $|e|^2 = \sum_{k=1}^s e_k^{\,2}(t)=1$.

We suppose that, for $x \in G$ and sufficiently small λ, there exists the mean value $M[x+\lambda e]$, $M = \underset{|e|=1}{M}$. If the limit

$$\Delta_{oo}F = 2s \lim_{0} \frac{MF[x+\lambda e]-F[x]}{\lambda^2}$$

exists, then it is called the *weak Laplace operator* of F at the point x. If $MF[x+\lambda e]=F[x]$ for each $x \in G$, then we shall say that F is a *weakly harmonic functional* in G.

We denote the classes of strongly harmonic functionals on D and G by $\mathcal{H}(D)$ and $\mathcal{H}(G)$, respectively. Similarly, the classes of weakly harmonic functionals in D and G are denoted by $\mathcal{H}_o(D)$ and $\mathcal{H}_o(G)$.

Lemma 4.1.1. If $F=F[x]$, $x \in A_s$,

$$F[x+\varepsilon\eta] = F[x] + \varepsilon\delta F + \frac{\varepsilon^2}{2}\delta^2 F + o(\varepsilon^2), \tag{3}$$

where δF and $\delta^2 F$ are of the form (1) and (2), respectively, and the estimate "o" is uniform with respect to the sphere $\|\eta\| = 1$, then

$$\Delta F = \Delta_o F. \tag{4}$$

Analogously, if (3) holds uniformly with respect to η on the sphere $|\eta| = 1$, then

$$\Delta F = \Delta_{oo} F. \tag{4'}$$

Proof. Averaging (3) over the sphere $\|\eta\| = 1$, we have

$$\mathfrak{M}(F[x+\eta] - F[x]) = \varepsilon\mathfrak{M}\delta F + \frac{\varepsilon^2}{2}\mathfrak{M}\delta^2 F + \mathfrak{M}o(\varepsilon^2). \tag{5}$$

Owing to formula (3) from 3.3, where x must be replaced by η, we get

$$\mathfrak{M}\delta F = 0, \quad \mathfrak{M}\delta^2 F = \mathfrak{M}\sum_{k=1}^{s}\int_a^b A_{1k}\eta^2 dt = \Delta F.$$

Dividing both sides of (5) by ε^2 and taking into account that

$$\left|\frac{\mathfrak{M}o(\varepsilon^2)}{\varepsilon^2}\right| \leqslant \sup_{\|\eta\|=1}\left|\frac{o(\varepsilon^2)}{\varepsilon^2}\right| = o(1)$$

for $\varepsilon \to 0$, we obtain $\Delta F = \Delta_o F$.

Arguing in the same way, from formula (1) of Section 3.1 (with η instead of x) we derive $\Delta F = \Delta_{oo} F$.

Lemma 4.1.2. (i) If, on the domain D, $H_n \rightrightarrows H$ and $H_n \in \mathcal{H}(D)$, then also $H \in \mathcal{H}(D)$.

(ii) If, on the domain D, $F_n \rightrightarrows F$ and $\Delta F_n \to \Phi$, then ΔF

exists and is equal to Φ . In particular, if $\Delta F_n=0$, then $\Delta F=0$.

In the conditions of the present lemma it is possible to substitute the normal domain D by a uniform domain G .

The proof of (i) follows immediately from the continuity of the operation $\mathfrak{M}$, while the proof of (ii) is the same as the proof of the classical theorem concerning the differentiability of a sequence of uniformly convergent functions. Therefore it is omitted here.

Let the function

$$f = f(t, \eta_1, \dots, \eta_m; \xi_1, \dots, \xi_n) \tag{6}$$

be given. We denote

$$\alpha_i = \frac{\partial f}{\partial \eta_i}, \quad \delta_k = \frac{\partial f}{\partial \xi_k}, \tag{7}$$

$$\alpha_{ij} = \frac{\partial^2 f}{\partial \eta_i \partial \eta_j}, \quad \beta_{ik} = \frac{\partial^2 f}{\partial \eta_i \partial \xi_k}, \quad \gamma_{kl} = \frac{\partial^2 f}{\partial \xi_k \partial \xi_l} . \tag{7'}$$

<u>Lemma 4.1.3</u>. Let the following conditions be satisfied:

(i) $x \in C_s[a,b]$, $a \leq a_o < b_o \leq b$, $a < a_i < b_i < b$;

(ii) the function (5) together with its derivatives (7) and (7') is continuous on the set

$$E: (a_o \leq t \leq b_o) \times (-\infty < \eta < \infty) \times (-\infty < \xi < \infty) = [a_o, b_o] \times E_{m+s} ;$$

(iii) for each $t \in [a_o, b_o]$, the variations δF and $\delta^2 F$ of the functionals $F_i[x|t]$ exist and have the form (1) and (2), respectively;

(iv) the operators $F_i[\overset{b_i}{\underset{a_i}{x}} | t]$, $\delta F_i[x|t]$, $\delta^2 F_i[x|t]$ act from $C_s[a_i, b_i]$ into $C[a_o, b_o]$:

$$F_i[\overset{b_i}{\underset{a_i}{x}} | t] \in \{ C_s[a_i, b_i] \longrightarrow C[a_o, b_o] \} , \quad \delta F_i \in \dots, \quad \delta^2 F_i \in \dots .$$

Finally, let

$$\Phi[x] = \int_{a_o}^{b_o} f(t, F_1[\overset{b_1}{\underset{a_1}{x}} | t], \dots, F_m[\overset{b_m}{\underset{a_m}{x}} | t], x(t)) dt \tag{8}$$

be a functional constructed on the basis of function (6).

Then the Laplacian $\Delta\Phi$ exists and is equal to

$$\Delta \Phi = \int_{a_o}^{b_o} \left(\sum_{i=1}^{m} \frac{\partial f}{\partial F_i} \Delta F_i + \sum_{k=1}^{s} \frac{\partial^2 f}{\partial x_k^2} \right) dt . \tag{9}$$

Proof. Under the conditions (i)-(iv), the existence of Φ is evident. Moreover, for any x, these conditions guarantee continuity of all integrands occurring below on $[a_o, b_o]$.

We vary x, changing its values on the interval $[a_o, b_o]$. In view of (ii), we have

$$\Phi[x+\varepsilon\eta] = \int_{a_o}^{b_o} f(t, F[x+\varepsilon\eta|t], x+\varepsilon\eta)dt$$

$$= \Phi[x] + \varepsilon\delta\Phi + o(\varepsilon)$$

$$= \Phi + \varepsilon \int_{a_o}^{b_o} (\sum_i \frac{\partial f}{\partial F_i}\delta F_i + \sum_k \frac{\partial f}{\partial x_k}\eta_k)dt + o(\varepsilon) .$$

Furthermore, taking into account (ii)-(iv), we get

$$\delta^2 F_i = \int_{a_o}^{b_o} \{ 2 \sum_{i,j=1}^{m} \frac{\partial^2 f}{\partial F_i \partial F_j}\delta F_i \delta F_j + 2 \sum_i \sum_k \frac{\partial^2 F}{\partial F_i \partial x_k}\delta F_i \eta_k$$

$$+ \sum_i \frac{\partial F}{\partial F_i}\delta^2 F_i + 2\sum_{k\neq l} \frac{\partial^2 f}{\partial x_k \partial x_l}\eta_k\eta_l + \sum_k \frac{\partial^2 f}{\partial x_k^2}\eta_k^2 \} dt ,$$

$$\delta F_i = \sum_k \int_{a_i}^{b_i} \frac{\delta F_i[x|t,t_1]}{\delta x_k(t_1)} \eta_k(t_1)dt_1 ,$$

$$\delta^2 F_i = \int_{a_i}^{b_i} \{ \sum_k \frac{\delta^2 F_i[x|t,t_1]}{\delta x_k^2(t_1)}\eta_k^2(t_1) + 2\sum_{k\neq l} \frac{\delta^2 F_i[x|t,t_1]}{\delta x_k(t_1)\delta x_l(t_1)}\eta_k(t_1)\eta_l(t_1)\} dt_1$$

$$+ 2\sum_{k,l} \int_{a_i}^{b_i}\int_{a_i}^{b_i} \frac{\delta^2 F_i[x|t;t_1,t_2]}{\delta x_k(t_1)\,\delta x_l(t_2)} \eta_k(t_1)\eta_l(t_2)dt_1 dt_2 .$$

In the expression of $\delta^2\Phi$ we are interested only in the terms containing η_k^2:

$$\sum_{k=1}^{s} \int_{a_o}^{b_o} \frac{\partial^2 f}{\partial x_k^2}\eta_k^2(t)dt + \sum_i \int_{a_o}^{b_o} \frac{\partial f}{\partial F_i}\{ \sum_k \int_{a_i}^{b_i} \frac{\delta^2 F}{\delta x_k^2(t_1)}\eta_k^2(t_1)dt_1\} dt .$$

Setting here $\eta \equiv 1$, we obtain

$$\Delta\Phi = \int_{a_o}^{b_o} \{ \sum_k \frac{\partial^2 f}{\partial x_k^2} + \sum_i \frac{\partial f}{\partial F_i}\Delta F_i \} dt ,$$

which was to be proved.

We focus our attention on two important special cases of the lemma:

1) Let $\Phi = \int_{a_o}^{b_o} f(x(t),t)dt .$

Then

$$\Delta\Phi = \int_{a_o}^{b_o} \sum_k \frac{\partial^2 f}{\partial x_k^2}\, dt \,. \tag{10}$$

2) If

$$\Phi = f(F_1,\dots,F_m)\,,$$

then

$$\Delta\Phi = \frac{\partial f}{\partial F_i}\,\Delta F_i \,. \tag{11}$$

Remark. The conditions of the lemma may be slightly weakened assuming f to be twice differentiable with respect to η not for all η but only for those which coincide with the values of $(F_1,\dots,F_m)$ if $x \in D$. Obviously, Lemma 3 is also correct if we consider F_i and Φ on a uniform domain G. If, in addition, this domain is bounded (i.e., $x \in D$ implies $|x| < B$, where B is some constant independent of x), it is sufficient for f to be twice continuously differentiable with respect to ξ on the ball $|\xi| < B$.

4.1.2. If $A_s = L_s{}^p(q)$ or $A_s = M_s(q)$, then Lemma 4.1.3 also remains valid. To justify this claim, we have merely to change conditions (i)-(iv) in the following way.

Lemma 4.1.3'. Assume the following conditions to be fulfilled:

(i) $F_i\left[\overset{b_i}{\underset{a_i}{x}}\middle| t\right]$, δF, $\delta^2 F \in \left\{ L_s{}^p(a_i,b_i) \longrightarrow L^p(a_o,b_o) \right\}$;

(ii) on the set E (see condition (ii) of Lemma 4.1.3), let $f(t,\xi,\eta)$ be a continuous function of ξ and η measurable with respect to t (Carathéodory condition). The derivatives (7) and (7') exist and satisfy the same condition;

(iii) on the set E, we have

$$|f| \le u(t) + \sum_{i=1}^{m} B_i |\eta_i|^p + \sum_{k=1}^{s} C_k |\xi_k|^p \,,$$

where $u > 0$, $u \in L(a_o,b_o)$ and B_i, C_k are positive constants. For d_i, δ_k, ..., γ_{kl} (see (7) and (7')) the estimates

$$|d_i| \le u_i(t) + \sum_{j=1}^{m} B_{ij} |\eta_j|^{p-1} + \sum_{k=1}^{s} C_{ik} |\xi_k|^{p-1}$$

with $u_i > 0$, $u_i \in L(a_o,b_o)$, B_{ij}, C_{ik} constants,

$$|\delta_k| \le \dots \text{ (analogously)} \,,$$

$$|d_{ij}| \le u_{ij}(t) + \sum_{q=1}^{m} B_{ijq} |\eta_q|^{p-2} + \sum_{l=1}^{s} C_{ijl} |\xi_l|^{p-2}$$

($u_{ij} > 0$, $u_{ij} \in L(a_o,b_o)$, B_{ijq}, C_{ijl} are constants) ,

$|\beta_{ik}|, |\gamma_{kl}| \leq \ldots$ (analogously) hold.

Then the functional $\Delta\Phi$ exists and relation (9) is valid.

If $A_s = M_s$, the former estimates can be weakened. In this case it is sufficient that, for each of the quantities $d_i, \delta_k, \ldots, \gamma_{kl}$, we have

$$|d_i| \leq u_i(t) + \sum_j b_{ij}\varphi_j(\eta_j) + \sum_k c_{ik}\psi_k(\xi_k),$$

$$\ldots, |\gamma_{kl}| \leq \ldots,$$

where $u_i \in L(a_o, b_o)$, b_{ij}, c_{ik} are some positive constants and φ as well as ψ are positive continuous functions.

As a consequence of Lemmas 4.1.1 and 4.1.3 we formulate

Lemma 4.1.4. If F_i and Φ satisfy the conditions of Lemmas 4.1.1 and 4.1.3, then

$$\Delta_o\Phi = \int_{a_o}^{b_o} \Big(\sum_i \frac{\partial f}{\partial F_i}\Delta_o F_i + \sum_k \frac{\partial^2 f}{\partial x_k^2}\Big)\,dt,$$

$$\Delta_{oo}\Phi = \int_{a_o}^{b_o} \Big(\sum_i \frac{\partial f}{\partial F_i}\Delta_{oo} F_i + \sum_k \frac{\partial^2 f}{\partial x_k^2}\Big)\,dt.$$

4.2. Spherical means and the Laplace operator in the Hilbert co-ordinate space l_2

4.2.1. Let H be an abstract real separable Hilbert space and $e_1, e_2, \ldots$ some complete orthonormal basis in H. Furthermore, let $x = \sum_k x_k e_k$ be the expansion of x with respect to this basis. The functional $F[x]$ defined on H can be represented as a function $f(x)$ of the point $x = (x_1, x_2, \ldots) \in l_2$:

$$F[x] = F\Big[\sum x_k e_k\Big] = f(x_1, x_2, \ldots). \tag{1}$$

Let P_n be the projector from l_2 to the subspace $x_{n+1}=0, x_{n+2}=0, \ldots$, i.e. $P_n x = (x_1, \ldots, x_n; 0, 0, \ldots)$. The projection of the sphere $\Omega_{a,R}$: $\|x-a\| = R$ is given by the relation

$$\Omega_n = P_n\Omega_{a,R}: \sum_{h=1}^{n} (x_h - a_h)^2 = R^2.$$

We form the mean μ_n of the function $f(P_n x)$ over this sphere. The limit $\lim_n \mu_n$ provided that it exists is called the mean of $f(x)$ over the Hilbert sphere $\Omega_{a,R}$.

4.2.2. Let f be twice differentiable with respect to each co-ordinate $x_1, x_2, \ldots$. We define the strong Laplace operator in l_2 by

$$\Delta^{o} f = \lim_{n} \frac{1}{n} \sum_{k=1}^{n} \frac{\partial^2 f}{\partial x_k^2} . \qquad (2)$$

4.2.3. We define the weak Laplace operator $\Delta^{oo} f$ at the point $a \in l_2$ in the following way:

$$\Delta^{oo} f = 2s \lim_{\lambda \to 0} \frac{M_{a,\lambda}\left[f(a+\lambda e) - f(a) \right]}{\lambda^2} . \qquad (3)$$

Now, the strong and weak harmonicity in l_2 are defined by the equations $\Delta^{o} f = 0$ and $\Delta^{oo} f = 0$, respectively.

4.2.4. Let H be a separable space $L^2(a,b)$, and let $\varphi_1(t), \varphi_2(t), \ldots$ be some orthonormal basis in it. Furthermore, let $F[x(t)]$ be a functional on $L^2(q)$. Starting from (1), (2), (3) and the definitions of Section 4.1, we can define the mean values and the Laplace operators

$$\mathfrak{M}_{a,R} F, \quad \Delta_{o} F, \quad \Delta_{oo} F, \quad \Delta^{o} F, \quad \Delta^{oo} F, \quad M_{a,R} F .$$

Under which conditions do the following equalities hold:

(*i*) $\mathfrak{M}_{a,R} F = M_{a,R} F$;

(*ii*) $\Delta_{o} F = \Delta^{o} F, \quad \Delta_{oo} F = \Delta^{oo} F$? (4)

Note that both the existence and the values of the quantities $M_{a,R} F$, (2) and (3) can depend upon the way of numeration of the co-ordinates. At the same time, it is always possible to choose a basis such that (4) is fulfilled (in case these operations exist). Such bases are called uniformly dense bases. There exist also uniformly dense bases for which everything said above is true independently of the order of numeration of the co-ordinates (concerning these problems, see LEVY [1,2]).

Certain conditions analogous to those formulated in Section 4.1 lead us to the relations $\Delta_{o} F = \Delta_{oo} F$, $\Delta^{o} F = \Delta^{oo} F$ and

$$\Delta^{o}(F_1 F_2) = F_1 \Delta^{o} F_2 + F_2 \Delta^{o} F_1 ,$$

where Δ^{o} can be replaced by Δ^{oo}.

In the sequel we use, in general, the unique notation Δ for the functional Laplace operator, but we shall exactly indicate which of the definitions applies.

CHAPTER 2. THE LAPLACE AND POISSON EQUATIONS FOR A NORMAL DOMAIN

In this chapter we consider Dirichlet's problem in a function space in the following setting. Let V be a normal domain in the space $L^2(q)$ bounded by the surface S. Find a functional $H[x]$ satisfying, for each sphere $\Omega_{a,R} \subset V$, the condition $\mathfrak{M}_{a,R}H = H[a]$ and taking on S the given value $F[x]$, where F is an element of the Gâteaux ring. The proofs are based on semigroup properties of the mean $\mathfrak{M}_{a,R}$. It is shown that the solution can be represented in a closed form if the "fundamental functional of the surface S" is known. This functional can be effectively found for surfaces which are called algebraic as well as in more general cases. Then the same idea is applied to the boundary value problem for Poisson's equation. The exterior Dirichlet problem is also examined. A complex domain is needed to cope with this problem, and additional conditions have to be imposed on the prescribed functions.

Furthermore, in this chapter the analogy of our formulae with the probability solutions of classical boundary value problems for elliptic equations is shown, and the properties of semigroups of continual means are studied.

At the end of the chapter some generalizations based on the utilization of the integral over a regular (especially, the Jessen) measure are established.

5. Boundary value problems for a normal domain with boundary values on the Gâteaux ring

5.1. Functional Laplace and Poisson equations

5.1.1. We shall now characterize the surface S on which the boundary values of the unknown functionals will be given for the problems discussed here.

We shall assume that the following conditions are satisfied:

(1°) S is a closed convex surface situated entirely in a finite part of the space $L^2(q)$.

(2°) S may be represented via the polar equation

$$S:\quad z=x+\varrho y, \quad x\in V, \quad z\in S, \quad \|y\|=1,$$

where z is a variable point on S, $\varrho = \varrho_x[y]$ is its polar radius-vector originating from the point x, and y is the unit vector defining the direction from x to z, i.e. the position of z.

Since S is a convex surface, it is clear that $\varrho_x[y]$ is a single-valued functional of y for each x.

(3°) For any $x \in V$, there exists

$$s[x] = \mathfrak{M}\, \varrho_x[y]\,, \quad \mathfrak{M} = \mathfrak{M}_{\|y\|=1} \,.$$

It is not hard to show that if S is the sphere $\|x\|=R$, then

$$s[x] = \sqrt{R^2 - \|x\|^2}\,.$$

We generalize this fact by requiring that:

(4°) $s[x] = \sqrt{\Gamma[x] - \|x\|^2}$, where $\Gamma[x]$ is a harmonic functional in V.

(5°) $s[x] = 0$ for $x \in S$.

In addition we suppose:

(6°) $\varrho_x[y]$ is uniformly continuous on the sphere $\|y\|=1$ for any x, and $s[x]$ is uniformly continuous on any sphere in V and continuous on $\bar{V} = V \cup S$.

The meaning of the requirements (1°), (2°), (3°), and (6°) is clear without any explanation. Furthermore, it can be shown that requirements (4°) and (5°) are also entirely natural in the theory considered here. In Section 5.2 it will be demonstrated that these conditions are satisfied for a very wide class of functionals when the surface S is given by the equation $U[x]=0$.

We shall say that S is a <u>surface of type</u> $\{S\}$, if conditions (1°)-(6°) are satisfied for it. The functional Γ is called a <u>fundamental functional</u> of the surface S.

Let the Gâteaux functional

$$F[x] = \int_{Q_m}\!\!\cdots\!\int g(x(t_1),\ldots,x(t_m);t_1,\ldots,t_m)\, dt^m \tag{1}$$

be given. For its generating function $g(\xi,t)$ the estimate

$$|g(\xi,t)| \leqslant a(t) + c\,\xi_1^2 \ldots \xi_m^2 \tag{2}$$

is assumed to hold, where $a \in L(Q_m)$, $a > 0$, $c=\text{const} > 0$, which implies the continuity and boundedness of (1) on every ball V_R: $\|x\| < R$ of the space $L^2(q)$:

$$\sup_{V_R} |F[x]| \leqslant \int_{Q_m} a(t)dt^m + cR^{2m}\,. \tag{3}$$

We choose an R such that $V \subset V_R$.

5.1.2. Theorem 5.1.1. If S is a surface of type $\{S\}$ and F is given by equation (1), then the functional

$$H[x] = \mathfrak{M} F[x+ \varrho_x[y]y] \tag{4}$$

is harmonic on V and the boundary condition

$$H\Big|_S = F[x]$$

holds.

Proof. First of all, we note that functional (4) can be written in the form

$$H[x] = \mathfrak{M} F[x+s[x]y] \tag{5}$$

or, equivalently,

$$H[x] = \mathfrak{M}_{x,s[x]} F . \tag{5'}$$

In fact, since $S \in \{S\}$, it follows that, for any $x \in V$, the mean $\mathfrak{M} \varrho_x[y]=s[x]$ exists and $\varrho_x[y]=s[x]$ almost everywhere on the sphere $\|y\|=1$.
From (2) we see that, for each fixed x , the mean $\mathfrak{M}_{x,s} F$ exists. In view of Lemma 3.2.1 (where x is replaced by y), the mean (4) also exists and is equal to (5).

Applying the Gâteaux formula to functional (1) (with $a=x$ and $R=s$), we obtain

$$H[x] = \mathfrak{M}_{x,s} F =$$

$$\left(\frac{1}{s[x]\sqrt{2\pi}}\right)^m \int\limits_{Q_m}\!\!\cdots\!\!\int dt^m \int\cdots\int g(\xi_1,\dots,\xi_m;t_1,\dots,t_m)\cdot$$

$$\cdot \prod_{k=1} \exp\left(-\frac{(\xi_k-x(t_k))^2}{2\, s^2[x]}\right) d\xi^m \tag{6}$$

or, in a shortened form,

$$H[x] = \left(\frac{1}{s\sqrt{2\pi}}\right)^m \int\limits_{Q_m} dt^m \int g(\xi,t)\exp\left(-\frac{|\xi-x(t)|^2}{2\, s^2}\right) d\xi^m . \tag{6'}$$

Next we shall prove that on any sphere $\Omega_{x,\lambda}$ lying in the domain V the equation $\mathfrak{M}_{x,\lambda} H=H[x]$ is satisfied.

Lemma 5.1.1. For any fixed values of x and λ and for variable y such that $x+\lambda y$ lies in the domain V , the formula

$$\mathfrak{M} s[x+\lambda y] = \sqrt{s^2[x]-\lambda^2}$$

holds true.

Proof. Owing to the formula $s[x]=\sqrt{\Gamma[x]-\|x\|^2}$, we can write

$$s^2[x+\lambda y] = \Gamma[x+\lambda y] - \|x+\lambda y\|^2$$
$$= \Gamma[x+\lambda y] - \|x\|^2 - 2\lambda(x,y) - \lambda^2\|y\|^2 .$$

Because Γ is a harmonic functional of x, for fixed x the functional $\Gamma[x+\lambda y]$ will be harmonic with respect to y. Thus

$$\mathfrak{M}\Gamma[x+\lambda y] = \Gamma[x] .$$

The scalar product (x,y) is a linear and, thus, a harmonic functional with respect to y. Therefore $\mathfrak{M}(x,y) = (x,0) = 0$.

Finally, taking into account that $\mathfrak{M}\|y\|^2 = \mathfrak{M}1 = 1$, we obtain

$$\mathfrak{M}s^2[x+\lambda y] = (\mathfrak{M}s[x+\lambda y])^2 = \Gamma[x]-\|x\|^2-\lambda^2 = s^2[x]-\lambda^2$$

and the lemma is proved.

From (6) it follows that

$$H[x+\lambda y]=\frac{1}{(s[x+\lambda y]\sqrt{2\pi})^m}\int_{Q_m} dt^m \int g(\xi,t)\exp\left(-\frac{|\xi-x(t)-\lambda y(t)|^2}{2s[x+\lambda y]^2}\right)d\xi^m. \quad (7)$$

Lemma 5.1.2. The following relation holds:

$$\mathfrak{M}H[x+\lambda y] = \frac{1}{(s_\lambda\sqrt{2\pi})^m}\mathfrak{M}\int\limits_{Q_m}\!\!\cdots\!\!\int dt_1\ldots dt_m \int\!\!\cdots\!\!\int g(\xi_1,\ldots,\xi_m;t_1,\ldots,t_m)\cdot$$
$$\cdot\prod_{k=1}\exp\left(-\frac{\xi_k-x(t_k)-\lambda y(t_k)}{2\,s_\lambda^2}\right)d\xi_1\ldots d\xi_m , \quad (8)$$

where

$$s_\lambda = \mathfrak{M}s[x+\lambda y] = \sqrt{s^2[x]-\lambda^2} . \quad (9)$$

Proof. We shall first show that for $x\in V$ and $x+\lambda y\in V$ (here x is fixed) the functional $H[x+\lambda y]$ is bounded.

In fact, as V is a domain, then, in view of the definition of $\rho_x[y]$, for every fixed x the functional $\rho_x[y]$ has a lower bound different from zero on the unit sphere. Putting $x+\lambda y=x_1$ and denoting $\inf_{\|y\|=1}\rho_x[y] = m$, we obtain

$$s[x+\lambda y] = s[x_1] = \mathfrak{M}\rho_{x_1}[y] \geqslant m > 0 .$$

In view of (7), this ensures the boundedness of $H[x+\lambda y]$.

Replacing in (7) $s[x+\lambda y]$ by the number s_λ (see (9)), we get the functional

$$H_\lambda = \left(\frac{1}{s_\lambda\sqrt{2\pi}}\right)^m \int_{Q_m} dt^m \int g(\xi,t)\exp\left(-\frac{|\xi - x(t) - \lambda y(t)|^2}{2\,s_\lambda^2}\right)d\xi^m\,, \qquad (10)$$

which is also bounded when x and $x+\lambda y$ lie in V. Since $s[x+\lambda y]$ is equal to s_λ almost everywhere, comparing (7) and (10), we observe that H_λ is equal to $H[x+\lambda y]$ almost everywhere. Consequently, the means of these functionals over the sphere $\|y\|=1$ are equal to each other. Thus the lemma is proved.

We shall now apply the Gâteaux formula once more to equation (10):

$$\mathfrak{M} H[x+\lambda y] = \left(\frac{1}{s_\lambda\sqrt{2\pi}}\right)^m\left(\frac{1}{\lambda\sqrt{2\pi}}\right)^m \int_{Q_m} dt^m \int\cdots\int \left\{ \int\cdots\int g(\xi_1,\ldots,\xi_m; t_1,\ldots,t_m) \prod_{i=1}^{m} \exp\left(-\frac{(\xi_i - x(t_i) - \lambda\eta(t_i))^2}{2\,s_\lambda^2}\right) d\xi_1\ldots d\xi_m \right\}$$

$$\exp\left(-\frac{\eta_1^2+\ldots+\eta_m^2}{2\lambda^2}\right) d\eta_1\ldots d\eta_m\,.$$

We transform this expression by applying the well-known relation

$$\frac{1}{2\pi\sigma_1\sigma_2}\int \exp\left(-\frac{\eta^2}{2\sigma_1^2}\right)\exp\left(-\frac{(\xi-\eta)^2}{2\sigma_2^2}\right)d\eta$$

$$= \frac{1}{\sqrt{2\pi(\sigma_1^2+\sigma_2^2)}}\exp\left(-\frac{\xi^2}{2(\sigma_1^2+\sigma_2^2)}\right)$$

m times and get

$$\mathfrak{M} H[x+\lambda y] = \left(\frac{1}{\sqrt{2\pi(s_\lambda^2+\lambda^2)}}\right)^m \int\cdots\int_{Q_m} dt^m \int\cdots\int g(\xi_1,\ldots,\xi_m; t_1,\ldots,t_m)\cdot$$

$$\cdot\prod_{i=1}^{m}\exp\left(-\frac{(\xi_i - x(t_i))^2}{2(s_\lambda^2+\lambda^2)}\right) d\xi^m\,.$$

By virtue of (9), $s_\lambda^2+\lambda^2 = s^2[x]$. Therefore

$$\mathfrak{M} H[x+\lambda y] =$$

$$\frac{1}{(s\sqrt{2\pi})^m}\int_{Q_m} dt^m \int g(\xi,t)\exp\left(-\frac{(\xi - x(t))^2}{2s^2}\right) dt^m = H[x]\,,$$

which proves the first part of the theorem.

It still has to be proved that $\lim_{x\to z} H[x] = F[z]$ for $z\in S$. For simplicity we shall suppose to start with that $m=1$ and that the function g does not contain t explicitly, i.e.

$$F = \int_0^1 g(x(t))dt .$$

Then

$$H[x] = \frac{1}{\sqrt{2\pi}} \int_0^1 dt \int g(x(t)+\xi s[x]) \exp(-\xi^2/2) \, d\xi .$$

In the case under consideration, $x \to z$ signifies that x tends to z in the mean, where $s[x] \to 0$ (see (5^0) from 5.1.1). Let x_n be some sequence such that $\| x_n - z \| \to 0$. Then, as is well-known, this sequence also converges in measure to z . Because $s[x_n]$ tends to zero, the sequence of functions $x_n(t)+\xi s[x_n]$ converges in measure to $z(t)$ for any value of ξ . Hence $g(x_n+\xi s[x_n])$ converges in measure to $g(z(t))$[1] .

From what has been said it follows that the sequence

$$\psi_n(t) = \int g(x_n(t)+\xi s[x_n]) \exp(-\xi^2/2) \, d\xi$$

also converges in measure, and from (2) we see that this sequence is bounded. Thus, using Lebesgue's theorem, we may proceed to the limit under the integral sign in the equation

$$H[x_n] = \frac{1}{\sqrt{2\pi}} \int_0^1 dt \int g(x_n(t)+\xi s[x_n]) \exp(-\xi^2/2) \, d\xi$$

and obtain

$$\lim_n H[x_n] = \frac{1}{\sqrt{2\pi}} \int_0^1 g(z(t))dt \int \exp(-\xi^2/2) d\xi = F[z] , \tag{11}$$

which was to be proved.

In complete analogy with this result we may prove that the relation

$$\lim_n H[x_n] =$$

$$\lim_n \left(\frac{1}{\sqrt{2\pi}\, s[x_n]}\right)^m \int_{Q_m} dt^m \int g(\xi, t) \exp\left(-\frac{|\xi - x_n(t)|^2}{2 s^2[x_n]}\right) d\xi^m = F[z]$$

is valid for the functional (1) in the case $m > 1$, too.

5.1.3. The functionals considered in the preceding theorem generate a ring $R(\overline{V})$: If $F', F'' \in R(\overline{V})$, then besides the additivity, we have also $F'F'' \in R(\overline{V})$.

In the following we denote

$$\mathfrak{M}_{x,s} F = \mathfrak{M}^s F .$$

---

[1] This follows from the continuity of the superposition operator.

Let $H = \mathfrak{M}^s F$. From the multiplicativity of the operator $\mathfrak{M}^s$ it follows that

$$\mathfrak{M}^s(F'F'') = \mathfrak{M}^s F' \mathfrak{M}^s F'' . \tag{12}$$

Therefore, the class $\mathfrak{M}^s F$ also generates a ring, which is denoted by $\mathcal{H}_0(\bar{V})$. We introduce on $R(\bar{V})$ and $\mathcal{H}_0(\bar{V})$ the uniform norms

$$\| F \| = \sup_{\bar{V}} |F| , \quad \| H \| = \sup_{\bar{V}} H .$$

Let $\bar{R}(\bar{V})$ and $\bar{\mathcal{H}}_0(\bar{V})$, respectively, be the closure of $R(\bar{V})$ and $\mathcal{H}_0(\bar{V})$ with regard to these norms. Since the operator $\mathfrak{M}^s$ is continuous with respect to the uniform norm (uniform convergence on the set $\bar{V}$), the mapping from R into $\mathcal{H}_0$ can be extended to a mapping from $\bar{R}$ into $\bar{\mathcal{H}}_0$:

$$H = \mathfrak{M}^s F, \quad H \in \bar{R}, \quad F \in \bar{\mathcal{H}}_0 .$$

On the boundary S of V both rings coincide.

Thus we are able to formulate

Theorem 5.1.1'. Let $F \in \bar{R}(\bar{V})$. Then the operator $\mathfrak{M}^s$ defines a functional H harmonic on the domain V with boundary values F .

5.1.4. Let us consider the functional **Poisson equation**

$$\Delta U + F[x] = 0 , \tag{13}$$

where the Laplace operator Δ is defined via

$$\Delta U = 2 \lim_{\lambda \to 0} \frac{\mathfrak{M} U[x+\lambda y] - U[x]}{\lambda^2} . \tag{14}$$

We introduce the notation

$$\mathfrak{N} F = \int_0^{s[x]} r \, \mathfrak{M} F[x+ry] \, dr . \tag{15}$$

Theorem 5.1.2. Let $F[x]$ be a functional defined on the set $\bar{V} = V \cup S$, where S is a surface of type $\{S\}$, and let F satisfy all the conditions of Theorem 5.1.1. Then, for any $x \in V$, the functional (15) exists and satisfies the equation

$$\Delta \mathfrak{N} F + F = 0 .$$

Proof. We start with the simple case, if $m=1$ and g does not contain the variable t explicitly. Thus, let

$$F = \int_0^1 g(x(t))dt .$$

Forming $\mathfrak{M}F$, we obtain

$$\mathfrak{M}F = \int_0^{s[x]} r\,\mathfrak{M}\int_0^1 g(x(t)+ry(t))dt .$$

In view of the Gâteaux formula, we get

$$\mathfrak{M}F = \frac{1}{\sqrt{2\pi}} \int_0^{s[x]} r \int_0^1 dt \int g(x(t)+r\xi)\,\exp(-\xi^2/2)d\xi dr . \qquad (16)$$

This functional will be denoted by $U[x]$. Then

$$U[x+\lambda y] = \frac{1}{\sqrt{2\pi}} \int_0^{s[x+\lambda y]} r \int_0^1 dt \int g(x(t)+r\xi+\lambda y(t))\exp(-\xi^2/2)d\xi dr . \qquad (17)$$

Lemma 5.1.3. The following equation holds:

$$\mathfrak{M}U[x+\lambda y] = \frac{1}{\sqrt{2\pi}} \int_0^{s_\lambda} r\,\mathfrak{M}\int_0^1 dt \int g(x(t)+r\xi+\lambda y(t))\exp(-\xi^2/2)d\xi dr , \qquad (18)$$

where, as above, $s_\lambda = \sqrt{s^2[x]-\lambda^2}$.

The proof of this lemma is not given, as it is essentially the same as the proof of Lemma 5.1.2.

Applying the Gâteaux formula to (18), we obtain

$$\mathfrak{M}U[x+\lambda y] =$$

$$\int_0^1 dt \int g(\eta)\left\{ \int_0^{s_\lambda} r\left(\frac{1}{2\pi\lambda r}\right) \int \exp\left(-\frac{(\eta-x(t)-\alpha)^2}{2r^2}\right)\exp\left(-\frac{\alpha^2}{2\lambda^2}\right)d\alpha dr \right\} d\eta .$$

Since

$$\frac{1}{2\pi\lambda r} \int \exp\left(-\frac{(\eta-x(t)-\alpha)^2}{2r^2}\right) \exp(-\alpha^2/2\lambda^2)d\alpha =$$

$$\frac{1}{\sqrt{2\pi}}\,\frac{1}{\sqrt{\lambda^2+r^2}}\exp\left(-\frac{(\eta-x(t))^2}{2(\lambda^2+r^2)}\right) ,$$

we have

$$\mathfrak{M}U[x+\lambda y] =$$

$$\frac{1}{\sqrt{2\pi}} \int_0^1 dt \int_0^{s_\lambda} \frac{rdr}{\sqrt{\lambda^2+r^2}} \int \exp\left(-\frac{(\eta-x(t))^2}{2(\lambda^2+r^2)}\right) g(\eta)d\eta ,$$

and after a change of variables $(\lambda^2+r^2=\beta^2)$, we get

$$\mathfrak{M}U[x+\lambda y] = \frac{1}{\sqrt{2\pi}} \int_0^1 dt \int_\lambda^{s[x]} d\beta \int \exp\left(-\frac{(\eta-x(t))^2}{2\beta^2}\right)g(\eta)d\eta .$$

In our case (see (16))

$$U[x] = \mathfrak{M}F = \frac{1}{\sqrt{2\pi}} \int_0^{s[x]} d\beta \int_0^1 dt \int g(\eta)\exp(-\frac{(\eta - x(t))^2}{2\beta^2})d\eta$$

and, therefore,

$$\mathfrak{M}U[x+\lambda y] - U[x] =$$

$$- \frac{1}{\sqrt{2\pi}} \int_0^1 dt \int_0^\lambda d\beta \int g(\eta) \exp(- \frac{(\eta - x(t))^2}{2\beta^2})d\eta \ .$$

Consequently

$$\frac{\mathfrak{M}U[x+\lambda y] - U[x]}{\lambda^2} =$$

$$- \frac{1}{\sqrt{2\pi}} \int_0^1 dt \frac{1}{\lambda^2} \int_0^\lambda d\beta \int g(\eta) \exp(- \frac{(\eta - x(t))^2}{2\beta^2})d\eta \ .$$

In order to justify the limiting procedure as $\lambda \to 0$, we introduce the notation

$$\frac{2}{\lambda^2} \int_0^\lambda \frac{1}{\sqrt{2\pi}} \exp(- \frac{(\eta - x(t))^2}{2\beta^2})d\beta = \varphi_\lambda(\eta, x) \ .$$

For any λ the function $\varphi_\lambda(\eta, x)$ is a monotonic majorant for itself (the function $\psi(\eta, x)$ is said to be a monotonic majorant of the function $\varphi(\eta, x)$ if $|\varphi(\eta, x)| < \psi(\eta, x)$ and if, for fixed x, the function ψ increases for $\eta < x$ and decreases in case $\eta > x$).
In fact, the function $\exp(- \frac{(\eta - x(t))^2}{2\beta^2})$ possesses this property for an arbitrary value of β. Hence the function $\varphi_\lambda(\eta, x)$ also possesses this property for every λ. On the other hand,

$$\int \varphi_\lambda(\eta, x)d\eta = \frac{2}{\lambda^2\sqrt{2\pi}} \int_0^\lambda d\beta \int \exp(- \frac{(\eta - x(t))^2}{2\beta^2})d\eta =$$

$$\frac{2}{\lambda^2} \int_0^\lambda d\beta \int \frac{1}{\sqrt{2\pi}} \exp(-\alpha^2/2)\beta \, d\alpha = 1 \ .$$

Consequently, by the theorem about a monotonic majorant (see NATANSON [1], Chap. 10), for almost all values of t $(0 < t < 1)$,

$$\lim_{\lambda \to 0} \int g(\eta)\varphi_\lambda(\eta, x(t))d\eta = g(x(t))$$

(the mentioned theorem is usually formulated for a finite interval $\eta_1 < \eta < \eta_2$. It may be applied in our case, however, as in virtue of (2), for any $\varepsilon > 0$ we can select a number N independent of the values of $x(t)$ such that

$$\left| \int_{|\eta| > N} g(\eta)\varphi_\lambda(\eta, x(t))d\eta \right| < \varepsilon \ .$$

As $g(x(t))$ is a summable function in the interval $0<t<1$ (since the functional F exists at the point x), then again in view of (2), we have

$$\lim_{\lambda\to 0}\int_0^1 dt\int g(\eta)\,\varphi_\lambda(\eta,x(t))\,d\eta = \int_0^1 g(x(t))\,dt = F[x],$$

which completes the proof in the case $m=1$. For $m>1$, analogous reasoning for the functional (1) leads to the equation

$$\Delta U = -\left(\frac{1}{\sqrt{2\pi}}\right)^m \lim_{\lambda\to 0}\int\cdots\int dt_1\ldots dt_m\int\cdots\int g(\eta_1,\ldots,\eta_m;t_1,\ldots,t_m)\cdot$$

$$\cdot\prod_{k=1}^{m}\frac{2}{\lambda^2}\int_0^\lambda \exp\left(-\frac{(\eta_k-x(t_k))^2}{2\beta^2}\right)\frac{d\beta}{\beta^{m-1}}\,d\eta_1\ldots d\eta_m\ .$$

Now we introduce the notation

$$\frac{2}{\lambda^2}\int_0^\lambda \beta^{-(m-1)}(\sqrt{2\pi})^{-m}\prod_{k=1}^{m}\exp\left(-\frac{(\eta_k-x(t_k))^2}{2\beta^2}\right)d\beta =$$

$$\varphi_\lambda(\eta_1,\ldots,\eta_m;x_1,\ldots,x_m)\ .$$

It is not difficult to see that

$$\int\cdots\int\varphi_\lambda(\eta_1,\ldots,\eta_m;x_1,\ldots,x_m)\,d\eta_1\ldots d\eta_m = 1\ .$$

Since the function $g(x(t_1),\ldots,x(t_m);t_1,\ldots,t_m)$ is summable over the cube Q_m, we have for almost all $t\in Q_m$

$$\lim_{\lambda\to 0}\int\cdots\int g(\eta_1,\ldots,\eta_m;t_1,\ldots,t_m)\,\varphi_\lambda(\eta_1,\ldots,\eta_m;x_1,\ldots,x_m)\,d\eta_1\ldots d\eta_m$$

$$= g(x(t_1),\ldots,x(t_m);t_1,\ldots,t_m)\ .$$

By virtue of Lebesgue's theorem on taking the limit under the integral sign, we have

$$\Delta U = -\lim_{\lambda\to 0}\int_{Q_m} dt^m\int_{E_m} g(\eta_1,\ldots,\eta_m;t_1,\ldots,t_m)\,\varphi_\lambda(\eta_1,\ldots,\eta_m;x(t_1),\ldots$$

$$\ldots x(t_m))\,d\eta^m = -\int_{Q_m} g(x(t),t)\,dt^m = -F[x]\ ,$$

which completes the proof of Theorem 5.1.2.

5.1.5. From the very definition of $\mathfrak{N}$ as an operator over the ring $R(\overline{V})$ the following properties immediately result:

(i) $\mathfrak{N}F\big|_S = 0$;

(ii) $\mathfrak{N}$ is an additive bounded operator:

$$\| \mathfrak{N} F \| \leq \frac{s^2}{2} \| F \| \leq \frac{d^2}{2} \| F \| ,$$

where d is the diameter of the domain V ;

(iii) if $F_n \in R(\overline{V})$ and $F_n \rightrightarrows F$ on the set $\overline{V}$, then on this set $\mathfrak{N} F_n \rightrightarrows \mathfrak{N} F$.

Theorem 5.1.2 can now be extended to the ring $\overline{R}(\overline{V})$.

<u>Theorem 5.1.2'</u>. Let $F \in \overline{R}(\overline{V})$, and let the equation

$$\Delta U + F = 0$$

be given. Its solution satisfying the boundary condition

$$U \big|_S = 0$$

is of the form

$$U = \mathfrak{N} F .$$

The class of solutions just mentioned can be described as follows. Let $R_1(\overline{V})$ be a ring characterized by the properties

(i) $R_1(\overline{V}) \subset \overline{R}(\overline{V})$,

(ii) if $F \in R_1(\overline{V})$, then ΔF exists and belongs to $R(V)$.

We introduce on R_1 the norm

$$\| F \|_{R_1} = \sup_{\overline{V}} |F| + \sup_{\overline{V}} |\Delta F| .$$

Let $\overline{R}_1(\overline{V})$ be the closure of R_1 according to this norm. Then $F \in \overline{R}(\overline{V})$ implies $\mathfrak{N} F \in \overline{R}_1(\overline{V})$.

We still note that, under the conditions of Theorem 5.1.2, the same operator $\mathfrak{N}$ can be expressed as

$$\mathfrak{N} F = \mathfrak{M} \int_0^{\rho_x[y]} rF[x+ry]\, dr . \qquad (15')$$

This can be proved using the reasoning of Subsection 5.1.2 when we changed over from (4) to (5). Furthermore, we have to take into account that the operations $\mathfrak{M}$ and $\int_0^{\rho} \ldots dr$ are interchangeable in the case considered here.

<u>5.1.6</u>. Theorems 5.1.1 and 5.1.2 remain valid in other function spaces, too. The difference consists in the conditions which have to be imposed upon the growth of $g(\xi, t)$ with respect to the variables ξ . For instance, if the space under consideration is $C[q]$ and F is a functional of the form (1), it is sufficient for g to be continuous on $E_m \times \overline{Q}_m$ and that, for some $\varepsilon > 0$,

$$|g(\xi_1,\ldots,\xi_m;t_1,\ldots,t_m)| < Ae^{a|\xi|^{2-\varepsilon}} + b(t) ,$$

where $A,a>0$, $b(t)\in L(Q_m)$, $b(t)>0$.

Under these conditions, F is continuous on the whole $C[\bar{q}]$ and bounded on any ball $\|x\|<R$. The means described above exist, and all the lemmas used above remain valid. Finally, it is not hard to understand that the boundary conditions are also fulfilled.

5.2. The fundamental functional of a surface S

Although the formulae obtained which yield solutions of the functional Dirichlet problem and Poisson's equation in the space L^2 were written above in an explicit form but without knowledge of the functional $s[x]$ (i.e., in essence, without knowledge of $\Gamma[x]$), it is impossible to regard these equations as completely solved. Meanwhile, until now the only values of $s[x]$ that have been studied have been those for the ellipsoid and, more particularly, for the sphere. This gap will be filled up now, and a general method will be demonstrated below for finding the functional s , starting from the equation of the surface S . In particular, it will be shown that both of the problems considered are effectively solvable in the space L^2 if S is an "algebraic" surface of any order.

The ideas are contained in the following. First of all, we establish the validity of conditions (4°) and (5°) from Section 5.1 for the case when the U which appears in the equation $U[x]=0$ of the surface S is a polynomial in $\|x\|^2$ with harmonic coefficients. At the same time, it will be proved that the problem of finding the functional s thereby reduces to the solution of an algebraic equation (for any x). Then a general formula is derived that can be used to approximate functionals by similar polynomials. The fact that this approximation is possible enables us to verify conditions (4°) and (5°) even for "transcendental" surfaces.

5.2.1. Let again S be a closed convex surface situated in a finite part of the space L^2 , and let V be the set of its inner points. We assume that the functionals $\varrho_x[y]$ and $s[x]$ have the same meanings as in 5.1 and that they satisfy the same conditions (apart from conditions (4°) and (5°), which will be proved here).

We shall use V to denote any domain in L^2 which possesses the property that, for arbitrary x and y ($x\in V$ and $\|y\|=1$), the point $x+s[x]y$ belongs to V . Because $|s[x]|<d$, where $d=\sup\|z'-z''\|$ $(z',z''\in S)$ is the diameter of the surface S , we may assume that the domain V lies entirely in a finite part of the space L^2 .

Theorem 5.2.1. If the equation of the surface S is of the form

$$X^m + H_1[x]X^{m-1} + \dots + H_m[x] = 0 , \qquad (1)$$

where $X = \|x\|^2/2$ and $H_1,\dots,H_m$ are uniformly continuous harmonic functionals in the domain $\overline{V}$, then the conditions (4°) and (5°) from 5.1.1 are satisfied.

Proof. For any y, $\|y\|=1$, the point $x+\rho_x[y]y$ lies on the surface S. Therefore, introducing the notation $\rho_x[y]=\rho$, from equation (1) we have

$$\left(\frac{\|x+\rho y\|^2}{2}\right)^m + H_1[x+\rho y]\left(\frac{\|x+\rho y\|^2}{2}\right)^{m-1} + \dots + H_m[x+\rho y] = 0 . \qquad (2)$$

Averaging this equation over the sphere $\|y\|=1$ and taking into account the multiplicativity of the operation $\mathfrak{M}$, we obtain

$$\left(\frac{\mathfrak{M}\|x+\rho y\|^2}{2}\right)^m + \mathfrak{M}H_1[x+\rho y]\left(\frac{\mathfrak{M}\|x+\rho y\|^2}{2}\right)^{m-1} + \dots$$

$$\dots + \mathfrak{M}H_m[x+\rho y] = 0 . \qquad (3)$$

But

$$\frac{1}{2}\mathfrak{M}\|x+\rho y\|^2 = \frac{1}{2}\mathfrak{M}(\|x\|^2+2\rho(x,y)+\rho^2\|y\|^2)$$

$$= \frac{\|x\|^2}{2} + \frac{1}{2}(\mathfrak{M}\rho)^2 = X + T[x] , \qquad (4)$$

where $T = s^2[x]/2$. Because $s\in\{S\}$, $\rho_x[y]=s[x]$ almost everywhere on the sphere $\|y\|=1$, under the conditions imposed on the functionals H_k and in view of Lemma 3.2.1, we have

$$\mathfrak{M}H_k[x+\rho_x[y]y] = \mathfrak{M}H_k[x+s[x]y] . \qquad (5)$$

From the definition of the domain V it follows that, for any fixed value of x, we can find an $\varepsilon(x)>0$ such that $H_k[x+s[x]y]=\Phi[y]$ is a harmonic functional on the ball $\|y\|<1+\varepsilon$ containing the sphere $\|y\|=1$. Consequently

$$\mathfrak{M}H_k[x+s[x]y] = \mathfrak{M}\Phi[y] = \Phi[0] = H_k[x] \qquad (6)$$

Taking into account (4)-(6) and using the notation introduced above, we may rewrite (3) in the form

$$(X+T)^m + H_1[x](X+T)^{m-1} + \dots + H_m[x] = 0 . \qquad (7)$$

We shall consider, along with (7), the equation

$$\mu^m + \mu^{m-1}H_1[x] + \dots + H_m[x] = 0 , \qquad (8)$$

which will be called the characteristic equation of the surface S. Generally speaking, equation (8) defines a multi-valued functional

$$\mu[x] = \Psi(H_1[x], \dots, H_m[x]) . \tag{9}$$

We shall prove that any branch of this functional is a harmonic functional in the domain V. This may be done by two methods.

1) Let $\Omega_{x,\lambda}$ be an arbitrary sphere in V, and let $p(H_1, \dots, H_m)$ be some polynomial in $H_1, \dots, H_m$. We consider the functional

$$P[x] = p(H_1, \dots, H_m) . \tag{10}$$

It follows immediately from the ring property of the symbol $\mathfrak{M}$ that the functional P is harmonic:

$$\mathfrak{M} P[x+\lambda y] = p(\mathfrak{M} H_1[x+\lambda y], \dots, \mathfrak{M} H_m[x+\lambda y]) = P[x] .$$

Let D be the range of values of the functionals $H_1, \dots, H_m$ on the sphere $\Omega_{x,\lambda}$. This range is bounded because each of the functionals H_k is uniformly continuous and therefore bounded on any sphere lying in the domain V. Thus, the functional (9) may be uniformly approximated on the sphere Ω_n by a sequence of functionals $P_n[x]$ each of which is a polynomial in $H_1, \dots, H_m$ and such that $\mathfrak{M} P_n[x+\lambda y] = P_n[x]$. Consequently, in view of (9),

$$\mathfrak{M} \mu[x+\lambda y] = \mathfrak{M} \lim_n P_n[x+\lambda y] = \lim_n \mathfrak{M} P_n[x+\lambda y] = \mu[x] .$$

2) Because of Lévy's theorem (3.2.2), we have $H_k[x+\lambda y] = \mathfrak{M} H_k[x+\lambda y]$ almost everywhere on the sphere $\|y\|=1$. But $\mathfrak{M} H_k[x+\lambda y] = H_k[x]$. Hence the relation $H_k[x+\lambda y] = H_k[x]$ also holds almost everywhere on this sphere. Thus

$$\mu(H_1[x+\lambda y], \dots, H_m[x+\lambda y]) = \mu(H_1[x], \dots, H_m[x])$$

a.e. on $\|y\|=1$ and

$$\mathfrak{M} \mu(H_1[x+\lambda y], \dots, H_m[x+\lambda y]) = \mu(H_1[x], \dots, H_m[x]) ,$$

$$\mathfrak{M} \Psi[x+\lambda y] = \Psi[x] .$$

Because S is a convex surface, the functional $\rho_x[y]$ has a unique value for any fixed x and y. Therefore $\mathfrak{M} \rho_x[y] = s[x]$ also has a unique and, moreover, real and positive value for every $x \in V$. Since equation (8) is a consequence of equation (1) which defines the surface S, there exists a unique branch of the functional (7) for which the functional $s[x]$, defined by the equation $X+T=\mu$, has a real positive value.

We shall denote this branch by $\frac{1}{2}\Gamma$. Thus $X+T = \frac{1}{2}\Gamma$ or, using the notation previously introduced, $\|x\|^2+s^2[x] = \Gamma[x]$.

Furthermore, equation (8) holds for $x \in V$ and equation (1) is valid for $x \in S$. Combining these equations and taking into account the continuity of all relevant functionals on the set $\bar{V}=V \cup S$, for $x \in S$ we obtain $T[x]=0$, which means that $s[x]=0$ if $x \in S$. The theorem is proved.

A simple, but nontrivial example of an algebraic surface of the type considered here provides the ellipsoid $\|kx\|=1$, where k is a bounded measurable function and $\|k\| \neq 0$. In this case

$$\Gamma = \|k\|^{-2} (1+ \|k\|^2 \|x\|^2 - \|kx\|^2) \ . \tag{11}$$

The proof that this ellipsoid is bounded, closed and convex is the same as for an n-dimensional ellipsoid. It is clear that the surface is algebraic, since its equation may, by virtue of (11), be rewritten in the form $X-\Gamma=0$. From the Gâteaux formula (3) of Section 3.3 it follows that the functional Γ is harmonic (it is obvious that $\Delta\Gamma=0$).

The preceding theorem can be generalized by approximating a continuous functional in the space L^2 by harmonic functionals and powers of $\|x\|$. In this connection we mention the following result.

Proposition 5.2.1.[1] Let V_R be the ball $\|x\| < R$ and $U[x] \in \bar{R}(\bar{V}_R)$ be a functional which is uniformly continuous on V_R . Furthermore, let the Dirichlet problem on $S \in \{S\}$ with the boundary values $U[x]$ be solvable. Then there exists a sequence of polynomials of the form

$$P_n[x] = H_0[x]X^n + H_1[x]X^{n-1} + \dots + H_n[x] \ , \tag{12}$$

$X=\|x\|^2/2$, $H_i \in \bar{R}(\bar{V}_R)$, $H_i \in \mathfrak{X}(V_R)$, $i=0,1,\dots,n$, such that

$$P_n[x] \rightrightarrows U[x] \ , \ x \in \bar{V}_R \ .$$

The classical Weierstrass theorem on the approximation of a continuous function by polynomials is a very simple case of this proposition and is obtained from it when $U=f(X)$, where f is a continuous function on the interval $0 \leq X \leq R^2/2$. In this case $H_1,\dots,H_n$ reduce to constants.

The statement of the following lemma differs only a little from that described above. It is presented here, however, as it seems to us to be of special interest.

---

[1] Compare with POLISHCHUK [3], where an analogous theorem is given on pp. 198-200.

As a preliminary we note the following. Let $U[x]$ be a functional defined on the ball $\overline{V}_R$. We write down the formal expansion

$$U[x] \sim \sum_{\nu=0}^{\infty} (\varrho - X)^{\nu} H_{\nu}[x], \tag{13}$$

where $\varrho = R^2/2$ and H_{ν} are functionals which are harmonic for $x \in V_R$.

Since $\Delta H_{\nu} = 0$ and $\Delta(\varrho - X)^{\nu} = (-1)^{\nu} \nu (\varrho - X)^{\nu - 1}$ (the latter relation results from equation (11) of Section 4.1), it follows that, applying the operator Δ term by term to the series (13) and designating the operation which yields the solution of the Dirichlet problem for the sphere $X = \varrho$ as $\mathfrak{M}^s$, we have

$$H_{\nu}[x] = (-1)^{\nu} \frac{\mathfrak{M}^s \Delta^{\nu} U}{\nu!} \tag{14}$$

for $X < \varrho$. Consequently

$$U[x] \sim \sum_{\nu=0}^{m} (-1)^{\nu} \frac{(\varrho - X)^{\nu}}{\nu!} \mathfrak{M}^s \Delta^{\nu} U[x] + o(\varrho - X)^{m+1}. \tag{15}$$

The problem of the remainder term in the expansion (15) and of the representation of the functional U by the series (13) is solved in the following way.

Lemma 5.2.1. If the functionals $\Delta U, \ldots, \Delta^{m+1} U$ exist for $X < \varrho$ and are uniformly continuous for $X \leq \varrho$ and if, for any ν, $\nu = 1, \ldots, m$, the Dirichlet problem with the boundary conditions

$$H\big|_{X=\varrho} = \Delta^{\nu} U$$

is solvable, then

$$U[x] = \sum_{\nu=0}^{m} (-1)^{\nu} \frac{(\varrho - X)^{\nu}}{\nu!} \mathfrak{M}^s \Delta^{\nu} U + \frac{(-1)^{m+1}}{m!} \int_0^{\varrho - X} t^m \Psi[x|t]\,dt, \tag{16}$$

where

$$\Psi[x|t] = \mathfrak{M} \Delta^{m+1} U[x + \sqrt{2t}\, y].$$

Proof. We shall start from the formula

$$\mathfrak{M}_{x,s[x]} U = U + \sum_{\nu=1}^{m} \left(\frac{s^2[x]}{2}\right)^{\nu} \frac{\Delta^{\nu} U}{\nu!} + R_m \tag{17}$$

with

$$R_m = \frac{\mathfrak{M}}{2^m m!} \int_0^{s[x]} r(s^2[x] - r^2)^m \Delta^{m+1} U[x + ry]\,dr, \tag{18}$$

which was proved in POLISHCHUK [2] for the space l_2 under analogous conditions. As mentioned in Section 4.2, the Laplacians in the spaces l_2 and L^2 coincide, if in L^2 a uniformly dense basis is chosen, which is always admissible. Hence, equation (17) is correct in the space L^2, too (in POLISHCHUK [2] the formula in question was established for any surface S of the type $\{S\}$; here it is needed only for the sphere). Recalling that

$$s[x] = \sqrt{R^2 - \|x\|^2}$$

for the sphere $\|x\|=R$, changing the variable in the integral (18) and using our notations, we may rewrite (17) as

$$\mathfrak{M}_{x,s[x]}U = \mathfrak{M}^s U =$$

$$U + \sum_{\nu=1}^{m} (\rho - X)^{\nu} \frac{\Delta^{\nu} U}{\nu!} + \frac{1}{m!} \int_0^{\rho - X} (\rho - X - t)^m \, \Psi[x|t] \, dt . \qquad (18^0)$$

Replacing here U successively by $\Delta U, \dots, \Delta^m U$ and reducing the number of terms on the right-hand side of (18^0) by unity every time, we obtain the following system of equations:

$$\mathfrak{M}^s \Delta U = \Delta U + \sum_{\nu=1}^{m-1} (\rho - X)^{\nu} \frac{\Delta^{\nu} U}{\nu!} + \frac{1}{(m-1)!} \int_0^{\rho - X} (\rho - X - t)^{m-1} \, \Psi[x|t] dt, \qquad (18^1)$$

$$\mathfrak{M}^s \Delta^2 U = \Delta^2 U + \sum_{\nu=1}^{m-2} (\rho - X)^{\nu} \frac{\Delta^{\nu} U}{\nu!} + \frac{1}{(m-2)!} \int_0^{\rho - X} (\rho - X - t)^{m-2} \, \Psi[x|t] dt, \qquad (18^2)$$

. . . .

$$\mathfrak{M}^s \Delta^m U = \Delta^m U + \int_0^{\rho - X} \Psi[x|t] \, dt . \qquad (18^m)$$

Multiplying equations $(18^0), \dots, (18^m)$, respectively, by $(-1)^{\nu} \frac{(\rho - X)^{\nu}}{\nu!}$, $\nu = 0, 1, \dots, m$, and adding them, we observe that the coefficients of $\Delta^{\nu} U$ $(1 \leq \nu \leq m-1)$ in the resulting sum are zero. The coefficient of $\Delta^m F$ is also zero. In fact, taking $(\rho - X)^m$ out of the brackets, we have $\sum_{\nu=0}^{m} (-1)^{\nu} C_m^{\nu} = 0$ in the brackets.

In each of the equations $(18^0), \dots, (18^m)$ we put the factor $(\rho - X)^{\nu}/\nu!$ under the integral sign. Then, after adding all the integrals, we get

$$\frac{1}{m!} \int_0^{\rho - X} \sum_{\nu=0}^{m-1} (-1)^{\nu} C_m^{\nu} (\rho - X - t)^{\nu} (\rho - X)^{m-\nu} \, \Psi[x|t] dt = \frac{(-1)^m}{m!} \int_0^{\rho - X} t^m \, \Psi[x|t] dt.$$

Thus equation (16) is proved.

Furthermore, the validity of the equation

$$\lim_m \frac{(-1)^m}{m!} \int_0^{\rho - X} t^m \, \Psi[x|t] dt = 0$$

uniformly for $X \leq \rho$ provides a condition that the functional H may be expanded in a uniformly convergent series of the form (13) (if, as was stipulated, all $\Delta^{\nu} U$ exist and $H_{\nu} = \mathfrak{M}^s \Delta^{\nu} U$ is a harmonic

functional and $H_\nu = \Delta^\nu U$ for $X = \varrho$).
The sum in (18^0) may be rearranged in powers of X to give

$$\sum_{\nu=0}^{m} \ldots = \Gamma_o + \Gamma_1 X + \ldots + \Gamma_m X^m , \qquad (19)$$

where Γ_i are harmonic functionals. If the equation of the surface S is given in the form $U[x]=0$ and the functional U satisfies the conditions of Lemma 5.2.1, then, approximating U by parts of the series (13), it is possible to find the functional $s[x]$ associated with the surface from the characteristic equation (8) and, by the same token, to obtain an approximate value of $s[x]$ for the surface S.

A more detailed justification of this statement will be given in the next subsection.

5.2.2. In order to find the functional $s[x]$ corresponding to the surface S, starting from its equation in the form $U[x]=0$, it is necessary to know its "polar equation" $\varrho = \varrho_x[y]$. Since ϱ satisfies the equation $U[x+\varrho y]=0$, the theorem on the existence of an implicit functional may be used. This theorem is a particular case of the following theorem on the existence of an abstract implicit functional.

Theorem 5.2.2 (KANTOROVICH and AKILOV [1]). Let the variables x_1, x_2 and x_3 lie in the Banach spaces X_1, X_2 and X_3, respectively. Furthermore, assume z to be a nonlinear operator mapping $X_1 \times X_2 \times X_3$ onto the Banach space Z, and let O_Z be the null element in Z. Then to solve the equation

$$z(x_1, x_2, x_3) = O_Z$$

relative to x_3 in a neighbourhood of the point (x_1^o, x_2^o, x_3^o) with $z(x_1^o, x_2^o, x_3^o) = O_Z$, it is necessary that the operation

$$z'_{x_3}(x_1^o, x_2^o, x_3^o) \in \{X_3 \longrightarrow Z\}$$

(z'_{x_3} denotes the Fréchet derivative with respect to x_3 in Z) should have an inverse

$$(z'_{x_3}(x_1^o, x_2^o, x_3^o))^{-1} \in \{Z \longrightarrow X_3\} . \qquad (20)$$

The continuity of z implies that the operator function $x_3 = x_3(x_1, x_2)$ is also continuous. In addition, the operator x_3 is uniquely defined by (20).

Returning to the equation $U[x+\varrho y]=0$, we note that in our case ϱ and U are scalar variables and the Fréchet derivative z'_{x_3} means $\partial U/\partial\varrho$. Thus, in order to solve this equation with respect to ϱ

in the neighbourhood of the values ρ_o, x_o, y_o it is sufficient that the partial derivative $\partial U[x+\rho y]/\partial\rho$ should exist and be nonzero for these values.

Let us consider a closed convex surface S given by the equation $U[x] = 0$ as well as a sequence of convex surfaces S_n defined via the equations $U_n[x] = 0$. The domains bounded by the surfaces S and S_n are denoted by V and V_n, respectively. Without loss of generality these domains are assumed to be described by the inequalities $U[x] < 0$ and $U_n[x] < 0$. We shall also assume that the functionals U and U_n are continuous on the sets $\overline{V} = V \cup S$ and $\overline{V}_n = V_n \cup S$. The surfaces S_n are said to be uniformly convergent to S if, for any $x \in V$ and $\mathcal{E} > 0$, the following conditions are satisfied for some value of n onwards:

(i) $x \in V_n$,

(ii) $| U[x] - U_n[x] | < \mathcal{E}$ for $x \in \overline{V \cap V_n}$

(the bar is used to denote the closure in the metric of L^2).

In order to find the "polar" functionals $\rho = \rho_x[y]$ and $\rho_n = \rho_{nx}[y]$ of the surfaces S and S_n from the equations $U[x+\rho y]=0$ and $U_n[x+\rho_n y]=0$, it is necessary that the derivatives $\frac{\partial U}{\partial \rho}$ and $\frac{\partial U_n}{\partial \rho}$ exist and be nonzero for $x+\rho y \in V$ and $x+\rho_n y \in V_n$.

From the theorem on the existence and continuity of an implicit function we conclude that the sequence $\rho_{nx}[y]$ converges uniformly to $\rho_x[y]$ with respect to x and with respect to y. In this case

$$\lim \mathfrak{M} \rho_{nx}[y] = \mathfrak{M} \rho_x[y]$$

also converges uniformly, or, what is the same thing,

$$s_n[x] \rightrightarrows s[x] , \quad x \in \overline{V} . \qquad (21)$$

We now suppose that S_n are surfaces of type $\{S\}$ and, hence, $s_n = \sqrt{\Gamma_n - \|x\|^2}$, where the $\Gamma_n[x]$ are harmonic functionals in V_n. From (21) it follows that on the set $\overline{V}$, $\Gamma_n[x] \rightrightarrows \Gamma[x]$. Consequently, Γ is also a harmonic functional.

Let $z \in S$, $z_n \in S_n$ and $z_n \longrightarrow z$. Since $s_n[z_n]=0$, from equation (21) and the continuity of s on the set S we get

$$s[z] = \lim_n s_n[z] = \lim_n s_n[z_n] = 0 .$$

In fact, we are able to formulate the following result:

Let S be a closed convex surface given by the equation $U[x] = 0$, and let S_n be a sequence of convex surfaces defined via the equations

$U_n[x] = 0$, which uniformly approximate the surface S . If the functionals U and U_n are continuous on the sets $\overline{V}$ and $\overline{V}_n$ and if the S_n are surfaces of type $\{S\}$, then S is also a surface of type $\{S\}$.

5.3. Examples

We intend to consider two interesting examples. The first is peculiar in that the solution of Dirichlet's problem is obtained using only one algebraic operation and the solution of Poisson's equation can be found via algebraic operations and quadrature. The second is related to the eigenvalues and eigenfunctionals of the operators $\mathfrak{M}^s$ and $\mathfrak{N}$ studied above.

5.3.1. Let the Dirichlet problem be posed in the form

$$F[x] = \sum_{i=0}^{n} G_i[x] \; \varphi_i(X) \; , \tag{1}$$

where $X=\|x\|^2/2$, the φ_i are continuous functions for $0 \leq X \leq d^2/2$, d is the diameter of the domain V , and the G_i are harmonic functionals continuous on the set $\overline{V} = V \cup S$. The surface S is of type $\{S\}$ and is given by the equation

$$\sum_{k=0}^{m} H_k[x] \; X^k = 0 \; , \tag{2}$$

where the H_k are harmonic functionals satisfying the conditions of Theorem 5.1.1.

The required harmonic functional H , which takes values equal to F on S , is defined by the equation

$$H = \mathfrak{M}^s F \; .$$

Using the ring properties of the operator $\mathfrak{M}^s$, we obtain

$$\mathfrak{M}^s F = \sum_i \mathfrak{M}^s G_i[x] \; \mathfrak{M}^s \varphi_i(X) \; .$$

The functionals G_i are harmonic, so that

$$\mathfrak{M}^s G_i[x] = G_i[x] \; .$$

It is easy to prove (initially for polynomials and later, by passing to the limit, for any continuous function) that

$$\mathfrak{M}^s \varphi_i(X) = \varphi_i(X + \frac{s^2[x]}{2}) \; .$$

Since $s=\sqrt{\Gamma - \|x\|^2}$, we can write $\mathfrak{M}^s \varphi_i = \varphi_i(\Gamma/2)$. Thus the solution can be finally written in the form

$$H[x] = \sum_i G_i[x]\, \varphi_i(\Gamma[x]/2) .$$

5.3.2. For the same surface S, the solution of the problem

$$\Delta U = F, \quad U\big|_S = 0$$

with F being a functional (1) is of the form

$$U = - \sum_i G_i[x] \int_{\chi}^{\frac{1}{2}\Gamma[x]} \varphi_i(t)dt .$$

5.3.3. We shall solve the Dirichlet problem under the conditions $S \in \{S\}$ and

$$F[x] = \int_{Q_m} \!\!\cdots\! \int k(t_1,\ldots,t_m) \Big\{ \prod_{j=1} \exp\,(i\,\lambda_j(t_1,\ldots,t_m)x(t_j))\Big\} dt_1 \ldots dt_m, \quad (3)$$

where the function $k(t_1,\ldots,t_m)$ is summable in the cube Q_m and the functions λ_j are measurable in this cube.

The generating function for this functional, namely

$$g(\xi,t) = k(t_1,\ldots,t_m) \prod_j \exp\,(i\,\lambda_j(t_1,\ldots,t_m)\,\xi_j) ,$$

ensures the existence of F in the whole space L^2.

Denoting the unknown functional by H, we obtain

$$H[x] = \mathfrak{M}^s F =$$

$$\mathfrak{M} \int_{Q_m} \!\!\cdots\! \int k(t_1,\ldots,t_m) \Big\{ \prod_j \exp\big(i\lambda_j(t_1,\ldots,t_m)(x(t_j)+s[x]y(t_j))\big)\Big\} dt_1 \ldots dt_m =$$

$$\frac{1}{(\sqrt{2\pi})^m} \int_{Q_m} \!\!\cdots\! \int k(t_1,\ldots,t_m) \Big\{ \int \!\cdots\! \int \prod_j \exp\big(i\,\lambda_j(t_1,\ldots,t_m)(x(t_j)+s[x]\,\xi_j)\big)$$

$$\cdot \exp(-\xi_j^2/2)\, d\xi_1 \ldots d\xi_m \Big\} dt_1 \ldots dt_m .$$

Using the well-known relation

$$\int \exp(iv\xi)\exp(-\xi^2/2)d\xi = \sqrt{2\pi}\,\exp(-v^2/2) ,$$

we may write

$$H[x] = \int_{Q_m} \!\!\cdots\! \int k(t_1,\ldots,t_m) \prod_j \exp(i\,\lambda_j(t_1,\ldots,t_m)x(t_j))\cdot$$

$$\cdot \exp(-\,s^2[x]\,\lambda_j^2(t_1,\ldots,t_m)/2)dt_1 \ldots dt_m . \quad (4)$$

Let the functions $\lambda_j(t_1,\dots,t_m)$ map the cube Q_m onto the sphere S_R: $\lambda_1^2+\dots+\lambda_m^2=R^2$. Then the preceding equation takes the form

$$\mathfrak{M}^s F = F \exp(- R^2 s^2/2) \ . \tag{5}$$

5.3.4. Let us solve the Poisson equation $\Delta U=F[x]$, where $F[x]$ is a functional defined by equation (3). From Theorem 5.1.2 we get

$$U = - \mathfrak{N} F = \int_0^{s[x]} r\, \mathfrak{M} F[x+ry]\,dr = \int_{Q_m}\!\!\dots\!\int k(t_1,\dots,t_m) \times$$

$$\frac{\exp(-\frac{s^2}{2} \sum_j \lambda_j^2(t_1,\dots,t_m))-1}{\sum_j \lambda_j^2(t_1,\dots,t_m)} \prod_j \exp(i\lambda_j(t_1,\dots,t_m)x(t_j)dt_1\dots dt_m \ .$$

If λ is a point on the sphere S_R , then

$$U = - \mathfrak{N} F = \frac{\exp(\frac{R^2 s^2}{2}) - 1}{R^2} F \ . \tag{6}$$

Equations (5) and (6) show that the functional F given by formula (3) is an eigenfunctional of the operators $\mathfrak{M}^s$ and $\mathfrak{N}$ corresponding to the eigenvalues

$$\exp(- R^2 s^2/2) \quad \text{and} \quad -R^{-2}(\exp(R^2 s^2/2)-1) \ ,$$

respectively.

Equations (5) and (6) also enable us to draw the following conclusion concerning the functional (3). It is possible to find $s[x]$ directly from (3) and (5) or (3) and (6). If S is the ellipsoid $\|kx\|=1$, then we can solve the "inverse problem of potential theory" in L^2 : knowing the density F and the "potential" $\mathfrak{M}^s F$ (or $\mathfrak{N} F$), the surface S can be reconstructed.

Actually, for the mentioned ellipsoid, we have

$$s[x] = \|k\|^{-1} \sqrt{1-\|kx\|^2} \ ,$$

and if the function k is normed, i.e. $\|k\|=1$, the given $s[x]$ determines the surface S uniquely.

5.4. The maximum principle and uniqueness of solutions

Since, for any $x \in V$, the relation $x+ \varrho_x[y]y=z \in S$ holds, the equation $H[x] = \mathfrak{M} F[x+ \varrho_x[y]y]$ shows that the obtained solution of the Dirichlet problem (Theorem 5.1.1') is the spherical mean of the boundary values of

F on S . Moreover, according to $H|_S = F$, we also have

$$\sup_V |H| \leq \sup_S |F| = \sup_S |H| .$$

Therefore, similarly to the classical theory of harmonic functions of n variables, H cannot attain its extremal values inside of the set V .

This yields directly the uniqueness of solutions of the boundary problem

$$\Delta U = Q[x] , \quad U|_S = 0 ; \quad Q \in \bar{R}(\bar{V}) , \quad S \in \{S\} ,$$

because if U_1 and U_2 are two solutions, then $U_1 - U_2$ is a solution of the Dirichlet problem with zero boundary values.

5.5. The exterior Dirichlet problem

We study the exterior Dirichlet problem in the space L^2 . Given a surface S it is required to find a functional H which is harmonic outside this surface and takes prescribed values on it. Note that the classical method of inversion for solving the exterior problem in a finite-dimensional space is not applicable here.

Instead, we use other concepts and show that the solution of this problem also may be obtained with the help of the operator $\mathfrak{M}_{x,s[x]}$, where, however, in the present case s is an imaginary variable. As long as $H = \mathfrak{M}_{x,s[x]}F$ is an even function of s , the functional H remains real. In accordance with this, all averaging will be carried out over a sphere of imaginary radius when we consider exterior problems. This means that the equation

$$\mathfrak{M}_{x,i\lambda} F = \mathfrak{M} F[x+i\lambda y] \tag{1}$$

holds true and harmonic functionals outside S will be subjected to the requirement

$$\mathfrak{M} H[x+i\lambda y] = H[x] . \tag{2}$$

More precisely, it will be shown that equation (2) is satisfied for the corresponding integral representation outside S and that H takes the given values F on S .

The definition of the surface S is refined in the following way: S is said to be a surface of type $\{S\}$, if S is a closed convex surface given by the equation $U[x]=0$, where U is a functional which is defined and uniformly continuous on any sphere $\|x\| < r$ in the space L^2 . Moreover, $U[x] < 0$ for interior (in relation to S) points x and $U[x] > 0$ for exterior points x.

Besides this, with a surface of type $\{S\}$ we associate a functional $s[x]$ uniformly continuous on any sphere $\|x\| < r$ and defined in the following way:

$$s[x] = \mathfrak{M} \varrho_x[y] = \sqrt{\Gamma[x] - \|x\|^2}$$

(cf. 5.1.1) if $x \in V$, and $s=0$ if $x \in S$. For exterior points, s is defined by the equation

$$s[x] = \sqrt{\tilde{\Gamma}[x] - \|x\|^2}, \qquad (3)$$

where $\tilde{\Gamma}$ is a harmonic functional outside the surface S being a continuous extension of Γ beyond the set S and satisfying the condition

$$\tilde{\Gamma}[x] - \|x\|^2 < 0, \quad x \in \tilde{V}.$$

By reason of what was said above, the functional s may, in the whole space, be written in the form

$$s[x] = \theta[x] \sqrt{-U[x]},$$

where θ is a functional defined and uniformly continuous on any sphere $\|x\| < r$ and takes only positive values.

As an example we may cite the ellipsoid $\|kx\| = 1$ mentioned above. For this ellipsoid we have

$$V: \ \|kx\| - 1 < 0, \quad \tilde{V}: \ \|kx\| - 1 > 0$$

and

$$s[x] = \|k\|^{-1} \sqrt{1 - \|kx\|^2}, \quad \theta[x] = \|k\|^{-1} = \text{const}.$$

The extension of the functional Γ onto the domain $\tilde{V}$ is clearly not unique, and we restrict ourselves to showing how for a class of "algebraic surfaces" (see 5.2) it is possible to select a "principal" extension Γ.

Let us suppose that S is given by equation (1) of Section 5.2:

$$X^m + H_1[x] X^{m-1} + \ldots + H_m[x] = 0.$$

Then we write the "characteristic equation" of this surface:

$$\mu^m + H_1[x] \mu^{m-1} + \ldots + H_m[x] = 0.$$

Any branch of the functional $\mu[x]$ determined by this equation is a harmonic functional in the domain V and vanishes on the surface S. In addition, we now assume that there exists a unique real branch

$\tilde{\mu}[x] = \tilde{\Gamma}$ of this functional such that $\tilde{\Gamma} < \|x\|^2$ for $x \in V$. This branch is taken as the principal extension of the functional Γ. In the sequel, we simply write Γ in place of $\tilde{\Gamma}$.

The solution of the exterior problem that is constructed below contains integrals of the generating function g of the functional F giving boundary values along straight lines parallel to the imaginary axes. This requires additional restrictions to be imposed on g.

We shall say that $g(\xi, t)$, $\xi \in E_m$, $t \in Q_m$ is a <u>function of class</u> $\{A\}$ in the variables ξ if, for almost all $t \in Q_m$, it can be extended with respect to the variables ξ_k, $k=1,\ldots,m$, into an m-dimensional complex plane $w_k = \xi_k + i\theta_k$ in such a way that $g(w_1,\ldots,w_m;\theta_1,\ldots,\theta_m)$ is an analytic function in all variables w_k and, for any number $a > 0$, the estimate

$$|g(\xi_1 + i\theta_1, \ldots, \xi_m + i\theta_m)| = o(|\theta_k| \exp(-\theta_k^2/2))$$

holds for $|\theta_k| \to \infty$, $k=1,\ldots,m$, in the strip $-a < \xi_k < a$ uniformly with respect to all other arguments on which the function $g(w_1,\ldots,w_m;\theta_1,\ldots,\theta_m)$ depends (see HIRSCHMAN and WIDDER [1], p. 180, where $m=1$).

<u>Theorem 5.5.1</u>. Let S be a surface of the type $\{S\}$ and F be the Gâteaux functional

$$F[x] = \int \cdots \int_{Q_m} g(x(t_1),\ldots,x(t_m);t_1,\ldots,t_m)dt_1\ldots dt_m . \tag{4}$$

We suppose that the generating function $g(\xi_1,\ldots,\xi_m;t_1,\ldots,t_m)$ of this functional fulfils all the conditions of Theorem 5.1.1. If, moreover, g belongs to class $\{A\}$ with respect to the variables ξ, then for $x \in \bar{V}$, there exists a $\lambda_0 = \lambda_0[x]$ such that, for any $0 < \lambda < \lambda_0$, the functional $H[x] = \mathfrak{M}_{x,S[x]}F$ satisfies the relations

$$\mathfrak{M}H[x+i\lambda y] = H[x]$$

and

$$\lim_{x \to z} H[x] = F[z] .$$

<u>Remark</u>. First of all, the theorem just stated will be proved for the case when the points x fill up some layer in $\tilde{V}$ the inner boundary of which is the surface S. After that a procedure will be indicated that permits the solution H obtained to be extended beyond the boundary of this layer. At the same time, an upper estimate for all λ_0 occurring in the formulation of the theorem will be derived.

<u>Proof</u>. For convenience of presentation, we examine the case $m=1$, $g=g(\xi)$, i.e. $F = \int_0^1 g(x(t))dt$.

Because of the Gâteaux formula, we have

$$H[x] = \frac{1}{\sqrt{2\pi}} \int_0^1 dt \int g(x(t)+s[x]\xi)\exp(-\xi^2/2)d\xi . \tag{5}$$

The latter equation can be written in the form

$$H[x] = \frac{1}{\sqrt{2\pi}} \int_0^1 dt \int g(x(t)+i\tilde{s}[x]\xi)\exp(-\xi^2/2)d\xi . \tag{6}$$

Here $\tilde{s}$ denotes the real quantity

$$\tilde{s}[x] = \sqrt{\|x\|^2 - \Gamma[x]} , \quad x \in \tilde{V} .$$

Lemma 5.5.1. If $g(\xi) \in \{A\}$, then the integral

$$\int_{d-i\infty}^{d+i\infty} g(w)\exp(\frac{(w-\eta)^2}{4\tau})dw$$

exists for $0 < \tau < 1$, $-\infty < \eta < \infty$ and does not depend on the value of d (for the proof, see HIRSCHMAN and WIDDER [1], p. 180).

According to this lemma, the functional (5) may be represented in the form

$$H[x] = \frac{1}{i\tilde{s}[x]\sqrt{2\pi}} \int_0^1 dt \int_{-i\infty}^{i\infty} g(w)\exp(\frac{(w-x(t))^2}{2\tilde{s}^2[x]})dw , \tag{7}$$

where the last integral exists if

$$0 < \tilde{s}^2[x] < 2 .$$

Using (7), we describe the expression $H[x+i\lambda y]$ and apply the operation $\mathfrak{M}$ to both sides of the resulting equation. Employing the Gâteaux formula and arguing analogously as in the proof of Theorem 5.1.1, we obtain

$$\mathfrak{M} H[x+i\lambda y] =$$

$$\frac{1}{2\pi i\tilde{s}_\lambda \lambda} \int_0^1 dt \int \left\{ \int_{-i\infty}^{i\infty} g(w)\exp(\frac{(w-x(t)-i\alpha)^2}{2\tilde{s}_\lambda^2})dw \right\} \exp(-\frac{\alpha^2}{2\lambda^2})d\alpha , \tag{8}$$

where (see Lemma 5.1.1)

$$\tilde{s}_\lambda^2 = \mathfrak{M}\tilde{s}^2[x+i\lambda y] =$$

$$\mathfrak{M}\|x+i\lambda y\|^2 - \mathfrak{M}\Gamma[x+i\lambda y] = \|x\|^2 - \Gamma[x] - \lambda^2 = \tilde{s}^2 - \lambda^2 . \tag{9}$$

On the basis of Lemma 5.5.1, the functional (7) exists if

$$0 < \tilde{s}_\lambda^2 < 2 . \tag{10}$$

After some elementary transformations, which are accomplished by use of (9) and the formula

$$\int \exp(-iv\alpha)\exp(-\frac{\alpha^2}{2\sigma^2})d\alpha = \sigma\sqrt{2\pi}\exp(-v^2\sigma^2/2) ,$$

we obtain

$$\mathfrak{M}H[x+i\lambda y] = \frac{1}{i\tilde{s}\sqrt{2\pi}}\int_0^1 dt \int_{-i\infty}^{i\infty} g(w)\exp(\frac{(w-x(t))^2}{2\tilde{s}^2})dw = H[x] .$$

Compared with the proof of Theorem 5.1.1 the proof of the relation $\lim_{x \to z} H[x] = F[z]$ does not require any significant changes.

In the case of an arbitrary functional of type (4) (if $m > 1$), all the reasoning is analogous.

The set of points for which the results derived above hold are characterized by inequality (10), which may be rewritten in the form

$$\Gamma[x] < \|x\|^2 < \Gamma[x]+2 .$$

We denote this "layer" by E_0 . Comparing (9) and (10), we see that $0 < \lambda < \lambda_0[x] < \tilde{s}[x]$, that is, $\sup_{E_0} \lambda_0 = \sqrt{2}$. It should be noted that this boundary depends neither on the functional F nor on the surface S . This concludes the proof of Theorem 5.5.1.

Now let S be a surface of type $\{S\}$ for which $s=s_1[x]=\sqrt{\|x\|^2-\Gamma_1[x]}$, where $\Gamma_1[x] = \Gamma[x]+2$. Applying the operation $\mathfrak{M}_{x,s_1[x]}$ to the functional F , we obtain a functional that is harmonic in the layer

$$\Gamma[x]+2 < \|x\|^2 < \Gamma[x]+4 .$$

Continuing this process, we extend H to the whole set $\tilde{V}$. It is not hard to see, however, that H will have discontinuities on the surfaces bounding these layers.

Under more restrictive conditions concerning the growth of $|g(w,t)|$, formula (7) represents a solution of the exterior Dirichlet problem even in the whole space L^2 . In this case we are able to state

<u>Theorem 5.5.2</u>. Let F be a functional of the form (4), the generating function $g(\xi,t)$ of which is continuous and bounded on the set $E_m \times Q_m$. Let, furthermore, the following conditions hold:

(i) For any $t \in Q_m$, the function $g(\xi,t)$ can be analytically continued with respect to the m variables ξ into an m-dimensional complex space $w_k = \xi_k + i\tau_k$, $k=1,\ldots,m$, as an entire function of the variables w_k .

(ii) There exist positive constants a and M such that

$$|g(w,t)| < M \exp(a(|w_1|+\ldots+|w_m|)) .$$

Then formula (7) yields a solution of the exterior Dirichlet problem.

Since simultaneously the conditions of Theorem 5.1.1 are also fulfilled, it follows that the right side of equation (7) represents a functional which is defined and harmonic in the whole space L^2.

We emphasize that there may be functionals harmonic and bounded in the whole space which are not constants (the functional $1/(1+l^2(x))$, where l is linear, provides a simple example). Thus, the well-known Liouville theorem on harmonic functions of a finite number of variables cannot be transferred to function spaces.

It is also common knowledge that a harmonic function whose values are all nonnegative reduces to a constant. For harmonic functionals this result fails to be valid, too.

5.6. The deviation H - F

Let V be a domain in a Hilbert space bounded by a surface S of the type $\{S\}$, and let H be the solution of the interior Dirichlet problem with boundary value $H = F$, where F is supposed to be known on the set $\overline{V} = V \cup S$. Under certain assumptions concerning the smoothness of F, we can go one step further and estimate the deviation $H - F$. Our smoothness assumptions suppose the existence of $\Delta^{\nu} F$ of all orders $\nu = 1,2,\ldots$. If the space in question is $L^2(a,b)$ and F is a Gâteaux functional with generating function $g(\xi,t)$, i.e. $F = \int_{Q_m} g(x,t)dt^m$, then $\Delta^{\nu} F = \int_{Q_m} \varphi_{\nu}(x,t)dt^m$, where $\varphi_{\nu}(\xi,t) = \Delta^{\nu}_{\xi} g(\xi,t)$ and Δ^{ν}_{ξ} are the iterated classical Laplace operators in E_m (see formula (10) of Section 4.1). Note that up to now we have not supposed the existence of the derivatives of $g(\xi,t)$ with respect to ξ. Moreover, for $\varphi_{\nu}(\xi,t)$ the conditions of existence of $\int_{Q_m} \varphi_{\nu}(x,t)dt^m$ now must be fulfilled.

It will be shown that, for every $\varepsilon > 0$, a layer $\Lambda_{\varepsilon} \subset \overline{V}$ bounded by two surfaces S and S_1 can be indicated such that

$$|H[x] - F[x]| < \varepsilon , \quad x \in \Lambda_{\varepsilon} . \tag{1}$$

The proof will be given for the sphere $S: \|x\| = R$, but it can be directly extended to an arbitrary surface $S \in \{S\}$. In the considered case, one has

$$\Lambda_{\varepsilon}: \sqrt{R^2 - u(\varepsilon)} \leq \|x\| \leq R ,$$

where $0 \leq u(\varepsilon) < R^2$, and the form of the function $u(\varepsilon)$ depends upon the restrictions on the growth of the sequence $|\Delta^{\nu} F|$, $x \in \overline{V}$, $\nu = 1,2,\ldots$.

5.6.1. We recall the formula

$$H = \mathfrak{M}^S F = F + \sum_{\nu=1}^{m} (\rho - X)^{\nu} \frac{\Delta^{\nu} F}{\nu!} + \mathcal{R}_m[x] ,$$

where

$$X = \frac{\|x\|^2}{2}, \quad \rho = \frac{R^2}{2}, \quad \mathcal{R}_m[x] = \frac{1}{m!} \int_0^{\rho - X} (\rho - X - t)^m \, \Psi[x|t] dt$$

and

$$\Psi[x|t] = \mathfrak{M} \Delta^{m+1} F[x + \sqrt{2t}\, y]$$

(see relations (17) and (18°) of Section 5.2). Let

$$|\Delta^{m+1} F[x + \sqrt{2t}\, y]| \leqslant (m+1)!\, M \frac{1}{R^{2m}} , \quad M = \text{const.}$$

Then, since $\mathfrak{M}$ is the averaging operation, we also have

$$|\Psi[x|t]| \leqslant (m+1)!\, M \frac{1}{R^{2m}} .$$

Hence, denoting $\rho - X = T$, we derive

$$|\mathcal{R}_m[x]| \leqslant \frac{(m+1)!}{m!} \frac{M}{R^{2m}} \int_0^T (T-t)^m dt = \frac{M}{R^{2m}} T^{m+1} \leqslant \frac{M R^2}{2^{m+1}} .$$

In this way, we see that the series

$$\sum_0^{\infty} \frac{T^{\nu}}{\nu!} \Delta^{\nu} F = e^{T\Delta} F \tag{2}$$

converges uniformly on $\bar{V}$. Applying the operator Δ term by term to (2), we get $\Delta e^{T\Delta} F = 0$. Since $T\big|_S = 0$, we conclude that

$$H = \sum_0^{\infty} \frac{T^{\nu}}{\nu!} \Delta^{\nu} F$$

represents the solution of Dirichlet's problem.

5.6.2. Now we specify two cases.

1) On the set $\bar{V}$, the inequality

$$|\Delta^{\nu} F| \leqslant M$$

holds. Then

$$|H - F| \leqslant \sum_1^{\infty} \frac{T^{\nu} M}{\nu!} \leqslant M(e^T - 1) .$$

Condition (1) will be fulfilled if

$$T \leqslant \ln\left(1 + \frac{\varepsilon}{M}\right) .$$

Consequently

$$\Lambda_\varepsilon : \sqrt{R^2 - 2\ln(1+\frac{\varepsilon}{M})} \leqslant \|x\| \leqslant R .$$

2) On the set $\overline{V}$, the relation

$$|\Delta^\nu F| \leqslant M\nu! \frac{2^\nu}{R^{2\nu}} q^\nu \quad , \quad 0 < q < 1$$

is valid. Then

$$|H-F| = \left| \sum_1^\infty \frac{T^\nu \Delta^\nu F}{\nu!} \right| \leqslant M \sum_1^\infty T^\nu \frac{2^\nu}{R^{2\nu}} q^\nu .$$

In this case, condition (1) will be true if

$$M \frac{2Tq}{R^2} \frac{1}{1 - \frac{2Tq}{R^2}} < \varepsilon ,$$

which implies

$$T \leqslant \frac{R^2}{2q(M+\varepsilon)} .$$

Hence

$$\|x\|^2 \geqslant R^2 - \frac{R^2 \varepsilon}{q(M+\varepsilon)}$$

and

$$\Lambda_\varepsilon : \quad R\sqrt{1 - \frac{\varepsilon}{q(M+\varepsilon)}} \leqslant \|x\| \leqslant R .$$

5.6.3. The general case $S \in \{S\}$ can be discussed along the same lines, if we replace R^2 by the functional $\Gamma[x]$ introduced in condition (4^0) of 5.1.1.

6. Semigroups of continual means. Relations to the probability solutions of classical boundary value problems. Applications of the integral over a regular measure

6.1. Semigroups of means over Hilbert spheres

Averaging repeatedly the Gâteaux functional over the sphere in the space L^2 , we obtain

$$\mathfrak{M}_{a,R_2}(\mathfrak{M}_{a,R_1} F) = \mathfrak{M}_{a,\sqrt{R_1^2+R_2^2}} F . \tag{1}$$

Setting here $R = \sqrt{2t}$, $\Phi[x] = \mathfrak{M}_{x,R} F = T_t F$, we get the relation

$$T_{t_2} T_{t_1} F = T_{t_1+t_2} F , \tag{2}$$

which holds for each functional of the Gâteaux ring.

Thus the means $\mathfrak{M}$ generate a semigroup[1], what was already used in Section 5. Note that in the literature this semigroup has not been examined hitherto. In order to outline how to embed it in the general Hille-Iosida theory of analytic semigroups, we have to construct a Banach space of functionals in which the means are linear operators satisfying the condition (2) for $t>0$. We shall indicate some possible variants of such a construction.

Let $R_o = R_o(L^2)$ be the Gâteaux ring with generators $F_m = \int_{Q_m} g(x,t)dt^m$, where $g(\xi,t)$ are bounded on the set $E_m \times Q_m$. We introduce the norm $\|F\| = \sup_{L^2} |F|$. For $F \in R_o(L^2)$, it is evident that

$$\mathfrak{M}_{x,R} F = T_t F \in R_o$$

and the same holds for any $F \in \overline{R}_o$, where $\overline{R}_o$ is the closure of R_o according to this norm.

Consequently, T_t is a linear operator on $\overline{R}_o$. It is also a contractive operator: $\| T_t F \| \leqslant \| F \|$. This results from the fact that T_t is an operator of averaging.

For any positive t_o and t , we have $\lim_{t \to t_o} \|(T_t - T_{t_o})F\| = 0$, i.e., the semigroup T_t is strongly continuous. At the same time, it is not uniformly continuous in general (see below).

Since, for $F \in R_o$, $T_t F$ can be represented by the Gâteaux formula, we deduce from the well-known properties of the kernel

$\frac{1}{\sqrt{2\pi t}} \exp(-(\xi-\eta)^2/2t)$ as well as the assumed conditions concerning the function $g(\xi,t)$ that T_t is continuous on $t \geqslant 0$ and $T_o F = F$. The same is valid for every $F \in \overline{R}_o$.

As can be seen from the equation

$$AF = \lim_{t\to 0} \frac{T_t F - F}{t} = 2 \lim_{R \to 0} \frac{\mathfrak{M} F[x+Ry] - F[x]}{R^2} , \qquad (3)$$

the weak functional Laplace operator is a generating operator A of this semigroup, if in (3) the limit is understood in the sense of the norm $\|\cdot\|$ introduced above. Of course, in this case the pointwise

---

[1] For spherical means in a finite-dimensional space this fact does not hold.

limit, i.e. the weak Laplacian defined above (see 4.1), also exists.

The harmonic functionals are invariant elements of the studied semi-group:

$$T_t H[x] = H[x] .$$

Due to the Hille-Iosida theorem, A has on $\overline{R}_o$ an everywhere dense domain of definition $D(A)$, and it is a closed operator.

In addition, if $F \in D(A)$, we have

$$\lim_{\varepsilon \to 0} \frac{(T_{t+\varepsilon} - T_t)F}{\varepsilon} = AT_t F - T_t AF .$$

The application of further results due to Hille enables us to write down different exponential formulae which express $T_t F$ by means of AF, powers of A and the passage to the limit with respect to the norm in $\overline{R}_o$.

One of these formulae reads as follows:

$$T_t F = \sum_{k=0}^{n-1} \frac{t^k}{k!} A^k F + \frac{1}{(n-1)!} \int_0^t (\tau - t)^{n-1} T_\tau A^n F d\tau , \qquad (4)$$

where $F \in D(A^n)$ and $\int_0^t \ldots$ has to be understood as the integral of a function with values in $\overline{R}_o$ in the sense of the norm introduced in $\overline{R}_o$.

The identification of A with the functional Laplace operator Δ shows that formula (4) coincides with equation (16) from 5.2, which was derived in POLISHCHUK [2] in a quite different way and under different assumptions.

We still note some other formulae. For instance, if $F \in \overline{R}_o$, one has:

1) $T_t F = \lim_n (I - t\Delta/n)^{-n} F$, $T_t F = \lim_n \exp(t \Delta_\eta) F$, $\Delta_\eta = (T_\eta - I)/\eta$.

Here I is the unit operator, and the limit is everywhere taken according to the norm in $\overline{R}_o$;

2) $$\int_0^t T_t F dt = \lim_{\omega \to \infty} \int_{\gamma - i\omega}^{\gamma + i\omega} e^{\lambda t} R(\lambda, \Delta) F \frac{d\lambda}{\lambda} , \quad t > 0 , \qquad (5)$$

where $R(\lambda, \Delta) = (\lambda I - \Delta)^{-1}$ is the resolvent of the operator Δ.
(In HILLE [1] it was shown that (5) holds if $\gamma > \max(0, \alpha)$, $\alpha = \lim_{\omega \to \infty} \frac{1}{\omega} \log \| T_\omega \|$.)

All these formulae can be rewritten, if we replace t by $R^2/2$, A by Δ and, after fixing in the Hilbert space L^2 the surface S, replace R by the functional $s[x]$ associated with S. After such a substitution, expression (5) becomes the operator $\mathfrak{N}$ which we have used above (see 5.2.2) for solving the functional Poisson equation.

Remark. Let us examine the semigroup T over the set of all functionals $F = \int_{Q_m} g(x,t)dt^m$, where $g(\xi,t)$ is bounded and m is a fixed number (a subsemigroup of the semigroup considered above). Let $\Phi = T_t F$. If we consider the restriction of F to the set of functions $\bar{x}$ which have constant values, then we get

$$T_t F = h(\eta) = \frac{1}{\sqrt{\pi t}} \int_{E_m} g(\xi) \exp(-\frac{|\xi-\eta|^2}{t}) d\xi^m , \quad \eta \in E_m .$$

This relation shows that, in Hille's terminology, T_t is a parabolic semigroup (see HILLE [1], Chap. XX).

As another example we shall consider the family of all functionals of the form $F = g(l_1(x),\dots,l_m(x),X)$, where $X = \|x\|^2/2$, $l_1,\dots,l_m$ are linear functionals and $g(\xi_1,\dots,\xi_m,\eta)$ is bounded on the set $E_m \times (\eta \geqslant 0)$. The set of all these functionals constitutes a ring with respect to the ordinary multiplication law. We denote this ring by $R_{oo}(L^2)$. Let $\bar{R}_{oo}$ be the closure of this ring with respect to the norm $\|F\| = \sup_{L^2} |F|$. From the relation

$$T_t g(l_1(x),\dots,l_m(x),X) = g(l_1(x),\dots,l_m(x),X+t)$$

we conclude that, for any $F \in \bar{R}_{oo}$, T_t is a translation operator on the half-line $t > 0$.

In this way, we have a simple example of a semigroup that is strongly but not uniformly continuous. The latter results immediately if we consider the restriction of this semigroup to the set of functionals of the form $F = g(X)$ (see HILLE [1], Chap. IX).

6.2. The operators $\mathfrak{M}^s$, $\mathfrak{N}$ and the probability solutions of classical boundary value problems in the space E_m

Let a linear elliptic equation in the space E_m be given. It is common knowledge that after the construction of the diffusion process by means of the operator occurring in this equation, one can describe the solution of the boundary value problem for this equation via integrals over the measure of the considered process and via quadrature, if the equation is not homogeneous.

Let us briefly explain the nature of the corresponding formulae and show that the solutions of the functional Laplace and Poisson equations obtained in Sections 5.1-5.4 can be described in a completely analogous form.

Let X_t be a random process with values in E_n and $x=x_t(u)$ its trajectories. As usual, let ω be points of the space Ω of elementary events on which a set of probability measures is given. Furthermore, let $A \subset \Omega$ and $P_x(A)$ be the probability measure of this process associated with the point $x \in E_n$.

If f is a measurable function of x, then $f(x_t)$ is a function of ω, i.e. a random value; $M_x(f(x_t))$ denotes its mathematical expectation understood as an integral over the measure P_x.

If the time t is also a random value, i.e. $t=\tau(\omega)$, then for the random value $f(x_{\tau(\omega)}(\omega)) = f(x_\tau)$ the symbol $M_x f(x_\tau)$ has the same meaning.

Now we suppose that X_t is a Markov process. Then

$$Mf(x_t) = T_t f(x),$$

where T_t is the semigroup operator of the process X_t (the same holds true if $t=\tau(\omega)$). Let, in addition, X_t be a diffusion process with the generating operator

$$L: \sum_{i,j=1}^{n} a_{ij}(x) \frac{\partial}{\partial x_i \partial x_j} + \sum_{i=1}^{n} b_i(x) \frac{\partial}{\partial x_i} - c(x),$$

$\sum a_{ij} \lambda_i \lambda_j \geqslant 0$ for arbitrary real λ.

Moreover, let G be a domain in E_n and G' its boundary. Then, under suitable conditions concerning G and the process X_t (i.e., concerning the coefficients a, b and c and the functions φ and g), the following results can be stated:

The solutions of the boundary value problems in E_n

A) $Lf = 0$, $x \in G$; $f(x) = \varphi(x)$, $x \in G'$;

B) $Lf = -g$, $x \in G$; $f(x) = 0$, $x \in G'$

are

A') $f(x) = M_x \varphi_\tau(x_\tau) = T_\tau(f(x_\tau))$;

B') $$f(x) = M_x \int_0^\tau g(x_t)dt = M_x \int_0^\tau T_t g(x)dt,$$

in which $\tau = \tau(\omega)$ is the instant of the first approaching of G' from the point x, and the symbols M and T are related to the process built according to the operator L.

If, in particular, $L = \Delta/2$ and Δ is the Laplace operator in E_n, then X is the Brownian movement and, for any x, M_x is equivalent to an integral over the Wiener measure.

All these formulae arise in the modern sophisticated theory of continuous Markov processes. But they become very clear after comparing them with the results of Section 5, as will be explained now.

For the boundary value problems in the space L^2

$$\text{C)}\quad \Delta H = 0,\quad H|_S = F,\quad F \in \overline{R}(\overline{V}),\quad S \in \{S\}$$

and

$$\text{D)}\quad \Delta U + F = 0,\quad U|_S = 0$$

in Section 5 we have obtained the solutions

$$\text{C')}\quad H = \mathfrak{M}^S F = \mathfrak{M} F[x + \rho_x[y] y] ;$$

$$\text{D')}\quad U = \mathfrak{N} F = \mathfrak{M} \int_0^{\rho_x[y]} rF[x+ry]dr = \int_0^{S[x]} r \mathfrak{M} F[x+ry]dr .$$

Let $x \in V$, and assume that the point x moves towards the boundary of this domain according to the law

$$\rho = \sqrt{2t} . \tag{1}$$

The vector y, $\|y\|=1$, will be called a <u>random direction</u> and $\rho_x[y]$ the <u>random distance</u> from $x \in V$ to the surface S in the direction y. We proceed from $\rho_x[y]$ to the random time $\tau_x[y]$ in accordance with the law (1).

Then instead of C') and D') we can write

$$\text{C")}\quad H = \mathfrak{M} F[x + \sqrt{2\tau_x[y]}\, y] ,$$

$$\text{D")}\quad U = \mathfrak{M} \int_0^{\tau_x[y]} F[x + \sqrt{2t}\, y] dt .$$

We define the translation operator

$$T_t F[x] = F[x + \sqrt{2t}\, y] ,$$

which can be considered as the semigroup operator having the weak functional Laplacian $\Delta/2$ as the generating operator (see 5.1).

Now formulae C") and D") may be written in the form

$$H = \mathfrak{M} T_{\tau_x[y]} F[x] ,$$

$$U = \mathfrak{M} \int_0^{\tau_x[y]} T_t F[x] dt ,$$

and we see that after the comparisons

$$y \sim \omega,\quad x \in L^2 \sim x \in E_n,\quad F[x] \sim f(x),\quad \mathfrak{M} \sim M_x$$

they are actually identical with the equations A') and B') presented above.

In the theory of Markov processes the mean time $m(x)$ of reaching the boundary G' of the domain G starting from the point x plays an important role:

$$m(x) = M_x \tau(\omega) \ , \quad x \in G \ .$$

What is known about the function $m(x)$? It turns out that, under appropriate conditions, for a continuous process the following statements are true:

(i) $m(x)$ is a subharmonic function on G ,

(ii) $\lim\limits_{x \to a} m(x) = 0 \ , \quad a \in G'$

(cf. DYNKIN [1], Theorem 13.7). In connection with equation (1), in our considerations the mean time $m(x)$ corresponds to the functional

$$T[x] = \mathfrak{M} \tau_x[y] = s^2[x]/2 \ .$$

Independently of the theory of Markov processes it was shown above (see Section 5.2) that for a wide class of surfaces the relation

$$T[x] = \frac{1}{2}(\Gamma[x] - \|x\|^2) \ , \quad x \in V$$

is valid, where Γ is a harmonic functional. Thus

$$\mathfrak{M} T[x+ \lambda y] = \frac{1}{2}(\Gamma[x] - \|x\|^2 - \lambda^2) < T[x] \ .$$

At the same place it was established that $T=0$ if $x \in S$.

In summary, under suitable conditions, the functional T has all the properties of the function mentioned above.

Returning to formulae C') and D'), we note that their right parts in Section 5 were expressed by means of $s[x]$. Therefore, we can rewrite them as follows:

$$\left. \begin{aligned} H &= \mathfrak{M} F[x+ \sqrt{2T[x]}\, y] = T_{T[x]} F \ , \\ U &= \int_0^{T[x]} F[x+ \sqrt{2t}\, y] dt = \int_0^{T[x]} T_t F dt \ . \end{aligned} \right\} \qquad (2)$$

This proved to be possible because of the properties of continual means (see 3.2) which fail to hold for integrals over measures of another kind. At the same time, the passage from A') and B') to formulae of the type (2) by replacing τ by the mean time $m(x)$ is impossible in general.

Under the same conditions concerning the operator L , the theory of random diffusion processes enables us to establish explicit expressions for the solution of problems more general than A) and B), respectively.

It can be proved that if $v(x) \geqslant 0$, φ is a continuous function on G, and if v and g satisfy a Hölder condition on G (see DYNKIN [1], Chap. 13), then the solution of the problem

$$Lf + v(x)f = -g(x), \quad x \in G,$$
$$\lim_{x \to a} f(x) = \varphi(a), \quad a \in G'$$

is of the form

$$f(x) = M_x \int_0^{\tau} e^{-\int_0^t v(x_s)ds} g(x_t)dt + M_x e^{-\int_0^{\tau} v(x_s)ds} \varphi(x_{\tau}) \tag{3}$$

(DYNKIN [1], Theorem 13.16).

The theory explained in Section 5 can be extended to the study of linear equations with a functional Laplace operator of a higher order and with variable coefficients (see POLISHCHUK [6]). In particular, for the equation

$$\Delta U + P[x]U = -\Phi[x], \quad P, \Phi \in \overline{R}(\overline{V}),$$
$$U\big|_S = A[x], \quad A \in \overline{R}(\overline{V})$$

the solution has a form similar to (3):

$$F = \mathfrak{M} \int_0^{\tau} e^{-\int_0^t P[x+ry]dr} Q[x+ty]dt + \mathfrak{M} e^{-\int_0^{\tau} P[x+ry]dr} A[x+\tau y], \tag{4}$$

$\tau = \tau_x[y]$. Under the same conditions as above, one can again replace τ by the mean time $T[x]$, however, in (3) it is impossible to substitute τ by m.

6.3. Regular measures and the extension of the Gâteaux ring

We intend now to indicate another way of extending the results of Section 5, which is based on the application of regular measures.

First of all, we state the principal properties of these measures.

6.3.1. Let R_{ω} be the space of sequences $\vec{\xi}$ of vectors:

$$R_{\omega}: \quad \vec{\xi} = (\vec{\xi}_1, \vec{\xi}_2, \dots),$$

where

$$\vec{\xi}_k = (\xi_k^1, \dots, \xi_k^s; t_k), \quad (\xi_k^1, \dots, \xi_k^s) \in E_s, \quad a < t_k < b.$$

It is evident that R_{ω} can be represented as $R_n \times R_{n,\omega}$, where R_n

is the space of vectors $(\vec{\xi}_1, \ldots, \vec{\xi}_n) = \vec{\eta}_n$ and $R_{n,\omega}$ is the space of sequences $(\vec{\xi}_{n+1}, \vec{\xi}_{n+2}, \ldots)$.

If $E \subset R_n$, then the product $E \times R_{n,\omega}$ is a cylinder having the base E in R_n . If the set $\mathfrak{I}$ is defined by the condition

$$\mathfrak{I} : \vec{A}_k < \vec{\xi}_k < \vec{B}_k , \quad k=1,\ldots,n,$$

$$\vec{A}_k = (A_k^{\,1}, \ldots, A_k^{\,s}; \alpha_k), \quad \vec{B}_k = (B_k^{\,1}, \ldots, B_k^{\,s}; \beta_k),$$

then the cylinder $Z = \mathfrak{I} \times R_{n,\omega}$ is said to be a <u>quasiinterval</u> in R_ω .

Let $p(\vec{\xi}_1, \ldots, \vec{\xi}_n) = p(\vec{\eta}_n)$ be a nonnegative function for which

$$\int_{R_n} p(\vec{\xi}_1, \ldots, \vec{\xi}_n) d\vec{\xi}_1 \ldots d\vec{\xi}_n = \int_{R_n} p(\vec{\eta}_n) d\vec{\eta}_n = 1 .$$

The expression

$$\mu_n(\mathfrak{I}) = \int_{\mathfrak{I}} p(\vec{\eta}_n) d\vec{\eta}_n$$

is called the <u>measure</u> of the quasiinterval $\mathfrak{I}$ with respect to the function p .

Thus, for each n , the countably additive measure $\mu_n(E)$ on the σ-ring of all Borel subsets E of R_n (the premeasure in R_ω) may be constructed. Simultaneously, the measurable functions $f(E)$ given on the subsets $E \subset R_n$ as well as the integrals

$$\int_E f(\vec{\eta}_n) \, d\mu_n$$

can be defined.

The measure is supposed to be continuous. Consequently, due to the well-known Kolmogorov theorem[1)], preserving the countable additivity, this measure can be extended to the σ-ring of B-sets in R_ω containing all cylindrical sets of R_ω - the "regular measure on R_ω ". In this way, in R_ω the measurable functions $f(\vec{\xi})$ and integrals

$$\int_M f(\vec{\xi}) \, d\mu , \quad M \subset R_\omega$$

(μ is the extension of the measure μ_n) are defined.

Note that if f_n is a cylindrical function (i.e., f_n depends only upon the co-ordinates related to vectors from R_n), then

$$\int_{R_n} f_n \, d\mu_n = \int_{R_\omega} f \, d\mu .$$

---

1) See KOLMOGOROV [1] (or the later english editions of this book), Chap. III, § 4.

In particular, if p does not depend on t and $s=1$, i.e. $p=p(\xi)$, we get the measure considered in SHILOV and FAN DYK TINH [1]. If

$p = \frac{1}{\sqrt{2\pi}} e^{-\xi^2/2}$, the measure is called normal. We denote it by ν.

If p does not depend on ξ, i.e. $p=p(t)$, and, moreover, $A = 0$, $B = 1$, then R_ω is the infinite-dimensional cube Q_ω: $0 < t_k < 1$, $k=1,2,\ldots$. If, in addition, the measure of a quasiinterval in Q_ω is defined by the equation $\mu_n = (\beta_1-\alpha_1)\ldots(\beta_n-\alpha_n)$, then μ is the measure examined by Jessen, which will be denoted by w.

The set of functions $f(\vec{\xi})$ for which $\int |f(\vec{\xi})|^p d\mu$, $p>0$ exists is a linear normed space $L^p(R_\omega, \mu)$.

6.3.2. We now formulate some lemmas about measures and integrals in R_ω. The proofs of Lemmas 6.3.1 and 6.3.2 (for the case $s=1$, $p=p(\xi)$) can be found in SHILOV and FAN DYK TINH [1]. Lemmas 6.3.3-6.3.5 (for the case when μ is a Jessen measure) are contained in JESSEN [1]. These proofs can be transferred to arbitrary regular measures μ on R_ω without essential modifications.

Lemma 6.3.1. For any function $f(\vec{\xi}) \in L^p(R_\omega, \mu)$ there exists a sequence of cylindrical functions f_n such that

$$\lim_n \| f - f_n \| = 0$$

($\|\cdot\|$ denotes the norm in $L^p(R_\omega, \mu)$). Moreover, one can take $f_n = \int_{R_{n,\omega}} f(\vec{\xi}) d\mu$.

We shall say that the function $f(\vec{\xi})$ has the K-property if its values remain fix under arbitrary changing a finite number of vectors of $\vec{\xi} = (\vec{\xi}_1, \vec{\xi}_2, \ldots)$. The set $E \subset R_\omega$ is called to have the K-property if, together with every point $\vec{\xi} \in E$, each other point differing from $\vec{\xi}$ by a finite number of vectors also belongs to E.

Lemma 6.3.2. If f has the K-property, then $f=\text{const}$ almost everywhere on R_ω. If the set E has the K-property, then $\mu(E) = 0$ or $\mu(E) = 1$.

Lemma 6.3.3. If $R_\omega = {}_1R_\omega \times {}_2R_\omega \times \ldots \times {}_nR_\omega$, where ${}_iR_\omega$ are the spaces of vector sequences, i.e. ${}_iR_\omega = ({}_i\vec{\xi}_1, {}_i\vec{\xi}_2, \ldots)$, and if ${}^1\mu$, ${}^2\mu$, ... are regular measures on ${}_1R_\omega$, ${}_2R_\omega$, ..., respectively, then the condition $f \in L({}_1R_\omega \times {}_2R_\omega \times \ldots \times {}_nR_\omega ; \mu)$ implies

$$\int_{R_\omega} f(\vec{\xi}) d\mu = \int_{{}_1R_\omega} d^1\mu \ldots d^n\mu \int_{{}_nR_\omega} f({}_1\vec{\xi}, \ldots, {}_n\vec{\xi}) .$$

Lemma 6.3.4. If $f(\vec{\xi}) \in L(R_\omega, \mu)$, then almost everywhere on R_ω ,

$$f(\vec{\xi}) = \lim_n \int_{R_{n,\omega}} f(\vec{\xi}) d\mu \quad .$$

Let $E_\omega : (\xi_1, \xi_2, \ldots)$; $Q_\omega : 0 < t_k < 1$, $k=1,2,\ldots$; $g=g(\xi, t)$, $\xi \in E_\omega$; $t \in Q_\omega$. As above we shall say that for $g(\xi, t)$ the Carathéodory condition holds if g is measurable with respect to t for each ξ and continuous in ξ almost everywhere on Q_ω .

Let x be a function on $A(q)$. We consider the superposition operator

$$hx = g(x(t_1), x(t_2), \ldots ; t_1, t_2, \ldots)$$

generated by the function g .

Lemma 6.3.5. If the function $g(\xi, t)$ satisfies the Carathéodory conditions and if, moreover, the estimate

$$|g(\xi, t)| \leq \left[\sum_{k=1}^{\infty} \lambda_k |\xi_k|^{p_2} + c(t) \right]^{1/p_1} , \quad p_1, p_2 > 0 \qquad (1)$$

holds, where

$$c(t) \in L(Q_\omega ; w), \quad \lambda_k > 0, \quad \sum_{k=1}^{\infty} \lambda_k < \infty , \qquad (2)$$

then h is a continuous operator acting from $L^{p_1}(0,1)$ into $L^{p_2}(Q_\omega ; w)$.

Proof. Let $x(t) \in L^{p_1}(0,1)$. We denote $\int_0^1 |x(t)|^{p_2} dt = \rho$ and consider the series

$$\sum_{k=1}^{\infty} \lambda_k |x(t_k)|^{p_2} \quad . \qquad (3)$$

In view of (1) it converges almost everywhere on Q_ω . In order to verify this, we use the following "three series theorem" due to Kolmogorov: Let θ_k be mutually independent nonnegative random values, $c > 0$, and assume $\theta_k(c) = \theta_k$ if $\theta_k \leq c$, $\theta_k(c) = 0$ if $\theta_k > c$. If, for some c , the following assertions are valid:

(i) the series $\sum_{k=1}^{\infty} \overline{\theta_k(c)}$ converges (the bar denotes the mean value),

(ii) $\sum_{k=1}^{\infty} P\{\theta_k \geq c\}$ converges,

then the series $\sum_{k=1}^{\infty} \theta_k$ converges with probability one.

Denote

$$\lambda_k |x(t_k)|^{p_2} = \theta_k \quad .$$

It is easy to see that the conditions of Kolmogorov's theorem are fulfilled for the series (3). Indeed, its terms depend on different t_k and, consequently, they are mutually independent with respect to the measure w in Q_ω. In addition, one has:

$$\sum_k \overline{\theta_k(c)} \leq \sum_k \overline{\theta}_k = \sum_k \lambda_k \int_{Q_\omega} |x(t_k)|^{p_2} dw = \varrho \sum_{k=1}^{\infty} \lambda_k < \infty .$$

From the well-known Chebyshev inequality it follows that

$$P\{\theta_k > \varrho\} \leq \lambda_k .$$

Hence both the conditions (i) and (ii) are valid for the series (3) and, thus, it converges almost everywhere on Q_ω. Denoting the sum of the series (3) by $\varphi(t)$ and its partial sums by S_n, we observe that the theorem on bounded convergence can be applied to S_n (here the convergence is even monotonic). Consequently

$$\int_{Q_\omega} \varphi(t) dw = \varrho \sum_{k=1}^{\infty} \lambda_k < \infty .$$

It remains to prove that $\varphi(t)$ is a measurable function on Q_ω. If g is a cylindrical function $g(\xi_1,\dots,\xi_n;t_1,\dots,t_n)$, this fact is a consequence of Carathéodory's theorem, according to which the superposition operator maps a measurable function into a measurable function. A careful examination of the proof of this theorem (see KRASNOSELSKIĬ et al. [1], Chap. V) shows that it is based on those properties of the classical Lebesgue measure which remain valid for regular measures in Q_ω, in particular, for the Jessen measure. Hence $\varphi(t)$ is measurable on Q_ω.

From (3) it can be seen that

$$\int_{Q_\omega} |\varphi(t)|^{p_2} dw \leq \varrho \sum_{k=1}^{\infty} \lambda_k + \int_{Q_\omega} c(t) dw .$$

Thus $h \in \{L^{p_1}(0,1) \longrightarrow L^{p_2}(Q_\omega; w)\}$. The continuity of the operator h can be proved in the same manner as in the case if g is a cylindrical function. The lemma has been completely proved.

As a consequence we conclude:

If $|g(\xi,t)| \leq \sum_{k=1}^{\infty} \lambda_k |\xi_k|^p + c(t)$, $c(t) \in L(Q_\omega, w)$, then the functional $F[x] = \int_{Q_\omega} g(x(t),t) dw$ exists on $L^p(0,1)$ and is continuous in the norm of this space.

<u>6.3.3.</u> Let $g(\xi,t)$ be a function defined on the set $E_\omega \times Q_\omega = R_\omega$. We suppose that g satisfies the Carathéodory conditions as well as the inequality

$$|g(\xi,t)| \leq u(t) + \sum_{k=1}^{\infty} \lambda_k \xi_k^2 \quad , \tag{4}$$

where

$$u(t) \in L(Q_\omega), \quad \lambda_k \geq 0, \quad \sum_{k=1}^{\infty} \lambda_k < \infty .$$

The former considerations allow us to construct the functional

$$F[x] = \int_{Q_\omega} g(x(t),t)dw \ , \tag{5}$$

which exists and is continuous on the space $L^2(q)$. Its mean value over the sphere $\Omega_{a,R}$ is defined by the formula

$$\mathfrak{M}_{a,R}F = \int_{Q_\omega} dw \int_{E_\omega} g(a(t)+\eta\sqrt{2R}\ ,t)d\nu = \int_{R_\omega} g(a(t)+\eta\sqrt{2R},t)d\mu \ , \tag{6}$$

where w is the Jessen measure on Q_ω and ν the normal measure on E_ω . For the functional $F_m = \int_{Q_m} g_m(x,t)dt^m$, equation (6) reduces to the Gâteaux formula (3) from 3.3.

Now we consider a normal domain V in $L^2(q)$ with the boundary S , $S \in \{S\}$.

Theorem 6.3.1. The Dirichlet problem with the boundary value (5) on the surface S of the type $\{S\}$ admits a solution in the form

$$H[x] = \mathfrak{M}F[x+\rho_x[y]y] \quad . \tag{7}$$

Proof. First of all, it should be noted that (7) can be expressed in the form

$$H[x] = \mathfrak{M}F[x+s[x]y] \quad . \tag{8}$$

This results from the same arguments which led us in 5.1 from (4) to (5).

Since, for any $x \in L^2(q)$, $g_n(x,t) \longrightarrow g(x,t)$ a.e. on Q_ω (Lemma 6.3.4), then for $\eta \in E_\omega$, one has

$$g_n(x(t)+\eta\sqrt{2s[x]}\ ,t) \longrightarrow g(x(t)+\eta\sqrt{2s[x]}\ ,t)$$

also almost everywhere on this set. As η is arbitrary here, the sequence $g_n(x(t)+\eta\sqrt{2s}\ ,t)$ considered as functions of η and t converges to the function $g(x(t)+\eta\sqrt{2s}\ ,t) = \Psi(\eta,t)$ in the measure $\mu = w \times \nu$ on R_ω .

From (4) we deduce that $g(\xi,t)$ is summable with respect to this measure on R_ω because

$$\int_{R_\omega} |g(\xi,t)|d\mu \leq \int_{Q_\omega} u(t)dw + \sum_{k=1}^{\infty} \lambda_k \quad .$$

Hence, denoting

$$\nu_n(a, d\xi, \sigma) = \frac{1}{(\sigma\sqrt{2\pi})^n} \exp\left(-\frac{(\xi_1-a)^2+\ldots+(\xi_n-a)^2}{2\sigma^2}\right) d\xi_1 \ldots d\xi_n$$

and using the Fubini theorem on iterated integrals (Lemma 6.3.3), we have

$$\int_{Q_\omega} dw \int_{E_\omega} g(x(t)+\eta\sqrt{2s}, t)\, \nu(1, d\eta, 0) = H[x];$$

$$H[x+\lambda y] = \lim_n H_n[x+\lambda y] =$$

$$\lim_n \int_{Q_n} g_n(\xi, t)\, \nu_n(s[x+\lambda y], d\xi, x+\lambda y)\, dt^n ;$$

$$\mathfrak{M} H[x+\lambda y] = \mathfrak{M} \int_{Q_\omega} dw \int_{E_\omega} g(\xi, t)\, \nu(s[x+\lambda y], d\xi, x+\lambda y) ;$$

$$\mathfrak{M} H[x+\lambda y] = \mathfrak{M} \int_{Q_\omega} dw \int_{E_\omega} g(\xi, t)\, \nu(s_\lambda, d\xi, x+\lambda y) =$$

$$\mathfrak{M} \lim_n \int_{Q_n} dt^n \int_{E_n} g_n(\xi, t)\, \nu_n(s_\lambda, d\xi, x+\lambda y) =$$

$$\lim_n \int_{E_n} d\eta^n \int_{Q_n} g_n(\xi, t)\, \nu_n(s_\lambda, d\xi, x+\lambda\eta)\, \nu_n(1, d\eta, 0) =$$

$$\lim_n \int_{Q_n} dt^n \int_{E_n} g_n(\xi, t)\, \nu_n(s[x], d\xi, x) =$$

$$\int_{R_\omega} g(\xi, t)\, \nu(s[x], d\xi, x)\, dw = H[x] .$$

Let now $x_m \in V$, $z \in S$, $\|x_m - z\| \longrightarrow 0$. Then, since $S \in \{S\}$, we have $s[x_m] \longrightarrow s[z] = 0$ and, for any $\xi \in E_\omega$, this implies $x_m + \xi s[x_m] \longrightarrow z$. With regard to the continuity of the superposition operator $hx = g(x,t)$, we have $g(x_m(t)+\xi, s[x_m]) \longrightarrow g(z(t))$ in the measure w on Q_ω . Therefore, taking into account (8), we obtain

$$\lim_m H[x_m] = \lim_m \int_{R_\omega} g(x_m + s[x_m]\xi, t)\, d\mu =$$

$$\int_{Q_\omega} g(z,t)\, dw \int_{E_\omega} \nu(1, d\xi, 0) = \int_{Q_\omega} g(z,t)\, dw = F[z] ,$$

which proves the theorem.

<u>Remark</u>. Condition (4) can be weakened, replacing it by

$$|g(\xi, t)| \leq u(t) + \sum_{k=1}^{\infty} \frac{\lambda^k \xi_1^2 \ldots \xi_n^2}{k!} ,$$

$$u(t) \in L(Q_\omega, w), \quad u \geqslant 0, \quad \lambda > 0 .$$

This implies the boundedness of F on any ball V_R: $\|x\| \leqslant R$:

$$\sup_{V_R} |F| \leqslant \int_{Q_\omega} u \, dw + e^{\lambda R^2} .$$

Therefore, the proof remains the same.

The unicity of the obtained solution in the class of functionals satisfying the conditions of the theorem follows directly from (7).

CHAPTER 3. THE FUNCTIONAL LAPLACE OPERATOR AND CLASSICAL DIFFUSION EQUATIONS. BOUNDARY VALUE PROBLEMS FOR UNIFORM DOMAINS. HARMONIC CONTROLLED SYSTEMS

7. Boundary value problems with strong Laplacian and their parallelism to classical parabolic equations

We deal here with boundary value problems for the equations

$$\Delta F = 0 , \quad \Delta U = F , \tag{1}$$

in which the operator Δ is defined as the iterated variational derivative, i.e. the strong Laplacian (see 4.1):

$$\Delta F = \int_a^b F''_{x^2(t)} \, dt \quad . \tag{2}$$

Our method is based on the application of the diffusion theory involving parabolic equations in a finite-dimensional space. After replacing in these equations the time τ by the functional $T[x]$ (the mean time of reaching the boundary S starting from the point x), the solutions of them are used as generating functions of the desired functional. This approach seems to be promising, however, it is worth mentioning that it does not give a deep inside into the problem under study. Everything related to the functionals $\rho_x[y]$, $\tau_x[y]$ considered in Sections 5 and 6 remains outside the "diffusion method". This method also fails to provide some information on how to find the functional T , whose definition from the very beginning was based on the spherical mean $\mathfrak{M}$. Here $T[x]$ is taken in a ready form. At the same time, the diffusion method permits us, starting from the classical equations

$$u'_\tau = \Delta u , \quad u'_\tau = \Delta u + g(\xi , \tau) , \tag{3}$$

to pose new problems which, together with the problems examined before, reveal a wide analogy between functional elliptic equations and classical parabolic equations. This analogy is even of a dual character as can be seen from the table contained in 7.2.

It turns out that for equations (1) it makes sense to set not only global conditions as in Section 5 but also local conditions, which express the values of the unknown functional at isolated points of the given domain. In such problems the functional $T = (R^2-\|x\|^2)/2$ (if we restrict ourselves to the case when S is a sphere) again plays the role of time, but in a different sense: now R is assumed to be variable and $\|x\|$ is constant. To give $\|x\|$ amounts to choose an initial reference.

7.1. The functional Laplacian and the classical parabolic operator

7.1.1. We suppose that the surface S on which the boundary values of the unknown functional are given belongs to the type $\{S\}$ (see Subsection 5.1.1), however, now we require only the conditions (1°), (2°) and (4°) to be fulfilled, where (4°) will be formulated in a slightly different form: There exists a functional $T[x]$ continuous on the set $\overline{V} = V \cup S$ such that δT and $\delta^2 T$ exist and are of the form (for $s=1$, see 4.1):

$$\delta T = \int_a^b A_0[x|t]\,\eta(t)dt = \int_a^b T'_{x(t)}\,\eta(t)dt\,, \tag{4}$$

$$\delta^2 T = \int_a^b A[x|t]\,\eta^2(t)dt + \iint_a^b B[x|t_1,t_2]\,\eta(t_1)\eta(t_2)dt_1dt_2$$

$$= \int_a^b T''_{x^2(t)}\,\eta^2(t)dt + \iint_a^b T''_{x(t_1)x(t_2)}\,\eta(t_1)\eta(t_2)dt_1dt_2\,. \tag{5}$$

Furthermore, suppose

$$\Delta T = \int_a^b T''_{x^2(t)}\,dt = -1, \quad x \in V, \quad T = 0, \quad x \in S, \tag{6}$$

and let, in addition,

$$T = \frac{1}{2(b-a)}\left(\Gamma[x] - \|x\|^2\right), \qquad \Gamma \in \mathcal{H}(V)\,. \tag{7}$$

(Note that from the harmonicity of Γ the equation $\Delta T = -1$ results immediately.)

7.1.2. Let the function $h(\xi,u,\alpha)$ of the variables

$$\xi = (\xi_1,\ldots,\xi_m), \quad \xi \in E_m\,; \quad u = (u_1,\ldots,u_m), \quad u \in Q_m$$

be given, which depends, moreover, on the parameter α and takes values on the interval

$$I: \quad \alpha_1 \leqslant \alpha \leqslant \alpha_2\,.$$

Furthermore, suppose that there exists the functional

$$F[x|\alpha] = \int_{Q_m} h(x(u),u,\alpha)\,du^m\,. \tag{8}$$

If the values of $T[x]$ for $x \in \overline{V}$ belong to the interval I, then the functional

$$H[x] = \int_{Q_m} h(x(u),u,T[x])\,du^m \tag{9}$$

exists along with (8).

We now are going to consider functionals on the space $L^2(0,1)$.

Lemma 7.1.1. Let $H[x]$ be a functional of the form (9), and assume the function $h(\xi,u,\alpha)$ to be twice continuously differentiable with respect to ξ and α and continuous in u. Then the functional ΔH exists and the equation

$$\Delta H = \int_{Q_m} \Delta h du + \Delta T \int_{Q_m} \frac{\partial H}{\partial T} du \tag{10}$$

is valid, where Δh is the Laplace operator with respect to the variables ξ.

The proof is omitted (cf. Lemma 4.1.3).

Since it was supposed that $\Delta T = -1$, we obtain

$$\Delta H = \int_{Q_m} (\Delta h - \frac{\partial h}{\partial T}) du . \tag{11}$$

7.1.3. Now we study the equation

$$\frac{\partial h}{\partial \tau} = \sum_{i=1}^{m} \frac{\partial^2 h}{\partial \xi_i^2} \tag{12}$$

with the initial condition

$$h\big|_{\tau=0} = g(\xi,u) \tag{13}$$

depending on a parameter u. The function g is assumed to be continuous and to satisfy condition (2) from 5.1. In this case, the solution of problem (11), (12) can be represented in the form

$$h(\xi,u,\tau) = \left(\frac{1}{2\sqrt{\pi\tau}}\right)^m \int_{E_m} g(\eta,u)\, e^{-\frac{|\xi-\eta|^2}{4\tau}} d\eta^m . \tag{14}$$

Let now H be a functional constructed by the generating function (14), in which τ is replaced by the functional $T[x]$. By virtue of Lemma 7.1.1, $\Delta H = 0$ on the set V.

The proof of the validity of the boundary conditions is the same as in Theorem 5.1.1.

7.1.4. Here we examine the inhomogeneous equation

$$\sum_{i=1}^{m} \frac{\partial^2 \varphi}{\partial \xi_i^2} = \frac{\partial \varphi}{\partial \tau} + g(\xi,u,\tau) \tag{15}$$

with the initial condition

$$\varphi\Big|_{\tau=0} = 0 \tag{16}$$

under the assumption that g satisfies the same conditions as in Subsection 7.1.3. The solution of problem (15), (16) may be represented as follows:

$$\varphi = \left(\frac{1}{2\sqrt{\pi}}\right)^m \int_0^\tau \left\{ \int_{E_m} g(\eta, u, \alpha)\, e^{-\frac{|\xi-\eta|^2}{4(\tau-\alpha)}}\, d\eta^m \right\} \frac{d\alpha}{(\tau-\alpha)^{m/2}} . \tag{17}$$

Now we write down the functional

$$U[x] = \left(\frac{1}{2\sqrt{\pi}}\right)^m \int_0^{T[x]} \left\{ \int_{Q_m} du^m \int_{E_m} g(\eta, u, \alpha) e^{-\frac{|x(u)-\eta|^2}{4(T[x]-\alpha)}}\, d\eta^m \right\} \frac{d\alpha}{(T[x]-\alpha)^{m/2}} . \tag{18}$$

It is built up by the generating function (17) with $\tau = T[x]$. Moreover, all the conditions of Lemma 7.1.1 are valid. Hence $U[x]$ satisfies the equation $\Delta U = F$ in which $F = \int_{Q_m} g(x,u,T[x])du^m$.

From (18) it also follows that $U\Big|_S = 0$.

Under the conditions just mentioned, the above considerations permit us to formulate the following

Theorem 7.1.1. Let S be a surface of the type $\{S\}$. Then the solution of the functional Dirichlet problem

$$\Delta H = 0, \quad x \in V, \quad H\Big|_S = \int_{Q_m} g(x,u,T)\, du^m$$

can be represented in the form (9), while the solution of the functional Poisson equation

$$\Delta U = \int_{Q_m} g(x,u,T)\, du^m , \qquad U\Big|_S = 0$$

may be expressed by formula (18).

Remark. If we study the problems mentioned above in the space $C[a,b]$, the conditions concerning the function g can be weakened (cf. 5.1.3).

7.1.5. Now we discuss the exterior Dirichlet problem. The set of points lying outside the surface S will be denoted by $\tilde{V}$. We suppose that there exists a functional $\tilde{T}[x]$ continuous on the set $\bar{\tilde{V}} = \tilde{V} \cup S$ and having the properties:

(i) $\tilde{T} > 0$ if $x \in \tilde{V}$,

(ii) $\delta\tilde{T}$ and $\delta^2\tilde{T}$ exist and are of the form (4) and (5), respectively.
In addition, we require $\Delta\tilde{T} = 1$ on $\tilde{V}$ and $\tilde{T} = 0$ on the surface S.

These requirements correspond to those from Section 5.5, where, in particular, the following example was cited:

$$S: \|kx\| = 1, \quad \tilde{V}: \|kx\| > 1, \quad \tilde{T} = \frac{1}{2}\|k\|^{-2}(\|k\|^2 - 1).$$

We formulate the inverse diffusion equation

$$\frac{\partial h}{\partial \tau} = -\sum_1^m \frac{\partial^2 h}{\partial \xi_i^2}$$

with the initial condition

$$h\Big|_{\tau=0} = g(\xi, u),$$

where u is a parameter and g belongs to the class $\{A\}$ (see Section 5.5).

The solution of this equation can be represented as follows (see HIRSCHMAN and WIDDER [1]):

$$h(\xi, u, t) = \frac{1}{(2\pi i)^m} \int_{d_1 - i\infty}^{d_1 + i\infty} \cdots \int_{d_m - i\infty}^{d_m + i\infty} g(w_1, \ldots, w_m; u_1, \ldots, u_m) \prod_{k=1}^m p(w_k - \xi_k; \tau)\, dw_k,$$

where

$$p(w; \tau) = (\pi/\tau)^{1/2} e^{w^2/4\tau}.$$

The condition $g \in \{A\}$ implies:

(i) h is a real function;
(ii) the integral on the right-hand side of the latter equation converges absolutely on the set $-\infty < \xi_k < \infty$, $0 < \tau < 1$ (diverges for $\tau \geq 1$) and does not depend on the values of d;
(iii) the function h is twice differentiable with respect to ξ and τ and continuous in u.

It follows from (i)-(iii) that the functional

$$H[x] = \frac{1}{(2\pi i)^m} \int_{Q_m} du \int_{d-i\infty}^{d+i\infty} g(w, u) \prod_{k=1}^m p(w_k - x(u_k); \tilde{T}[x])\, dw^m \tag{19}$$

exists provided that $0 < \tilde{T} < 1$.

We also see that Lemma 7.1.1 remains valid in the case under study. Hence

$$\Delta H = \int_{Q_m} \Delta h\, du^m + \Delta\tilde{T} \int_{Q_m} \frac{\partial h}{\partial \tilde{T}}\, du^m.$$

In view of $\Delta\tilde{T} = 1$ this yields $\Delta H = 0$ on the set $\tilde{V}$. The proof of the relation $H\big|_S = F$ remains unchanged in comparison with the interior Dirichlet problem.

Summarizing, Theorem 7.1.1 can be supplemented by the following statement: Under the condition $g \in \{A\}$, the functional (19) expresses the solution of the exterior Dirichlet problem for a surface of type $\{S\}$ on the subset $0 < \tilde{T} < 1$ of $\tilde{V}$.

Remark. The coincidence of the solutions obtained in this section and the solutions of Section 5 is a consequence of the fact that, under the conditions formulated in 5.1, the weak harmonicity implies the strong one. Applying, however, the superposition operator, we discover a difference between them. So, for instance, if $H_1 \in \mathcal{H}_0$, $H_2 \in \mathcal{H}_0$ and f is a continuous function, we also have $f(H_1,H_2) \in \mathcal{H}_0$. At the same time, if $\Delta H_1 = 0$, $\Delta H_2 = 0$ (strong harmonicity), then for the validity of $\Delta f(H_1,H_2) = 0$ it is necessary for f to be a twice continuously differentiable function.

7.2. Dual problems and an analogy table

We now intend to demonstrate that to the most important classical heat equations with initial as well as boundary conditions there may be assigned some dual problems for functional elliptic equations.

We shall use some expressions which could be called the functional heat potentials. In order to obtain an analogue of the classical problem in E_1

$$u'_\tau = u''_{\xi\xi} \; ; \quad u(0,\tau) = \omega_1(\tau), \quad u(1,\tau) = \omega_2(\tau) \, , \qquad (*)$$

it proves to be natural to consider in the function space $A(q)$ not only a single sphere S_R: $\|x\| = R$, but a family of spheres S_R, $0 < R < \infty$.

The assignment of the functional H to the two points $x_0, x \in S_R$ corresponds to the boundary conditions in (*). The same applies to the functional analogue of problems (3) in E_1 with the conditions $u(0,t) = \omega_1(t)$, $u'_\xi(1,t) = \omega_2(t)$. However, in this case the derivative u'_ξ corresponds to the functional derivative of U in a direction tangent to S_R.

Here we limit ourselves to fixing the boundary values of the unknown functionals on the sphere and deal only with the simplest case, namely heat equations on the line. It is not difficult, however, to show that our approach presented below can be extended to parabolic equations of much more general types maintaining the same laws.

The function space considered here is $C[a,b]$, but the results may be formulated in other spaces $A(a,b)$, too.

We use the usual notations: $x(u)\uparrow$ and $x(u)\downarrow$ means the monotonic and, consequently, the uniform convergence (since the x_n are supposed to be continuous), $(x,y) = \int_a^b x(u)y(u)du$.

Let V_R be the ball $\|x\| < R$ and G_o a set of functions such that:

(i) $G_o \subset V_R$,

(ii) $G_o \subset C[a,b]$,

(iii) if $x \in G_o$, the set of all u for which $x(u)=0$ has the measure zero.

We need the following modification of Lemma 7.1.1.

> Lemma 7.2.1. Let $g(\xi, u, \alpha)$ be a function satisfying the conditions of Lemma 7.1.1 and, in addition, the following assumptions:
>
> (i) g is continuously differentiable with respect to ξ everywhere with the exception of $\xi = 0$,
>
> (ii) there exist the limit values $g(-0,u,\alpha)$ and $g(+0,u,\alpha)$,
>
> (iii) the function g is, together with g'_ξ and g'_α , continuous with respect to u .
>
> Then on the set G_o equation (10) is fulfilled and the limits
>
> $$H[+0] = \int_a^b g(+0,u,T[0])du, \quad H[-0] = \int_a^b g(-0,u,T[0])du$$
>
> exist if $x \downarrow 0$ and $x \uparrow 0$, respectively.

We leave the proof of this lemma to the interested reader and merely note that the only difference to Lemma 7.1.1 consists in the fact that, for $x \downarrow 0$ and $x \uparrow 0$, the expressions $g(x(u),u,T)$ and $g'_x(x(u),u,T)$ may have discontinuities for those values of u where $x(u)=0$. However, since the set of these values is of measure zero, the functional derivatives and, in particular, the Laplacian exist on the set G_o and have the same form as under the conditions of Lemma 7.1.1.

Remark. To differentiate a functional on the set G_o means that, at a point $x \in G_o$, we consider only such increments η that $x+\eta$ belongs also to G_o .

It is well-known that the heat potential giving the solution of the heat equation on a finite interval is a function with discontinuities at the ends of this interval. In accordance with this, the "functional heat potentials" used below will be considered on a set of functions which we define as follows. Suppose again V_R to be the ball $\|x\| < R$, and let the function $x_o(u) > 0$ be given. Let, furthermore, G be the set of functions $x(u)$ satisfying the properties: (i) $G \subset V_R$, (ii) the equations $x(u)=0$, $x(u)=x_o(u)$ can be fulfilled only on a set of zero measure.

Problem 1. Find a functional $H[x|R]$ depending on the parameter R, $0<R<\infty$, which, for each fixed R, satisfies the conditions

1) $\Delta H = 0$ if $x \in G$,

2) $\lim_{x \downarrow 0} H[x|R] = \omega_1(R)$, $\lim_{x \uparrow x_0} H[x|R] = \omega_2(R)$

(ω_1, ω_2 are given functions continuous on the half-line $[0,\infty]$).

3) $H[x|R] = 0$ if $\|x\| = R$.

Thus, in analogy with the classical heat equation $\Delta H = 0 \sim u_\tau' - k^2 u_{\xi\xi}'' = 0$, condition 3) plays the role of an initial condition, and the set G corresponds to the whole axis $-\infty < \xi < \infty$ with the excluded points $\xi = 0$ and $\xi = 1$.

Theorem 7.2.1. Problem 1 is solvable, and $H[x|R]$ may be represented in the form

$$H[x|R] = \int_a^b du \int_0^T \frac{\varphi(\tau)}{2k\sqrt{\pi}(T-\tau)^{3/2}} x(u) \exp\left(-\frac{x^2(u)}{4k^2(T-\tau)}\right) d\tau$$

$$- \int_a^b du \int_0^T \frac{\psi(\tau)}{2k\sqrt{\pi}(T-\tau)^{3/2}} (x_0(u)-x(u)) \exp\left(-\frac{(x_0(u)-x(u))^2}{4k^2(T-\tau)}\right) d\tau, \quad (20)$$

where

$$T = T[x] = \frac{1}{2}(R^2 - \|x\|^2), \quad k^2 = (b-a)^{-1} \quad (21)$$

and φ, ψ are continuous functions being solutions of a system of singular Volterra equations with the kernels $k_1 = k_2 = q(u)/u^{3/2}$, $u = t-\tau$.
(This system will be obtained in the proof.)

Proof. First of all, we note that

$$\Delta T = -(b-a). \quad (22)$$

Now, let $0 < \xi < 1$, and let $u(\xi, t)$ be the heat potential (cf. KRZYŻAŃSKI [1], Chap. IX):

$$u(\xi,t) = \int_0^t \frac{\varphi(\tau)}{2k\sqrt{\pi}(t-\tau)^{3/2}} \xi \exp\left(-\frac{\xi^2}{4k^2(t-\tau)}\right) d\tau$$

$$- \int_0^t \frac{\psi(\tau)(1-\xi)}{2k\sqrt{\pi}(t-\tau)^{3/2}} \exp\left(-\frac{(1-\xi)^2}{4k^2(t-\tau)}\right) d\tau. \quad (23)$$

This function satisfies the equation $u_t' = k^2 u_{\xi\xi}''$. Comparing equations (20) and (23), we see that $u(\xi,t)$ is the generating function of the functional $H[x|R]$, where the parameter t is replaced by T and the constant 1 is replaced by the function $x_o(u)$. In virtue of Lemma 7.2.1 as well as relations (20) and (22), we conclude that $\Delta H = 0$ on the set G . It is well-known that for the function $u(\xi, t)$ the limits $u(+0,t)$ and $u(1-0,t)$ exist if φ and ψ are continuous.

Suppose $0 < x(u) < x_o(u)$, and let $x(u)$ successively tend to the bounds of this beam in a monotonic way. Since the convergence is assumed to be uniform, we can pass to the limit in the integrals occurring in (20). Taking into account requirement 2) of Problem 1, we obtain

$$(b-a)\varphi(t) - \int_a^b du \int_0^t \frac{\psi(\tau)}{2k\sqrt{\pi}\,(t-\tau)^{3/2}}\, x_o(u)\, \exp\left(-\frac{x_o^2(u)}{4k^2(t-\tau)}\right) d\tau = \omega_1(\sqrt{2t}) , \quad (24)$$

$$-(b-a)\psi(t-d) + \int_a^b du \int_0^{t-d} \frac{\varphi(\tau)x_o(u)}{2k\sqrt{\pi}(t-d-\tau)^{3/2}} \exp\left(-\frac{x_o^2(u)}{4k^2(t-d-\tau)}\right) d\tau = \omega_2(\sqrt{2t}) , \quad (25)$$

where $t = R^2/2$, $d = \|x_o\|^2$.

Changing here the order of integration with respect to τ and u , which is clearly possible, and setting

$$\frac{1}{2\sqrt{\pi}} \int_a^b x_o(u)\, \exp\left(-\frac{x_o^2(u)}{4k^2(t-\tau)}\right) du = q(t-\tau) ,$$

we get the system of equations

$$\varphi(t) - \int_0^t \frac{\psi(\tau)}{(t-\tau)^{3/2}}\, q(t-\tau)d\tau = k^2\omega_1(\sqrt{2t}) , \quad (26)$$

$$-\psi(t) + \int_0^t \frac{\varphi(\tau)}{(t-\tau)^{3/2}}\, q(t-\tau)d\tau = k^2\,\omega_2(\sqrt{2(t+d)}) , \quad (27)$$

where $q(t-\tau)$ is a continuous function for $0 \le \tau \le t < \infty$. If φ and ψ are solutions of these equations, then they satisfy, for $d \le t < \infty$, also the system (24), (25).

The fact that (20) vanishes on the sphere $\|x\| = R$ results directly from (21). The theorem has been proved.

Note that the generating functions φ and ψ of the functional (20) are uniquely determined by the given functions ω_1 and ω_2 .

Let now condition 3) of Problem 1 be replaced by the following assumption:

3') $H[x|R] = \int_{Q_m}\!\!\ldots\!\int f(x(u),u)\, du^m , \quad \|x\| = R ,$ (✱)

where $f(\xi,u)$ is a continuous function bounded on the set $\bar{E}_m \times \bar{Q}_m$. As was shown above, the formula

$$\Gamma[x] = \left(\frac{1}{2\sqrt{\pi T}}\right)^m \int_{Q_m}\!\!\ldots\!\int du^m \int_{E_m} f(\xi,u) \prod_{k=1}^{m} \exp\left(\frac{(x(u_k)-\xi_k)^2}{4T}\right) d\xi^m \quad (✱✱)$$

defines a functional Γ that is harmonic on the ball $\|x\| < R$. This functional is continuous for $\|x\| \leq R$ and takes the values (✱) on the sphere $\|x\| = R$. Repeating arguments similar to those used in the theory of differential equations, we thus can pass from condition 3') to the zero condition 3) of Problem 1.

It would be natural to expect that in constructing an analogue to the classical problem

$$u_\tau' = k^2 u_{\xi\xi}'' , \quad u(0,\tau) = \varphi(\xi), \quad u_\xi'(0,\tau) = \psi(\tau) ,$$

the value of u_ξ' will correspond to the functional derivative of the unknown functional U with respect to x. This way of reasoning, however, fails to be successful because, together with U, we must also vary the functional T, since T itself depends upon x. In order to avoid this difficulty, we shall suppose that, for every x, the functional derivative is taken along a direction tangent to the sphere $\|x\| = R$ and passing through this point, i.e. tangent to the corresponding level surface of the functional $T[x]$.

In the function space L^2 we fix now a direction defined by the vector $e(u)$, $\|e\| = 1$, which is supposed to be a continuous function.

Let F_e' be the functional derivative of F in the direction e. This derivative is defined via

$$F_e' = \int_a^b F_{x(u)}' \, e(u)\, du ,$$

where $F_{x(u)}'$ is the first functional derivative with respect to $x(u)$, $u \in [a,b]$. If the function $g(\xi,u,\alpha)$ is continuous and has continuous derivatives with respect to ξ and α, then the derivative of the functional $F = \int_a^b g(x(u),u,\Phi)du$ in the direction e is of the form

$$F_e' = \int_a^b g_{x(u)}' \, e(u)\, du + \Phi_e' \int_a^b \frac{\partial g}{\partial \Phi} du \quad (28)$$

(cf. Lemma 7.1.1).

If we replace here Φ by the functional T and take into consideration that $T_e' = -(x,e)$, then under the condition $(x,e) = 0$, which henceforth is supposed to be satisfied, we obtain

$$F_e' = \int_a^b g'_{x(u)}\, e(u)\, du . \tag{29}$$

Problem 2. Find a functional $H[x|R]$ depending on the parameter R, $0 < R < \infty$, and satisfying the conditions

1) $\Delta H = 0$, $x \in G$;

2') $\lim\limits_{x \downarrow 0} H[x|R] = \omega_1(R)$;

2") $\lim\limits_{x \uparrow x_0} H_e'[x|R] = \omega_2(R)$;

3) $H[x|R] = 0$ if $\|x\| = R$,

where all notations have the same meaning as above and all functions are subject to the same conditions.

Theorem 7.2.2. The solution of Problem 2 can be represented in the form

$$H = \int_a^b du \int_0^T \frac{\varphi(\tau)}{2k\sqrt{\pi}\,(T-\tau)^{3/2}}\, x(u) \exp\left(-\frac{x^2(u)}{4k^2(T-\tau)}\right) d\tau$$

$$+ \int_a^b du \int_0^T \frac{k\,\psi(\tau)}{\sqrt{\pi}\sqrt{T-\tau}} \exp\left(-\frac{(x_0(u)-x(u))^2}{4k^2(T-\tau)}\right) d\tau , \tag{30}$$

where φ and ψ are the solutions of a system of singular Volterra integral equations with kernels of the form

$$k_1 = \frac{q(u)}{u^{1/2}}, \quad k_2 = \frac{q(u)}{u^{3/2}}, \quad u = t-\tau, \quad q(u) \in C[a,b] .$$

Proof. The fact that functional (30), which has the sum of a dipole and a simple source with the heat densities φ and ψ as a generating function, satisfies the equation $\Delta H = 0$ results, as above, from Lemma 7.2.1. Condition 2') implies

$$(b-a)\,\varphi(t) + \int_a^b du \int_0^t \frac{k \exp\left(-\frac{x_0^2(u)}{4k^2(t-\tau)}\right)}{\sqrt{\pi}\sqrt{t-\tau}}\, \psi(\tau)\, d\tau = \omega_1\sqrt{2t} . \tag{31}$$

Computing the functional derivative of H at the point x in the direction e orthogonal to x and taking into consideration that in such a differentiation T behaves as a constant, we have

$$H_e' = \int_a^b du \int_0^T \frac{\varphi(\tau)}{2k\sqrt{\pi}\,(T-\tau)^{3/2}} \exp\left(-\frac{x^2(u)}{4k^2(T-\tau)}\right) e(u)\, d\tau$$

$$- \int_a^b du \int_0^T \frac{\varphi(\tau)}{4k^3\sqrt{\pi}\,(T-\tau)^{5/2}}\, x^2(u) \exp\left(- \frac{x^2(u)}{4k^2(T-\tau)}\right) e(u)\, d\tau$$

$$+ \int_a^b du \int_0^T \frac{\psi(\tau)}{2k\sqrt{\pi}\,(T-\tau)^{3/2}} (x_o(u)-x(u)) \exp\left(- \frac{(x_o(u)-x(u))^2}{4k^2(T-\tau)}\right) e(u)\, d\tau .$$

Passing here to the limit for $x \uparrow x_o$ and preserving the condition $(x,e)=0$, from 2") we obtain

$$(b-a)\,\psi(t-d) + \int_a^b du \int_0^{t-d} \frac{\exp\left(- \frac{x_o^2(u)}{4k^2(t-d-\tau)}\right)}{2k\sqrt{\pi}\,(t-d-\tau)^{3/2}}\, e(u)\, \varphi(\tau)\, d\tau$$

$$- \int_a^b du \int_0^{t-d} \frac{\exp\left(- \frac{x_o^2(u)}{4k^2(t-d-\tau)}\right)}{4k^3\sqrt{\pi}\,(t-d-\tau)^{5/2}}\, x_o^2(u)\, \varphi(\tau)\, d\tau = \omega_2(\sqrt{2t}) . \qquad (32)$$

Setting here

$$\frac{1}{2k\sqrt{\pi}} \int_a^b \exp\left(- \frac{x_o^2(u)}{4k^2(t-\tau)}\right) du = q_o(t-\tau) ,$$

$$\frac{1}{2k\sqrt{\pi}} \int_a^b e(u) \exp\left(- \frac{x_o^2(u)}{4k^2(t-\tau)}\right) du = q_1(t-\tau) ,$$

$$\frac{1}{4k^3\sqrt{\pi}} \int_a^b e(u) x_o^2(u) \exp\left(- \frac{x_o^2(u)}{4k^2(t-\tau)}\right) du = q_2(t-\tau)$$

and recalling that $k^2 = (b-a)^{-1}$, we come to the system of Volterra equations

$$\psi(t) + 2k^4 \int_0^t \frac{\psi(\tau) q_o(t-\tau)}{\sqrt{t-\tau}}\, d\tau = k^2\, \omega_1(\sqrt{2t}) , \qquad (33)$$

$$\psi(t) + k^2 \int_0^t \frac{\varphi(\tau) q_1(t-\tau)}{(t-\tau)^{3/2}} d\tau - k^2 \int_0^t \frac{\varphi(\tau) q_2(t-\tau)}{(t-\tau)^{5/2}} d\tau$$

$$= k^2\, \omega_2(\sqrt{2(t+d)}) . \qquad (34)$$

For $d \leq t < \infty$, the solutions φ and ψ of this system satisfy the system (31), (32). The validity of condition 3) is evident. The theorem is completely proved.

We select some special cases, in which system (33), (34) is essentially simplified.

(i) $q_0 \equiv 0$. We immediately get $\varphi = k^2\,\omega_1(\sqrt{2t})$, and from the second equation we find ψ by means of the known functions φ, q_1 and q_2 .

(ii) $q_2 \equiv 0$. The order of the singularity in the second equation decreases from 5/2 to 3/2 .

(iii) $q_1 \equiv 0$, $q_2 \equiv 0$ (this case holds, for example, if $a = -b$, x_0 is an even function on $[-b,b]$ and $e(u)$ is an odd function on the same interval). The functions φ and ψ can be expressed by ω_1 and ω_2 in a direct way.

We sum up the previous explanations in the overleaf table, which includes the results of Section 7.1, too.

It goes without saying that this table does not exhaust all the variety of possible analogies between the two classes of equations. Thus, for instance, it is clear that the specification of an initial condition 5) and one of the two boundary conditions 6) (heat equation on the semi-axis) has the boundary value problem 5) with a local condition 6) as a functional analogue. In contrast with Problem 1, the solution of the latter problem reduces to only one integral equation.

Problems 1 and 2 may be generalized in various directions. In particular, it is not hard to generalize Problem 1 by constructing functional analogues of one-dimensional heat equations with boundary conditions depending on time.

ANALOGY TABLE

Classical diffusion equations	Functional elliptic equations
1) Space: E_m: $-\infty < \xi_k < \infty$, $k=1,\dots,m$	1) Space: $A(a,b)$ ($L^2(a,b)$, $C[a,b]$, ...)
2) Time: τ	2) Functional: $T[x]$ (in boundary value problems)
3) Equations in E_m:	3) Equation and domain:
a) direct: $u'_\tau = k^2 \Delta u$	a) $\Delta U = 0$, $\Vert x\Vert < R$
b) inverse: $u'_\tau = -k^2 \Delta u$	b) $\Delta U = 0$, $\Vert x\Vert > R$
c) inhomogeneous: $u'_\tau = k^2 \Delta u + q(\xi,\tau)$	c) $\Delta U = Q[x]$, $\Vert x\Vert < R$
4) Diffusion coefficient: k	4) $(b-a)^{-1}$
5) Initial condition: $u(x,0) = \varphi(x)$	5) Boundary condition: $U[x] = F[x]$, $\Vert x\Vert = R$
6) One-dimensional heat equation, boundary value problems on E_1: $u(\xi,\tau)$, $\tau > 0$	6) $H[x\vert R]$, $R > 0$ variable
6_1) Axis $-\infty < \xi < \infty$ with excluded points $\xi = 0$, $\xi = l_0$	6_1) Set G: (i) $x \in C[a,b]$ (ii) $\operatorname{mes}_{[a,b]} \{x(u)=0\} = 0$ (iii) $\operatorname{mes}_{[a,b]} \{x(u)=x_0(u)\} = 0$
6_2) Time: τ	6_2) $R^2/2$
6_3) $u'_\tau = k^2 u''_{\xi\xi}$	6_3) $\Delta H[x\vert R] = 0$, $x \in G$
a) $u(+0,\tau) = \varphi_1(\tau)$, $u(l-0,\tau) = \varphi_2(\tau)$	a) $\lim_{x \downarrow 0} H[x\vert R] = \omega_1(R)$, $\lim_{x \uparrow x_0} H[x\vert R] = \omega_2(R)$
b) $u(+0,\tau) = \varphi_1(\tau)$, $u'_\xi(l-0,\tau) = \varphi_2(\tau)$	b) $\lim_{x \downarrow 0} H[x\vert R] = \omega_1(R)$, $\lim_{x \uparrow x_0} H'_e[x\vert R] = \omega_2(R)$, $(x,e) = 0$

8. Boundary value problems for uniform domains

The Dirichlet problem for a uniform domain differs from the functional Dirichlet problem examined in Sections 5-7 in many aspects. It can be considered as an intermediate problem between the functional and the classical Dirichlet problem. We shall see that in a certain sense the latter problem is a degenerated Dirichlet problem for a uniform domain. The same is true for classical boundary value problems of other types.

8.1. Functional and classical Dirichlet problems

Let $G = G(\sum_t, A_s(q))$, $q=(a,b)$ be a uniform function domain and $G' = G'(\sum_t, A_s(q))$ its boundary (see Section 2.1). As in 4.1, we shall denote the class of functionals weakly harmonic in the domain G by $\mathcal{H}_0 = \mathcal{H}_0(G)$.

We study the following problems:

Problem I. Find a functional $H[x]$ satisfying the conditions

$$H[x] \in \mathcal{H}_0(G), \quad H[x] = \Psi[x], \quad x \in G',$$

where Ψ is given.

Problem II. Given F find a functional $H[x]$ for which

$$H[x] \in \mathcal{H}_0(G), \quad \frac{dH}{dn}\Big|_{G'} = F[x] .$$

Problem III. Find a functional $\Phi[x]$ fulfilling the conditions

$$\Delta \Phi = F[x], \quad x \in G, \quad \Phi\Big|_{G'} = 0$$

with given $F[x]$.

All these problems may be considered in different function spaces and for various functional classes. The boundary conditions mean that, if $x_n \in G$, $z \in G'$ and $x_n \to z$ in the topology of $A_s(q)$, then $H[x_n] \to H[x]$.

We consider Problems I-III on the set $G(\sum_t, C_s[\bar{q}])$ with boundary values in the Gâteaux ring.

8.1.1. Let us begin with the Dirichlet problem I under the assumption

$$\Psi[x] = f(F_1, \ldots, F_N) , \tag{1}$$

where $x(t) = (x_1(t), \ldots, x_s(t))$ and

$$F_j = \int\cdots\int_{Q_m} g_j(x(t_1),\ldots,x(t_m);t_1,\ldots,t_m)dt^m = \int_{Q_m} g_j(X(t),t)dt^m. \quad (2)$$

Recall that $\sum_t(\zeta)$ is a family of domains in E_s, and ζ designates the values of vector functions $(x_1(t),\ldots,x_s(t))$, $t \in \bar{q}$, constituting the functional domain G.

We introduce the notations

$$\Sigma_{t_1}(\zeta_1)\times\ldots\times\Sigma_{t_m}(\zeta_m) = \Sigma_{m,t}, \quad (3)$$

$$\Sigma'_{t_1}(\zeta_1)\times\ldots\times\Sigma'_{t_m}(\zeta_m) = \Sigma'_{m,t} \quad (4)$$

(each factor on the left side of (3) and (4) is one and the same set, while "x" means the direct product).

<u>Theorem 8.1.1</u>. Let the functions $g_j(\zeta_1,\ldots,\zeta_m;t_1,\ldots,t_m)$, $j=1,\ldots,N$, be continuous on the set $\Sigma'_{m,t}$ and f (see (1)) be continuous on the set

$$\mathcal{G}: m_j(b-a)^m \leq F_j \leq M_j(b-a)^m, \quad j=1,\ldots,N,$$

where

$$\left.\begin{aligned} m_j &= \min_{\Sigma'_{m,t}} g_j(\zeta_1,\ldots,\zeta_m;t_1,\ldots,t_m), \\ M_j &= \max_{\Sigma'_{m,t}} g_j(\zeta_1,\ldots,\zeta_m;t_1,\ldots,t_m). \end{aligned}\right\} \quad (5)$$

For Problem I, (1), (2) to be solvable it is sufficient that there exist functions h_j satisfying the conditions

$$\begin{aligned} &\Delta_\alpha h_j = 0, \quad \alpha = 1,\ldots,m; \\ &h_j\Big|_{\Sigma'_{m,t}} = g_j(\zeta_1,\ldots,\zeta_m;t_1,\ldots,t_m) \end{aligned} \quad (6)$$

(Δ_α means the classical Laplacian with respect to the arguments of the vector ζ_α).

If (6) is fulfilled, the solution can be represented as

$$\Psi[x] = f(H_1[x],\ldots,H_N[x]), \quad (7)$$

where

$$H_j = \int\cdots\int_{Q_m} h_j(x(t_1),\ldots,x(t_m);t_1,\ldots,t_m)dt^m = \int_{Q_m} h_j(X(t),t)dt^m. \quad (8)$$

<u>Proof</u>. To start with, let the problem

$$H\Big|_G \in \mathcal{H}_0, \quad H\Big|_{G'} = F[x] = \int_{Q_m} g(X(t),t)dt^m \quad (9)$$

under the conditions mentioned above be given.

Let

$$\Delta_\alpha h = 0, \quad h\Big|_{\Sigma^{\cdot}_{m,t}} = g(\zeta_1,\dots,\zeta_m;t_1,\dots,t_m)$$

and

$$H = \int\limits_{Q_m} h(X(t),t)dt^m . \tag{10}$$

According to the general formula (1) from 3.1, we have

$$\underset{Z}{M}H = \int\limits_{Q_m}\dots\int \frac{dt_1\dots dt_m}{|S_{t_1}|\dots|S_{t_m}|}\int\limits_{S_{m,t}}\dots\int h(\zeta_1,\dots,\zeta_m;t_1,\dots,t_m)ds_{t_1}\dots ds_{t_m}, \tag{11}$$

where

$$S_{t_i}: \ |\zeta_i - \underset{o}{x}(t_o)| < \varrho(t_i); \quad S_{m,t}: \prod_{i=1}^{m} S_{t_i}; \quad Z = Z(S_t;C_s[q]) .$$

Since h is harmonic with respect to each vector ζ_α, $\alpha=1,\dots,m$, from the last equation we conclude that

$$\underset{Z}{M}H = \int\limits_{Q_m} h(\underset{o}{x}(t_1),\dots,\underset{o}{x}(t_m);t_1,\dots,t_m)dt^m = \int\limits_{Q_m} h(\underset{o}{X}(t),t)dt^m = H[\underset{o}{x}],$$

i.e. $H \in \mathcal{H}_o$.

If $\underset{\nu}{x} \rightrightarrows z$ converges uniformly on $C_s[\overline{q}]$, then from the continuity of g and h on the set $\overline{\Sigma}_{m,t} = \Sigma_{m,t} \cup \Sigma'_{m,t}$ and the fact that $g(\cdot) = h(\cdot)$ on the set $\Sigma^{\cdot}_{m,t}$, we conclude

$$\lim_{\nu} h(\underset{\nu}{x}(t_1),\dots,\underset{\nu}{x}(t_m);t_1,\dots,t_m) = g(z(t_1),\dots,z(t_m);t_1,\dots,t_m)$$

uniformly on $\overline{Q}_m$. Thus

$$H\Big|_{G'} = F .$$

For the general case, if the boundary conditions are of the form (1), we use a lemma, which we already met above in a similar form.

<u>Lemma 8.1.1</u>. Let $\mathcal{G}$ be the domain of values of $\Phi_1,\dots,\Phi_N$ when $x \in \overline{G}$. If $\overline{\mathcal{G}}$ is a bounded set and f is continuous on $\overline{\mathcal{G}}$, then for any sphere (or ball) Ω in G, the relation

$$\underset{\Omega}{M}f(\Phi_1,\dots,\Phi_N) = f(\underset{\Omega}{M}\Phi_1,\dots,\underset{\Omega}{M}\Phi_N)$$

holds provided that the means $\underset{\Omega}{M}\Phi_j$ exist.

<u>Corollary 8.1.1</u>. If $\Phi_j \in \mathcal{H}_o$, then also $f(\Phi_1,\dots,\Phi_N) \in \mathcal{H}_o$.

Since the functions h_j (see (6)) are harmonic on the set $\Sigma_{m,t}$ ($\Delta h = \sum_\alpha \Delta_\alpha h$), then, for $t \in \overline{Q}_m$, in view of the maximum principle we can write

$$\inf_{G'} g_j(X(t),t) \leq \inf_{G} h_j(X(t),t) \leq h_j(X(t),t)$$

$$\leq \sup_{G} h_j(X(t),t) \leq \sup_{G'} g_j(X(t),t) \ , \quad t \in Q_m \ .$$

Consequently

$$\min_{\overline{Q}_m} \inf_{G'} g_j(X(t),t) \leq h_j(X(t),t) \leq \max_{\overline{Q}_m} \sup_{G'} g_j(X(t),t) \ .$$

The extreme terms of these inequalities are m_j and M_j, respectively, indicated in (5). Integrating over Q_m, we obtain

$$m_j(b-a)^m \leq \int_{Q_m} h_j(X(t),t)dt^m \leq M_j(b-a)^m \ , \quad x \in \overline{G} \ .$$

Thus, on the basis of Lemma 8.1.1, the relation

$$\underset{Z}{M}\Psi = \underset{Z}{M}f(H_1,\dots,H_N) = f(\underset{Z}{M}H_1,\dots,\underset{Z}{M}H_N) = f(H_1[\underset{o}{x}],\dots,H_N[\underset{o}{x}]) = \Psi[\underset{o}{x}]$$

holds true. The validity of the boundary conditions results from the continuity of the function f on the set $\mathcal{G}$. The theorem is proved.

<u>8.1.2</u>. The proof of the unicity theorem will be based on the following

<u>Lemma 8.1.2</u>. Let $G(\Sigma_t, C_s[\overline{q}])$ be a function domain constructed by the family of domains $\Sigma_t \subset E_s$ of dimension ν, $1 \leq \nu \leq s$. If $g(\zeta_1,\dots,\zeta_m;t)$ is continuous on the set $\Sigma_{m,t}$ and

$$F = \int_{Q_m} g(X(t),t)dt^m = 0 \quad \text{for} \quad x \in G \ ,$$

then g does not depend upon $\zeta_1,\dots,\zeta_m$, i.e. $g = g(t)$.

We intend to prove this lemma for $m=1$. The case $m>1$ will be proved under the additional condition of analyticity of g with respect to ζ.

<u>Proof</u>. (i) Assume $m=1$, and let the relations

$$x_1 = f_1(u_1(t),\dots,u_\nu(t);t), \ \dots, \ x_s = f_s(u_1(t),\dots,u_\nu(t);t) \ ,$$
$$a_i(t) \leq u_i \leq b_i(t), \quad b_i - a_i = \delta_i(t) > 0, \quad i=1,\dots,\nu \qquad (12)$$

form a parametric representation of the domain G.

We set $v_i = u_i - \delta_i/2$ and rewrite equations (12) in the form

$$x_i = f_i(u-\tfrac{\delta}{2},t) = \tilde{f}_i(v,t), \quad -\delta_i/2 < v_i < \delta_i/2 \ . \qquad (13)$$

In this way,

$$F[x] = \int_q g(\tilde{f}_1(v,t),\ldots,\tilde{f}_s(v,t);t)dt = \int_q \gamma(v_1,\ldots,v_\nu;t)dt, \quad (14)$$

where with regard to the continuity of g and f, the function γ can also be considered as continuous.

The lemma will be verified if we establish that, for $|v_i| < \delta_i/2$, relation (14) implies the independence of the function γ of v. Without loss of generality we may assume that $\gamma(0,t) = 0$.

From the continuity of γ it follows that (14) is also true on the set of all step functions $\bar{v}$ for which $|\bar{v}_i| < \delta_i/2$.

In contrast to our assertion, let γ depend on v. Then we can indicate an interval Δ, scalar-valued vectors $\eta' = (\eta'_1,\ldots,\eta'_\nu)$, $\eta'' = (\eta''_1,\ldots,\eta''_\nu)$ as well as a number $\varepsilon > 0$ such that on Δ:

a) $\gamma(\eta',t) - \gamma(\eta'',t) > \varepsilon$,

b) $|\eta'_i|, |\eta''_i| < \delta_i(t)/2$.

Let χ_Δ be the characteristic function of the interval Δ. Evidently, for $v' = \eta'\chi_\Delta$, $v'' = \eta''\chi_\Delta$, the vectors $(x_1,\ldots,x_s)$ defined via (13) belong to the domain G. Now we have

$$\int_q (\gamma(v',t) - \gamma(v'',t))dt = \int_\Delta (\gamma(\eta',t) - \gamma(\eta'',t))dt > \varepsilon|\Delta|,$$

which contradicts the assumption of the lemma.

(ii) Let $m > 1$. We assume that the domain G is star-shaped near every point belonging to G [1] (this restriction is not essential, see the remark at the end of the proof). At first, we suppose that $s=1$ and, consequently, the dimension of $\Sigma_{m,t}$ is equal to m.

In accordance with this, all arguments ξ of the function $g(\xi_1,\ldots,\xi_m;t)$ are regarded as scalars. As already mentioned in Section 1, we assume that g is a symmetric function with respect to the indices $1,\ldots,m$ (without this assumption the lemma fails to be valid; for instance, with $g(\xi_1,\xi_2) = \xi_1 - \xi_2$, we get $F = \iint_{Q_2} x(t_1)dt_1dt_2 - \iint_{Q_2} x(t_2)dt_1dt_2 = 0$).

Since g was supposed to be an analytic function, we can write

---

[1] A domain G in a linear space is said to be star-shaped near the point $x_0 \in G$ if $x_0 + x \in G$ implies $x_0 + \lambda x \in G$ for any λ, $|\lambda| < 1$.

$$g(\xi,t) = \sum_{\nu=0}^{\infty} \sum_{\alpha_1+\dots+\alpha_\nu=\nu} C_{\alpha_1\dots\alpha_\nu}(t)\,\xi_1^{\alpha_1}\dots\xi_m^{\alpha_\nu}, \tag{15}$$

and, for $t \in q$, this series converges on $\sum_{m,t}$.

Due to the symmetry of g, the coefficients $C_{\alpha_1\dots\alpha_\nu}$ can also be assumed to be symmetric functions of their indices.

From (15), we deduce

$$F[x] = \sum_{\nu=0}^{\infty} \sum_{\alpha_1+\dots+\alpha_\nu=\nu} \int_{Q_m} C_{\alpha_1\dots\alpha_\nu}(t)x^{\alpha_1}(t_1)\dots x^{\alpha_\nu}(t_m)dt^m = 0. \tag{16}$$

We take an arbitrary but fixed function $x \in G$. Then, since G is a star-shaped domain, for some interval $0 < \lambda < \lambda_0 \leq 1$ we will have $\lambda x \in G$ and thus $F[\lambda x] = 0$. From (16) then the relations

$$\sum_{\alpha_1+\dots+\alpha_\nu=\nu} \int_{Q_m} C_{\alpha_1\dots\alpha_\nu}(t)x^{\alpha_1}(t_1)\dots x^{\alpha_\nu}(t_m)dt^m = 0, \quad \nu=1,2,\dots$$

result. We now want to show that these equations imply $C_{\alpha_1\dots\alpha_\nu} = 0$ for any α and ν. For $\nu=1$, this is evident. For the sake of brevity, we will prove the claim for $\nu=2$ (in the case $\nu>2$ the argument is the same).

Thus, we suppose

$$\Phi_2[x] = \int_q C_2(t)x^2(t)dt + \int_q\int_q C_{12}(t_1,t_2)x(t_1)x(t_2)dt_1dt_2 = 0.$$

In contrast to our assertion, let $C_2(t) \neq 0$ on a set $E \subset q$ of positive measure $|E|$. We can suppose that $C_2(t) > 0$ on this set. In this case we are able to find an interval $\Delta \subset E$, $|\Delta| = \delta$ such that $\inf_\Delta C_2 = m > 0$ and to indicate a function $x_\delta(t)$ with the properties

$$x_\delta(t) = h > 0, \quad t \in \Delta; \quad x_\delta(t) = 0, \quad t \bar{\in} \Delta.$$

Now we have

$$\int_q C_2(t)x_\delta^2(t)dt = \int_\Delta C_2(t)x_\delta^2(t)dt \geqslant \delta h^2 m$$

and

$$\left|\int_q\int_q C_{12}(t_1,t_2)x_\delta(t_1)x_\delta(t_2)dt_1dt_2\right| = \left|\int_\Delta\int_\Delta \dots dt_1dt_2\right| \leq Mh^2\delta^2,$$

where $M = \sup_{\Delta\times\Delta} |C_{12}(t_1,t_2)|$.

It follows that, for δ sufficiently small; $\Phi_2[x_\delta] \neq 0$, which contradicts the fact that $\Phi_2[x_\delta] = 0$. Hence $C_2(t) = 0$ almost everywhere on q.

Repeating the same arguments, we can show that $C_{12}(t_1,t_2) = 0$ almost everywhere on $q \times q$.

Consequently, the term of second order in (15) is equal to zero. In the same manner we may show that all the other terms in (15) containing ξ reduce to zero. Thus $g = g(t)$.

In the case $s > 1$, we write $g(\zeta_1,\ldots,\zeta_m;t) = g(\xi_{11},\ldots,\xi_{1s},\ldots,\xi_{m1},\ldots,\xi_{ms};t)$ and, after fixing $x_2(t),\ldots,x_s(t)$, we can show that g does not depend on $\zeta_1 = (\xi_{11},\ldots,\xi_{1s})$. Then, fixing $x_3(t),\ldots x_s(t)$, we show that g does not depend on ζ_1, ζ_2 etc. (the conclusion results also from the symmetry of g with respect to $\zeta_1,\ldots \zeta_m$). Thus $g = g(t)$.

If G is star-shaped around the point $\underset{0}{x}$, then with the aid of the translation $\eta = \xi - \underset{0}{x}$, we can transform Σ_t into a star $\tilde{\Sigma}_t$ around zero, and from the established independence of the function $g(\eta+\underset{0}{x},t)$ of η it follows that the function $g(\xi,t)$ is independent of ξ on the set Σ_t. If the domain G is given by the parametric equations (12), then expanding $\tilde{f}_i$ in a power series of the parameters v^j and repeating the previous arguments, we can prove that g does not depend upon ζ. Since in (12) we can regard u as local co-ordinates, the requirement of (global) star-shapedness of G may be assumed to hold without loss of generality. The lemma is completely proved.

<u>Theorem 8.1.2</u>. Let for the set $\Sigma'_{m,t}$ (see (4)) and the function g the conditions of Lemma 8.1.2 be fulfilled. If the system (6) has a unique solution in the class of functions mentioned in this lemma, then $H = \int_{Q_m} h\, dt^m$ is the unique functional of Gâteaux type being a solution of problem (9).

In fact, if $F = \int_{Q_m} h dt^m$, $\tilde{F} = \int_{Q_m} \tilde{h} dt^m$ and on the set G' the equality $F = \tilde{F}$ holds, then owing to Lemma 8.1.2, the generating function φ of the functional $F-\tilde{F}$ has the form $\varphi(t)$ and we can suppose that $\varphi = 0$. In view of the unique solvability of problem (6) assumed above, we then have $h = \tilde{h}$ on the set $\Sigma_{m,t}$. Hence $F = \tilde{F}$ if $x \in G$.

<u>Remark</u>. The analyticity of the function $g(\xi,t)$ with respect to the arguments of the vector ξ used in the proof of Lemma 8.1.2 is obvious because $h(\xi,t)$ is a harmonic function of the same arguments and it is well-known that a harmonic function is analytic as well.

8.1.3. Looking back on the considerations explained in 8.1.1 and 8.1.2, we observe that Problem I, (9) is related to the standard classical problem if $m=1$. For $m>1$, we encounter the problem of finding an m-harmonic function on Σ_m by its values on the m(s-1)-dimensional skeleton $\Sigma_m^{\cdot}$. In some important special cases problems of this kind are solvable. Let e.g. the domain $G: x^2(t)+y^2(t)<1$ be given and the boundary values be defined by the functional

$$F = \int_q \int_q g(w(t_1),w(t_2);t_1,t_2)dt_1dt_2 ,$$

where $g = g(\zeta_1,\zeta_2;t_1,t_2)$ and $g(\cdot)$ is an analytic function with respect to ζ_1 and ζ_2. Setting $\zeta_1 = \xi_1+i\eta_1$, $\zeta_2 = \xi_2+i\eta_2$, we get the problem

$$\frac{\partial^2 h}{\partial \xi_1^2} + \frac{\partial^2 h}{\partial \eta_1^2} = 0, \quad \frac{\partial^2 h}{\partial \xi_2^2} + \frac{\partial^2 h}{\partial \eta_2^2} = 0; \quad |\zeta_1| < 1, \quad |\zeta_2| < 1,$$

$$h(\xi_1,\eta_1;\xi_2,\eta_2;t_1,t_2) = g(\xi_1,\eta_1;\xi_2,\eta_2;t_1,t_2); \; |\zeta_1|=1, \; |\zeta_2|=1,$$

the solution of which is obtained by means of a double Poisson integral.

At the same time, it is not hard to understand why the introduction of superposition operators does not lead to additional difficulties. Let, for example, $s=2$, $m=2$; $F = \int_q g_1 dt \cdot \int_q g_2 dt$. In this case the problem reduces to the pair of usual problems in different spaces

$$\Delta h_1(\xi_1,\eta_1) = 0, \quad h_1\Big|_l = g_1(\xi_1,\eta_1,t) ;$$

$$\Delta h_2(\xi_2,\eta_2) = 0, \quad h_2\Big|_l = g_2(\xi_2,\eta_2;t)$$

(l is a closed contour in the ξ,η-plane).

The same applies if the boundary conditions are given in the form

$$F = f(\int_q g_1 dt, \ldots, \int_q g_N dt) ,$$

where f is a continuous function.

Up to now we dealt with the weak Dirichlet problem. Obviously, the functional (10) is strongly harmonic:

$$\Delta H = \Delta \int_{Q_m} h dt^m = \int_{Q_m} \sum \Delta_k h dt^m = 0 .$$

The same is true for the functional (7) if f is a differentiable function in the range of $H_1,\dots,H_N$.

It is easy to see that the strong Dirichlet problem $\Delta H = 0$, $H|_{G'} = \int_{Q_m} g(X(t),t)dt^m$ can be incorrect for $m>1$. It leads us to the classical problem $\Delta h = 0$, $h|_{\Sigma'_{m,t}} = g$, which is superdefinite: the number of arguments ξ of h is ms, while the dimension of $\Sigma'_{m,t}$ is equal to $ms-s$.

All this is a natural consequence of the fact that the dimension of the boundary of the domain under study is less than $m(s-1)$ if $m>1$. Thus, in the simplest case $G: u(t)<x(t)<v(t)$, the strong Dirichlet problem is correct only if the boundary values are given in the form $\int_q g(x(t),t)dt$ (or as a function of functionals of this kind), and in this case the solution process reduces to the linear interpolation of the function $g(\zeta,t)$ with two nodes $\zeta = u(t)$, $\zeta = v(t)$.

In order to solve Problem I (see Subsection 8.1.1) under the conditions (1) and (2) in the case $m=1$, it was sufficient to solve N times the classical Dirichlet problem and to compose the desired functional. It is very interesting that, in its turn, the classical Dirichlet problem can be considered as a degeneration of the investigated functional Dirichlet problem for a uniform domain. Let us explain this fact in more detail.

Assume that Σ_t does not depend on t. Therefore $G = G(\Sigma, C_s[\bar{q}])$ is a domain of the first kind. From the very definition of the domain G it follows that any vector $\zeta \in \Sigma$ considered as a function $x(t)$, which takes the constant value ζ, belongs to Σ. Let G_0 be the set of such vectors. Clearly, this set can be identified with Σ.

Let $H = \int_a^b h(x(t))dt$ be the solution of the Dirichlet problem for G with the boundary value $F = \int_a^b g(x(t))dt$. As the restriction of these expressions to the set G_0 we can write

$$H|_{G_0} = h(\zeta), \quad F|_{G_0} = g(\zeta).$$

Since $\Delta H = \int_a^b \Delta h dt$, $\Delta H|_{G_0} = \Delta_\xi h$, we see that the functional Dirichlet problem reduces to the equations

$$\sum_1^s \frac{\partial^2 h}{\partial \xi_k^2} = 0, \quad \zeta \in \Sigma; \quad h|_{\Sigma'} = g(\zeta),$$

which proves our assertion.

The situation can be visualized as follows:

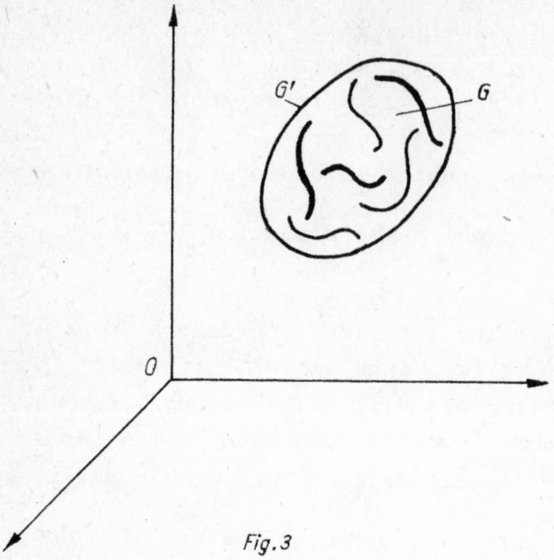

Fig.3

Dirichlet problem for a uniform domain $G(\Sigma, C_3[\overline{q}])$ with boundary surface Σ'. Thin lines - trajectories on Σ, bold lines - trajectories in the interior of Σ.

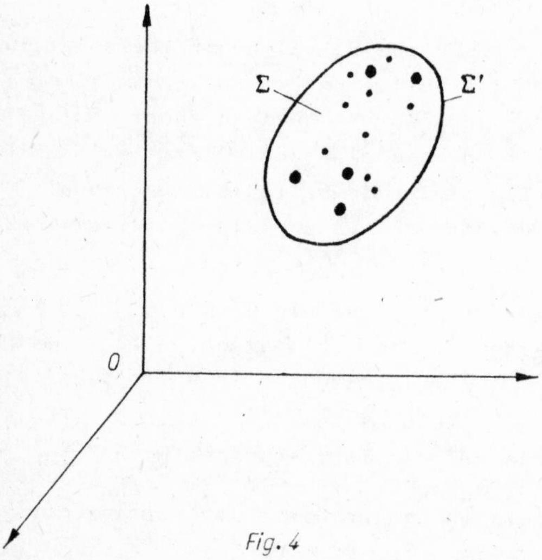

Fig. 4

Degeneration into a classical Dirichlet problem in E_3

8.2. The Dirichlet problem for operators

Now we study the question of extending the results derived above to the solution of Problem I, (1), (2) in the Lebesgue spaces $L_s^{\alpha}(q)$ consisting of vector functions $x = (x_1(t),\dots,x_s(t))$ summable to the α-th power, $\alpha > 0$ (where the norm in L_s^{α} is defined via $\|x\|_{\alpha} =$

$= \left(\sum_{1}^{s} \int_{q} |x_k(t)|^{\alpha} dt)^{1/\alpha} \right)$. In this setting it makes sense to pass from functionals to operators. Let $G(\sum_t, L_s^{\alpha}(q))$ and $G'(\sum_t, L_s^{\alpha}(q))$ be a uniform domain in the space $L_s^{\alpha}(q)$ and its boundary, respectively. The Dirichlet problem for operators can be formulated as follows:

Let q^* be some interval on the axis $-\infty < u < \infty$. Find an operator $H \in \{L_s^{\alpha}(q) \longrightarrow L_s^{\beta}(q^*)\}$ such that $\Delta H = 0$ on the set G and, for $\underset{n}{x} \in G$, $z \in G'$, the relation $\| \underset{n}{x} - z \|_{\alpha} \longrightarrow 0$ implies $\| H\underset{n}{x} - Fz \| \longrightarrow 0$. The Laplacian of the operator is defined by $\Delta = \sum_{1}^{s} \frac{\partial^2}{\partial x_k \partial x_k}$, where $\frac{\partial}{\partial x_k \partial x_k}$ is the iterated partial Fréchet derivative with respect to x_k. The given operator F belongs to $\{L_s^{\alpha}(q) \longrightarrow L_s^{\beta}(q)\}$, $\beta > 0$.

We come to this problem in a natural way assuming that in (2) the functions g_j depend, apart from ξ and t, on a parameter $u \in q^*$. In accordance with this, (6) will also be a function of u and the functionals (1), (2), (7), (8) become operators:

$$F_j x = \int_{q} g_j(x(t), t, u) dt, \quad H_j x = \int_{q} h_j(x(t), t, u) du, \tag{17}$$

$$\Psi x = f(H_1 x, \dots, H_N x) . \tag{18}$$

We restrict ourselves to the study of the case $m=1$, where g_j are assumed to possess the form

$$g_j = g_j(\xi, t) k_j(t, u) .$$

Correspondingly

$$h_j = h_j(\xi, t) k_j(t, u) .$$

Reckoning that, for each pair (t,u), h_j results from g_j as above by the solution of the classical Dirichlet problem, our aim consists in clarifying the conditions under which the operators H_j and Ψ yield the solution of the Dirichlet problem for the domain $G(\sum_t, L_s^{\alpha}(q))$. Since we now deal with unbounded functions, these conditions will be expressed by means of estimates of the growth of the functions h_j and f (and their derivatives) with respect to ξ (the restrictions on h_j are, actually, restrictions on g_j because h_j are determined by g_j in a quite definite manner).

In the sequel, we suppose that all functions and their partial derivatives satisfy the Carathéodory conditions on their domains of definition.

We shall employ the following theorems (KRASNOSELSKIĬ et al. [1], Chap. V):

Theorem 8.2.1. If $fx = f(x(t),t)$ and f is a superposition operator on $L_s^\alpha(q)$, $\alpha > 0$, such that on the strip $\Pi : E_s \times q$ the estimate

$$|f(\zeta,t)| \le a(t) + b|\zeta|^{\sigma/\alpha}, \quad \sigma > 0, \quad b = \text{const} > 0, \quad a \in L^\sigma(q)$$

holds, then

$$f \in \{ L_s^\alpha(q) \longrightarrow L_s^\sigma(q) \} .$$

Theorem 8.2.2. Suppose $f \in \{ L_s^\alpha(q) \longrightarrow L_s^\sigma(q) \}$, $0 < \alpha < \sigma$, and let f'_{ξ_i} exist on Π. For the existence of the derivative of the operator f at any point $x \in L_s^\alpha$ it is necessary and sufficient that

$$f'_{x_i}(x(t),t) \in \{ L_s^\alpha(q) \longrightarrow L_s^{\sigma-\alpha}(q) \} .$$

Theorem 8.2.3. Let

$$\mathfrak{A}x = \int_q k(t,u) f(x(t),t)dt ,$$

and let the linear operators

$$k_j \varphi = \int_q k_j(t,u)\, \varphi(t)dt$$

belong to $\{ L^\alpha(q) \longrightarrow L^\tau(q^*) \}$, $\tau > 0$. If the conditions of Theorems 8.2.1 and 8.2.2 hold, then $\mathfrak{A}$ is a differentiable operator and

$$\mathfrak{A}'_{x_i} x = \int_q k(t,u) f'_{x_i}(x,t)dt \in \{ L_s^\alpha(q) \longrightarrow L_s^{\sigma-\alpha}(q^*) \} .$$

Now we are prepared to formulate

Theorem 8.2.4. Suppose $\alpha > 0$, $\beta > 0$, and let positive constants σ, τ, $\sigma > 2\alpha$, $0 < \tau < \beta$, $c_0, c_1, c_2, c_3, c_4 > 0$ exist such that the following conditions be fulfilled:

(i) $|h_j(\zeta,t)| \le b_0(t) + c_0|\zeta|^{\sigma/\alpha}$, $b_0 \in L^\sigma(q)$;

(ii) $\left| \dfrac{\partial h_j}{\partial \xi_k} \right| \le b_1(t) + c_1|\zeta|^{\frac{\sigma-\alpha}{\alpha}}$, $b_1 \in L^{\sigma-\alpha}(q)$;

(iii) $\left| \dfrac{\partial^2 h_j}{\partial \xi_k\, \partial \xi_k} \right| \le b_2(t) + c_2|\zeta|^{\frac{\sigma-2\alpha}{\alpha}}$, $b_2 \in L^{\sigma-2\alpha}(q)$;

(iv) $k_j(u,t)$ are linear operators: $k_j \in \{ L^\sigma(q) \longrightarrow L^\tau(q^*) \}$;

(v) the function $f(\eta_1,\dots,\eta_N;u) = f(\eta,u)$ is twice continuously differentiable with respect to the arguments $\eta_1,\dots,\eta_N$ on the strip $\Pi = E_N \times q$, where the estimates

$$|f| \le b_3(u) + c_3|\eta|^{\beta/\tau}, \quad b_3(u) \in L^\beta(q^*) ,$$

$$\left|\frac{\partial f}{\partial \eta_i}\right| \leq b_4(u)+c_4|\eta|^{\frac{\beta-\tau}{\tau}}, \quad b_4(u) \in L^{\beta-\tau}(q^*)$$

hold. Then the operator solution of the functional Dirichlet problem is of the form

$$\Psi x = f(H_1x,\dots,H_Nx) ,$$

where

$$H_j = \int_q h_j(x,t)k_j(t,u)dt$$

and $h_j(\zeta,t)k_j(t,u)$ considered as a function of ζ is almost everywhere on $q \times q^*$ a solution of the classical Dirichlet problem in the domain Σ_t with boundary values $g_j(\zeta,t)k_j(t,u)$ on the set $\Sigma_t^{\cdot}$.

The proof follows immediately from the properties of continuity and differentiability of the operators involved in Theorems 8.2.1-8.2.3.

It should be noted that almost everywhere on $q \times q^*$ the derivatives $\frac{\partial h_j}{\partial \xi_k}$, $\frac{\partial^2 h_j}{\partial \xi_k \partial \xi_k}$ exist. Furthermore, in view of Theorems 8.2.1 and 8.2.2, the Fréchet derivatives $\frac{\partial h_j}{\partial x_k}$ and $\frac{\partial^2 h_j}{\partial x_k \partial x_k}$ of the operators h_j with respect to x_k exist on the set G . Omitting the indices at x , we can state

$$\frac{\partial h_j}{\partial x} \in \left\{L_s^{\alpha}(q) \longrightarrow L_s^{\sigma-\alpha}(q)\right\}, \quad \frac{\partial^2 h_j}{\partial x\, \partial x} \in \left\{L_s^{\alpha}(q) \longrightarrow L_s^{\sigma-2\alpha}(q)\right\} .$$

Theorem 8.2.3 implies that the operators

$$H_jx = \int_q h_j(x(t),t)k_j(u,t)dt$$

are twice differentiable on the space $L^{\alpha}(q)$ and, in addition, $H \in \left\{L^{\alpha}(q) \longrightarrow L^{\tau}(q^*)\right\}$. Again omitting the indices at x , for the first and second derivatives H_x' , H_{xx}'' we can write

$$H_x' = kh_x' \in \left\{L_s^{\alpha}(q) \longrightarrow L_s^{\sigma-\alpha}(q)\right\} ,$$

$$H_{xx}'' = kh_{xx}'' \in \left\{L_s^{\alpha}(q) \longrightarrow L_s^{\sigma-\alpha}(q) \longrightarrow L_s^{\tau}(q)\right\} .$$

With regard to (v), we have

$$\Psi = f(H_1x,\dots,H_Nx;u) \in \left\{L_s^{\tau}(q^*) \longrightarrow L^{\beta}(q^*)\right\} .$$

Moreover, again by virtue of (v), the relation

$$\Delta \Psi x = \left[\sum_1^N \left(\frac{\partial f}{\partial H_j}\right) x\right] \Delta H_jx$$

holds for $x \in L_s^\alpha$. Since $\Delta H_j = 0$ on the set G , we obtain on this set $\Delta \Psi x = 0$.

All operators considered here are strongly continuous. Hence $\| x-z \|_\alpha \xrightarrow[n]{} 0$ implies $\| H_{j_n} x - H_j z \|_\beta \longrightarrow 0$, i.e.

$$H_j \big|_{G'} = F_j \big|_{G'} .$$

From (v) we conclude that in (18) Ψ is also a continuous operator. Consequently, on the set G' , one has

$$\Psi(H_1,\ldots,H_j) = \Psi(F_1,\ldots,F_j) ,$$

which completes the proof of the theorem.

8.3. The functional Neumann problem

The functional Neumann problem for a uniform domain with boundary values in the Gâteaux ring (see 8.1, Problem II) has common traits with the Dirichlet problem considered in Section 8.1.

Let $G(\sum_t, C_s[\bar{q}])$, $s > 1$, be a uniform domain with smooth boundary (smooth skeleton boundary) $G'(\sum_t, C_s[\bar{q}])$. By the *derivative of the functional* $H = \int_{Q_m} h(X(t),t)dt^m$ at the point $x \in G'$ we understand the functional $\Phi = \int_{Q_m} \varphi dt^m$ constructed via the generating function $\varphi(\zeta_1,\ldots,\zeta_m;t)$, which is the derivative of $h(\zeta_1,\ldots,\zeta_m;t)$ in direction of the normal to the boundary (normal to the skeleton boundary):

$$\varphi(\zeta,t) = \frac{dh}{dn} = \sum_\alpha \frac{dh}{dn_\alpha} = \sum_{\alpha=1}^{m} \sum_{k=1}^{s} \frac{\partial h}{\partial \xi_{\alpha k}} \cos \theta_{\alpha k} , \quad t \in Q_m .$$

(For each $\xi_{\alpha k}$, $\cos \theta_{\alpha k}$ defines the normal direction to $\dot{\sum}_{m,t}$ at the point $\xi_{\alpha k}$. Since $\dot{\sum}_{m,t}$ is symmetric with respect to the pair (ζ_α, t_α) , they have the same expression for $\alpha = 1,\ldots,m$.)

As a matter of course, this definition is in accordance with the general definition of the directional derivative of F in direction of the corresponding unit vector e , $|e(t)| = 1$:

$$\frac{dF}{de} = \frac{dF[x+\lambda e]}{d\lambda}\bigg|_{\lambda=0} .$$

<u>Theorem 8.3.1</u>. Let $g(\zeta_1,\ldots,\zeta_m;t)$ be a continuous function on the set $\sum_{m,t}$ analytic with respect to the variables $\xi_{\alpha k}$, $\alpha = 1,\ldots,m;$

$k=1,\ldots,s$. If there exists a function $h(\zeta_1,\ldots,\zeta_m;t)$ satisfying the equations

$$\Delta_\alpha h\Big|_{\Sigma_{m,t}} = 0\,, \quad \frac{dh}{dn}\Big|_{\Sigma^{\cdot}_{m,t}} = g\,,$$

then the functional $H = \int\limits_{Q_m} h(X(t),t)dt^m$ provides the solution of the functional Neumann problem

$$H \in \mathcal{H}_0(G)\,, \quad \frac{dH}{dn}\Big|_{G'} = F = \int\limits_{Q_m} g(X(t),t)dt^m\,.$$

Up to an additive constant C this solution is unique in the class of Gâteaux functionals constructed by those generating functions which satisfy the conditions of the theorem.

We leave the proof to the reader because it is entirely analogous to the proof of Theorem 8.1.1. We shall make only one remark concerning the unicity of the solution for the case $m=1$.

Let $\Phi = \int\limits_q \varphi(x(t),t)dt$, and let $\varphi(\zeta,t)$ be analytic with respect to ξ_k and continuous on the set $E_s \times \bar{q}$. Furthermore, suppose $\frac{d\Phi}{dn}\Big|_{G'} = 0$. Since the generating function of $\frac{d\Phi}{dn}$ is $\frac{d\varphi(\zeta,t)}{dn}$, $\zeta \in \Sigma^{\cdot}_t$, then from the previous equation and Lemma 8.1.2 we conclude that $\frac{d\varphi(\zeta,t)}{dn} = \gamma(t)$ on $\Sigma^{\cdot}_t$. We can suppose that $\gamma(t) \equiv 0$. Using the well-known formula

$$\int\limits_{\Sigma'_t} \frac{d_\zeta\varphi}{dn}\, d_\zeta\sigma = \int\limits_{\Sigma_t} |\nabla_\zeta\varphi|\, d_\zeta v\,,$$

we notice that $\nabla_\zeta\varphi(\zeta,t) = 0$, $\zeta \in \Sigma_t$. Hence $\varphi = \psi(t)$ and $\Phi = \int\limits_q \psi(t)dt = \text{const.}$

8.4. Properties of the Poisson equation

Here we intend to sketch the properties of Problem III from Section 8.1. They will be formulated only briefly for the case $m=1$.

Let $F = \int\limits_q g(x(t),t)dt$. If the function $g(\zeta,t)$, $t \in \bar{q}$, $\zeta \in E_s$, satisfies some Hölder conditions on Σ_t and is continuous on $\overline{\Sigma}_t$, then the functional $U = \int\limits_q f(x(t),t)dt$, where

$$f(\zeta,t) = \int_{\Sigma_t} g(\zeta,\eta)k(\zeta,\eta,t)d\eta$$

and $k(\zeta,\eta,t)$ is the Green function of the domain Σ_t, possesses the properties:

(i) U satisfies the equation $\Delta U = F[x]$, $x \in G$;
(ii) $U = 0$ on G';
(iii) U is continuous on $\overline{\Sigma}_t$ in the topology of the space $C_s[\overline{q}]$.

Unlike the Dirichlet problem, Problems II and III become essentially more complicated if we replace in them the functional $F[x]$ by the functional $f(F)$ because the solutions of the resulting problems cannot be expressed as the superpositions of solutions to problems with boundary values F, as it was the case in Subsection 8.1.1.

As for the rest, if $m=1$, Problems I, II and III are of the same type, and from the previous considerations it is clear that, under appropriate restrictions, they are well-posed. If the domain G is of the first kind, $m=1$, and $g(\zeta,t)$ does not depend on t, i.e. $g = g(\zeta)$, then on the set of vector functions G_0 with constant components, Problems II and III reduce to the classical problems of the same name (cf. the end of Section 8.1).

9. Harmonic control systems

In this section we discuss the functional Dirichlet problem in connection with continuous control systems. We deal with ordinary differential equations containing function parameters (control parameters) which vary in some domain $\mathcal{G}$ (control domain). Integrals of these equations are functionals belonging to the Volterra or Picard classes (see 1.1).

We pose the functional Dirichlet problem with the boundary values f on $\mathcal{G}$. In the case if $\mathcal{G}$ is a normal domain, the solution is obtained using the classical diffusion equations and with the aid of an iterative process corresponding to the original differential equation.

A similar situation arises if $\mathcal{G}$ is a uniform domain, however, the auxiliary classical equations are now elliptic.

The solutions obtained permit us to replace the system in question by a "harmonic system" having some new important properties compared with the original one.

9.1. Normal control domain

Let the equation

$$\frac{dy}{dt} = f(t,y,x) \tag{1}$$

be given, which involves control parameters $x(t) = (x_1(t),\dots,x_s(t))$ belonging to the set $\overline{D} = D \cup D'$, where D is a normal domain in the space $A_s(q)$, $q = (a,b)$.

Parallelly to (1), we study the equation

$$\frac{dy}{dt} = f(t,y,\lambda_1,\dots,\lambda_s) ,$$

where the parameters $\lambda_1,\dots,\lambda_s$ are scalars. Let for this equation the initial condition $y|_{t_o} = y_o$ be given.

In several applied problems y_o is regarded as a function of λ. In accordance with this, it will be supposed that the choice of the initial value in (1) is defined by the function $x(t)$. Varying $x(t)$ in the domain $\overline{D}$, the integral of equation (1) becomes a functional $Y[x|t]$ of x ("Volterra functional"). Furthermore, it is assumed that Y_o is also a functional: $Y_o = Y_o[x]$.

We shall refer to Y_o as an initial functional. Generally speaking, Y_o depends on all values of t from the interval $(-\infty, t_o)$: $Y_o = Y_o\left[\overset{t_o}{\underset{-\infty}{x}}\right]$. In the present book all functionals depend on functions defined on finite intervals. Hence we suppose $Y_o = Y_o\left[\overset{t_o}{\underset{a}{x}}\right]$, where a is one and the same for all x and $-\infty < a < t_o$.

Another natural assumption is the following:

$$Y_o = \int_a^{t_o} f_o(x(t),t)\,dt \tag{2}$$

(Y_o is a Gâteaux functional).

9.1.1. Thus we start with the differential equation

$$\frac{dY}{dt} = f(t,Y[x|t],x(t)) , \quad a \leq t \leq b , \tag{3}$$

where Y is a Volterra functional satisfying the initial condition

$$Y[x|t_o] = Y_o \tag{3'}$$

with Y_o defined via (2).

Furthermore, we form the Picard functional

$$\Phi[x] = \int_a^b g(t, Y[x|t]; x(t))dt \tag{4}$$

and pose the following functional Dirichlet problem:

Find a functional Ψ such that

$$\Psi \in \mathcal{H}(D) \ , \quad D = D(A_s(a,b)) \ ; \quad \Psi\Big|_{D'} = \Phi[x] \ .$$

As above the validity of the boundary conditions means that $\Psi[x_n] \longrightarrow \Psi[z]$ if $x_n \in D$, $z \in D'$, $x_n \to z$.

We shall study this problem in the space $C_s[a,b]$. Under evident modifications, the following results remain also valid for functionals in the spaces $A_s = L_s^p$, $p \geqslant 2$ and $A_s = M_s$. Of course, in these cases, $Y[x|t]$, regarded as a function of t , is defined almost everywhere on the interval (a,b) .

Let the following assumptions be valid:

(i) The generating function $f_0(\xi_1, \dots, \xi_s; t) = f(\zeta, t)$ of Y_0 (see (2)) is continuous on the set

$$(-\infty < \xi_k < \infty) \times [a \leq t \leq t_0] = E_s \times [a, t_0]$$

and

$$|f_0(\zeta, t)| \leq A_0 + B_0 |\zeta|^2, \quad A_0, B_0 = \text{const} > 0 \ .$$

(ii) Let E be the set

$$(a \leqslant t \leqslant b) \times (-\infty < \eta < \infty) \times (-\infty < \xi_k < \infty) = [a,b] \times E_1 \times E_s \ .$$

We suppose that $f(t, \eta, \zeta)$ (see (1) and (3)) is a continuous function on E having on this set continuous derivatives with respect to η and ξ_k , where

$$|f'_\eta| \leq M|\zeta| \ , \quad M = \text{const} \ .$$

(iii) $g(t, \eta, \zeta)$ (see (4)) is a continuous and bounded function on E .

In addition, we formulate conditions concerning the domain D .

(iv) The domain D is supposed to be bounded, i.e., there exists a ball K_R: $\|x\| < R$ with $K_R \supset \overline{D}$. Moreover it is supposed that there exists a functional $T[\overset{b}{\underset{a}{x}}] = T$ having variations δT, $\delta^2 T$ of the form (4) and (5), respectively, from Section 7.1 as well as the properties

(iv') $T[x] > 0$ if $x \in D$, $T[x] = 0$ if $x \in D'$;

(iv") $\Delta T[x] = -s(b-a)$.

Since
$$\Delta \|x\|^2 = \sum_1^s \Delta_j \int_a^b \sum x_j^2(t)dt = 2s(b-a) ,$$
the conditions (iv") and (iv') mean that

$$T[x] = \frac{1}{2}(\Gamma[x]-\|x\|^2), \quad \Delta\Gamma = 0, \quad x \in D,$$
$$\Gamma[x] = \|x\|^2, \quad x \in D' .$$

Theorem 9.1.1. Let $\Phi[x]$ be the Picard functional (4), and assume the conditions (i)-(iv) to be fulfilled. Then the solution of the functional Dirichlet problem with the boundary values $\Phi[x]$ on the set D' has the form

$$\Psi[x] = \int_a^b h(t,H[x|t],x(t),T[x])dt , \tag{5}$$

where $h(t,H[x|t],\zeta,T[x])$ is a solution of the diffusion equation

$$\frac{\partial h}{\partial T} = s^{-1}(b-a)^{-1} \sum_1^s \frac{\partial^2 h}{\partial \xi_k^2}$$

with the initial value

$$h\Big|_{T=0} = g(t,H[x|t],\zeta) .$$

Here H is a harmonic functional, i.e.

$$H \in \mathcal{H}(D), \quad H\Big|_{D'} = Y[x|t] ,$$

constructed via the solution of the diffusion equation and an iterative procedure associated with equation (1), while $Y[x|t]$ is the Volterra functional obtained from (3), (3') and (2).

Proof. The functional (5) will be constructed successively in three steps: 1) Solution of a Dirichlet problem with boundary values $Y_o[x]$; 2) the same with boundary values $Y[x|t]$; 3) the same with boundary values $\Phi[x]$.

1) Let $h_o(\zeta,t,\tau)$ be the solution of the diffusion equation

$$\frac{\partial h_o}{\partial \tau} = \Delta_\zeta h_o ; \quad h_o(\zeta,t,0) = f_o(\zeta,t) .$$

We form the functional

$$H_o[x] = \int_a^{t_o} h_o(x(t),t,T[x])dt . \tag{6}$$

The function h_o is continuous and twice continuously differentiable with respect to ξ_k and τ for $\tau > 0$. Hence, due to Lemma 4.1.3 (cf. formula (9) of 4.1),

$$\Delta H_o = \int_a^{t_o} \left(\sum_1^s \frac{\partial h_o}{\partial x_k^2} + \frac{\partial h_o}{\partial T} \Delta T \right) dt \; .$$

If $x \in D$, then in view of (iv"), we can write

$$\Delta H_o = \int_a^{t_o} \sum_1^s \left(s(b-a) \frac{\partial^2 h_o}{\partial x_k^2} - \frac{\partial h_o}{\partial T} \right) dt = 0 \; . \qquad (7)$$

In addition, from (2), (6), (iv'), (iv") we get for $x_n \in D$, $z \in D'$, $x_n \rightrightarrows z$:

$$\lim_n H_o[x_n] = \int_a^{t_o} f_o(z(t),t)dt = Y_o[z] \; . \qquad (8)$$

In this way, functional (6) satisfies the two conditions (7) and (8).

2) Now we construct the functional

$$H[x|t] \in \mathcal{H}(D), \quad H[x|t]\Big|_{D'} = Y[x|t] \; .$$

Let $x \in \overline{D}$ and $y_o, y_1, \ldots$ be the sequence of Picard iterations of equation (1) corresponding to this function. Let, furthermore, $Y_o[x]$, $Y_1[x|t], \ldots$ be the following sequence of iterations, which is obtained if x varies on the set $\overline{D}$:

$$Y_{n+1}[x|t] = Y_o[x] + \int_{t_o}^{t} f(u, Y_n[x|u], x(u))du \; .$$

In particular

$$Y_1[x|t] = Y_o[x] + \int_{t_o}^{t} f(u, Y_o[x|u], x(u))du \; .$$

We form the functional

$$H_1[x|t] = H_o[x] + \int_{t_o}^{t} h(u, H_o[x], x(u), T[x])du \; , \qquad (9)$$

where $h(t, H_o, \zeta, T)$ is a solution of the problem

$$\frac{\partial h}{\partial T} = (\Delta_\zeta h)s^{-1}(b-a)^{-1}, \quad h(t,H_o,\zeta,0) = f(t,H_o,\zeta) \; .$$

Because of Lemma 4.1.3, which is obviously applicable here, one has

$$\Delta H_1 = \Delta H_o + \int_{t_o}^{t} \left(\sum_1^s \frac{\partial^2 h}{\partial x_k^2} + \frac{\partial h}{\partial H_o} \Delta H_o + \frac{\partial h}{\partial T} \Delta T \right) dt \; .$$

Taking into account (iv") as well as the equation $\Delta H_o = 0$ for $x \in D$, we get

$$\Delta H_1 = \int_{t_o}^{t} \left(\sum_1^s \frac{\partial^2 h}{\partial x_k^2} - s(b-a) \frac{\partial h}{\partial T} \right) du = 0 \; .$$

Moreover, if $x \in D'$, the relation

$$H_1[z|t] = H_o[z] + \int_{t_o}^{t} f(u,H_o[z],z(u))du$$

$$= Y_o[z] + \int_{t_o}^{t} f(u,Y_o[z],z(u))du = Y_1[z|t]$$

holds true. If we repeat the same, then in the next iteration we obtain

$$H_2[x|t] = H_o[x] + \int_{t_o}^{t} h(u,H_1[x|u],x(u),T[x])du ,$$

where

$$\frac{\partial h(t,H_1,\zeta,T)}{\partial T} = s^{-1}(b-a)^{-1} \Delta_\zeta h, \quad h\Big|_{T=0} = f(t,H_1,\zeta) .$$

For $h(u,H_1,\zeta,T)$ regarded as a function of u and ζ all conditions of Lemma 4.1.3 are satisfied.

Repeating this process, we obtain two functional sequences $Y_n[x|t]$ and $H_n[x|t]$, $n=0,1,2,\ldots,$ such that

$$H_{n+1}[x|t] = H_o[x] + \int_{t_o}^{t} h(u,H_n[x|u],x(u),T[x])du , \tag{10}$$

$$H_n \in \mathcal{H}(D), \quad H_n[x|t] = Y_n[x|t] \text{ if } x \in D', \quad H_n[x|t_o] = H_o[x] .$$

As a result of the existence and unicity theorem of a solution of equation (1), the limit

$$Y[x|t] = \lim_n Y_n[x|t] , \quad x \in \overline{D}$$

exists for $t \in [a,b]$, where

$$\frac{dY[x|t]}{dt} = f(t,Y[x|t],x(t)), \quad Y[x|t_o] = Y_o[x] .$$

Now we want to show that the sequence Y_n converges uniformly on $\overline{D}$. From (i) and (ii) we deduce

$$|Y_1-Y_o| \leq \int_{t_o}^{t} |f(u,x(u))|du \leq \int_{t_o}^{t} A_o du + \int_{t_o}^{t} B_o \sum_1^s x_k^2(u)du$$

$$\leq A_o(b-a) + B_o(b-a)R^2 = A_1 + B_1R^2 = K = \text{const} .$$

Taking into account (ii), we can write

$$|Y_2-Y_1| \leq \int_{t_o}^{t} |f(u,Y_1[x|u],x(u))-f(u,Y_o[x],x(u))| du$$

$$\leq \int_{t_o}^{t} MK\sqrt{\sum x_k^2(u)} du \leq MK(t-t_o)^{1/2}R ;$$

$$\left|Y_3-Y_2\right| = \int_{t_0}^{t} \left|f(u,Y_2[x|u],x(u))-f(u,Y_1[x|u],x(u))\right| du$$

$$\leq MKR \left[\int_{t_0}^{t} (t-t_0)dt \right]^{1/2} \left[\int_{t_0}^{t} \sum x_k^2(u)du \right]^{1/2} = \frac{t-t_0}{\sqrt{2}} M^2KR .$$

Consequently, for $n=1,2,\dots,$ we obtain

$$\left| Y_{n+1}[x|t]-Y_n[x|t]\right| \leq M^nKR\sqrt{\frac{(t-t_0)^n}{n!}} .$$

Whence

$$Y_n[x|t] \rightrightarrows Y[x|t] , \quad x \in \overline{D} .$$

This implies that the sequence $H_n[x|t]$ also converges uniformly: $H_n \rightrightarrows H$, $x \in \overline{D}$. This fact can be justified by establishing an explicit relation between the generating functions f and h of the functionals Y_n and H_n , respectively,

$$h(.,\zeta,..,T) = \left(\frac{s(b-a)}{4\pi T}\right)^{s/2} \int_{E_s}\!\!\dots\!\!\int f(.,\eta,..)\, e^{-\frac{s(b-a)|\zeta-\eta|^2}{4T}} d\eta^s$$

(the "Weierstrass transform") and making use of the properties of the kernel

$$K(\zeta,\eta;T) = \frac{1}{2\sqrt{\pi T}} e^{-\frac{|\zeta-\eta|^2}{4T}} .$$

However, the same can be proved in a simpler way if we have in mind that, because of the Gâteaux formula (for $m=1$, see formula (3) from 3.3) and the harmonicity of $H_n[x|t]$ both in the strong and the weak sense, the relation

$$H_n[x|t] = \underset{\Omega}{\mathfrak{M}} Y_n[x|t]$$

holds, where Ω is the Hilbert sphere with centre at x and radius $\sqrt{2T[x]}$. This implies

$$\left|H_{n+1}[x|t]-H_n[x|t]\right| = \left| \underset{\Omega}{\mathfrak{M}}(Y_{n+1}[x|t]-Y_n[x|t])\right|$$

$$\leq \sup_{\Omega} \left| Y_{n+1}-Y_n\right| \leq M^nRK\sqrt{\frac{(t-t_0)^n}{n!}} .$$

If $x \in D'$, then $Y_n = H_n$ and hence

$$\left| H_{n+1}-H_n\right| \leq M^nRK\sqrt{\frac{(t-t_0)^n}{n!}} .$$

Consequently

$$H_n \rightrightarrows H \quad \text{if} \quad x \in \overline{D} .$$

From Lemma 4.1.2 it follows that, for $x \in D$,

$$\lim_n \Delta H_n = \Delta \lim_n H_n = \Delta H = 0 .$$

In addition, for $x_n \in D$, $z \in D'$, $\lim_n x_n = z$, we get

$$\lim_n H[x_n | t] = \lim_n \lim_m H_m[x_n] = \lim_m \lim_n H_m[x_n] = \lim_m H_m[z] = Y[z] .$$

3) Now we turn to the expression (4) and form the functional

$$\Psi[x] = \int_a^b h_1(t, H[x|t], x(t); T[x])dt , \qquad (11)$$

where

$$\frac{\partial h_1(t, H, \zeta, T)}{\partial T} = s^{-1}(b-a)^{-1} \Delta_\zeta h_1, \quad h_1(t, H, \zeta, 0) = g(t, H, \zeta) .$$

Taking into account the equations $\Delta H = 0$ and $H|_{D'} = Y$, conditions (iv') and (iv") as well as Lemma 4.1.3, after repeating the previous arguments, we obtain

$$\Delta \Psi = 0 \quad \text{if} \quad x \in D \quad (\text{i.e.} \quad \Psi \in \mathcal{H}(D)) ,$$

$$\Psi[z] = \int_a^b g(t, H[z|t], z(t))dt = \Phi[z] \quad \text{if} \quad z \in D' .$$

Thus (11) is the desired functional and the theorem is proved.

9.1.2. If we restrict ourselves to the Dirichlet problem with boundary values $Y[x|t]$, it seems to be natural to consider the domain D_t consisting of functions defined on the interval $a \leq u \leq t$. In this case all arguments remain the same as above, however, instead of the functional $T = T[\overset{b}{\underset{a}{x}}]$ we have to use the functional $\tilde{T} = \tilde{T}[\overset{t}{\underset{a}{x}}]$ satisfying the conditions

$$\tilde{T} > 0 \quad \text{if} \quad x \in D_t , \quad \tilde{T} = 0 \quad \text{if} \quad x \in D_t' , \quad \Delta \tilde{T} = s(t-a) .$$

The solution of the problem $\Delta \tilde{H} = 0$, $\tilde{H}|_{D_t'} = Y$ is obtained as the uniform limit $\tilde{H} = \lim_n \tilde{H}_n$, where $\tilde{H}_n$ differs from H_n only by the fact that the corresponding functional T is replaced by $\tilde{T}$.

If in $\tilde{H}$ and $\tilde{Y}$ the value t is assumed to be variable (i.e., if we consider the Dirichlet problem for a family of domains D_u, $a < u < t$), then we have

$$\tilde{T} = \frac{1}{2} (\Gamma[x|t] - \int_a^t x^2(u)du) \quad \text{for} \quad x \in \overline{D}_t$$

and

$$\Gamma[x|t] = \int_a^t \sum_1^s x_k^2(u)du \quad \text{on } D_t' ,$$

so that we obtain

$$\sum_1^s x_k^2(t) = \frac{d\Gamma[x|t]}{dt} , \quad x \in D_t' .$$

This means a restriction on the values of the functions at separated points, which corresponds to the definition of a uniform domain.

9.1.3. We now suppose that the boundary D' of the domain D is a convex surface S and recall the definition of a surface of the type $\{S\}$:

(i) for each $x \in D$, S can be represented by the equation $z = x + \varrho e$, where $\varrho = \varrho_x[e]$ is the polar radius from x in the direction defined by the unit vector e , $\|e\| = 1$;

(ii) there exists the functional $\underset{\|e\|=1}{\mathfrak{M}} \varrho_x[e]$ taking the values $\sqrt{2T[x]}$, where $T\left[\begin{smallmatrix} b \\ x \\ a \end{smallmatrix}\right]$ is the functional introduced in Subsection 9.1.1.

Theorem 9.1.2. Let S be a surface of the type $\{S\}$ and $H[x|t]$, $\Psi[x]$ be the solutions of the functional Dirichlet problem with the boundary values $Y[x|t]$ and $\Phi[x]$, respectively, on S satisfying the conditions of Theorem 9.1.1. Then H and Ψ can be described in the form

$$H[x|t] = \mathfrak{M}\, Y[x+ \varrho_x[e]e|t] , \tag{12}$$

$$\Psi[x] = \mathfrak{M}\, \Phi[x+ \varrho_x[e]|e] . \tag{13}$$

We do not go into details of the proof of this theorem and confine ourselves to the following explanations.

As in 5.1, with the aid of P. Lévy's theorem, we prove that, for $S \in \{S\}$ and for each iteration,

$$\mathfrak{M} Y_n[x+ \varrho_x[e]e|t] = \mathfrak{M}\, Y_n[x+\sqrt{2T[x]}\, e|t] , \qquad x \in \bar{D}$$

(cf. relations (4) and (5) from 5.1). Since $Y_n \rightrightarrows Y$ for $x \in \bar{D}$, this means

$$\mathfrak{M}\, Y[x+ \varrho_x[e]e|t] = \mathfrak{M} Y[x+\sqrt{2T[x]}\, e|t] .$$

Taking into account the explicit expression of the functionals $\mathfrak{M} Y_n[x+\sqrt{2T[x]}\, e]$ and the Gâteaux formula (3) of Section 3.3 for $a=x$, $R = \sqrt{2T}$, $m=1$, we have

$$\mathfrak{M} Y_n[x+\sqrt{2T[x]}\, e|t] = H_n[x|t] .$$

Since $Y_n[x|t] = H_n[x|t]$ on the set D', we may write

$$\mathfrak{M} Y[x+\sqrt{2T[x]}\, e|t] = H[x|t] \quad .$$

The latter coincides with the required representation. Formula (13) can be proved along the same lines.

Remark. Lévy's theorem mentioned above is based on the assumption of uniform continuity of the considered functional. This assumption was included in the definition of the type $\{S\}$. In the paper POLISHCHUK [11,II] Theorem 9.1.2 was proved without this requirement and in a slightly different manner.

9.1.4. We now indicate important conclusions of the representations (12) and (13).

1) For any fixed $t \in [a,b]$, the functional $H[x|t]$ (the functional Ψ) cannot attain its extreme values inside of the domain D (maximum principle).

2) Let $H|_{D'} = 0$. Since, for each x, $H[x|t]$ can be represented as the mean of the values of $Y[x|t]$ on the surface S, we see that $H[x|t] = 0$ for $x \in D$, too, i.e., the obtained solution is unique in the class of functionals satisfying the indicated demands.

3) The functional $H[x|t]$ obtained in Subsection 9.1.1 has the properties $\Delta H = 0$, $H|_{D'} = Y$ and satisfies the equation

$$\frac{dH[x|t]}{dt} = h(t, H[x|t], x(t), T\,[\overset{b}{\underset{a}{x}}]) \,,$$

which, setting $H[x|t] = u$, can be rewritten in the form

$$\frac{du}{dt} = h(t,u,x,T[x]) \,. \tag{14}$$

Now we compare the two control systems described by equations (1) and (14). We interpret y and u as state vectors and $\frac{dy}{dt}$, $\frac{du}{dt}$ as their velocities. The principal difference between them consists in the following. In contrast with the velocity $\frac{dy}{dt}$, at each instant the velocity $\frac{du}{dt}$ depends not only upon t, but it also depends on all the history of the control parameter x because $T = T\,[\overset{b}{\underset{a}{x}}]$.

4) Unlike y, for u the maximum principle holds.

5) If, in addition to the conditions mentioned in (i) and (ii) of 9.1.1, the generating functions $f_o(\zeta, t)$ and $f(t, \eta, \zeta)$ of the functionals

Y_o and Y, respectively (see (2), (3)), are entire functions of ξ and η, ξ, then the Laplacians $\Delta^{\nu} Y$ of all orders $\nu = 1,2,\dots$ exist and, under the same assumptions as in 5.6, we can estimate the deviation $H[x|t] - Y[x|t]$ in some layer $\Lambda_{\varepsilon} \subset \bar{D}$ bounded by D'.

9.2. Uniform control domain

9.2.1. Let $G = G(\Sigma_t, C_s[a,b])$ be a uniform domain and $G' = G'(\Sigma'_t, C_s[a,b])$ its boundary. The problem is to find a functional $U[x]$ satisfying the conditions $\Delta U = 0$ if $x \in G$; $U|_{G'} = \Phi[x]$, where $\Phi[x]$ is the Picard functional defined by formula (4) from 9.1 with Y being a Volterra functional such that

$$\frac{dY[x|t]}{dt} = f(t, Y[x|t], x(t)), \quad x \in \bar{G}, \quad \bar{G} = G \cup G'$$

and

$$Y[x|t_o] = \int_a^{t_o} f_o(t, x(t))dt = Y_o[x], \quad a < t_o < b,$$

where f, f_o and g are given functions.

The validity of the boundary conditions is here understood in the sense that $x_n \in G$, $z \in G'$ and $x_n \rightrightarrows z$ (i.e. uniform convergence with respect to the metric in $C_s[a,b]$) implies $U[x_n] \longrightarrow \Phi[x]$.

We suppose that, for every $t \in [a,b]$, Σ'_t is a closed smooth oriented surface lying entirely in the interior of the ball V_R,

$$\bar{V}_R: \quad |\zeta| \le R, \quad \Sigma'_t \subset V_R. \tag{1}$$

Theorem 9.2.1. Let the functions $f_o(t, \zeta)$, $f(t, \eta, \zeta)$, $g(t, \eta, \zeta)$ be continuous on the set $[a \le t \le b] \times (-\infty < \eta < \infty) \times V_R$ and the following conditions be fulfilled:

(i) $|f_o(t, \zeta)| \le A_o + B_o |\zeta|^2$, $A_o, B_o = \text{const} > 0$;

(ii) f is continuously differentiable with respect to η, where

$$|f'_\eta| < M|\zeta|.$$

If the Dirichlet problem for Σ_t with boundary conditions f_o, f, g on Σ'_t is solvable, then the solution of the functional Dirichlet problem $\Delta U = 0$, $U|_{G'} = \Phi$ with Φ defined by relation (4) from 9.1 may be obtained by solving the classical Dirichlet problem for Σ'_t and using the Picard iteration process corresponding to equation (1) of Section 9.1.

In addition, it will be shown that the solution obtained is weakly harmonic, i.e., for every sphere $S = S_{x_o, \rho} : |x-x_o| = \rho(t)$, $S \subset G$, the relation

$$M U = U[x_o]$$
$$S$$

holds.

<u>Proof.</u> Let $\varphi_o(t, \zeta)$ be a solution of the problem

$$\Delta_\zeta \varphi_o = 0, \quad \varphi_o \Big|_{\Sigma_t'} = f_o(t, \zeta).$$

Then for the functional

$$\Gamma_o[x] = \int_a^{t_o} \varphi_o(t, x(t)) dt,$$

by Lemma 4.1.3, we have

$$\Delta \Gamma_o = \int_a^{t_o} \sum_k \frac{\partial^2 \varphi}{\partial x_k^2} dt = 0, \quad \Gamma_o \Big|_{\Sigma'} = Y_o.$$

The same arguments (conditions on f_o, f and Σ_t as well as the application of the same lemma) show that the solution $\Gamma_1[x|t]$ of the Dirichlet problem for G with the boundary value

$$Y_1[x|t] = Y_o[x] + \int_{t_o}^t f(u, \Gamma_o[x], x(u)) du$$

is of the form

$$\Gamma_1[x|t] = \Gamma_o[x] + \int_{t_o}^t \varphi(u, \Gamma_o[u], x(u)) du, \tag{2}$$

where

$$\Delta_\zeta \varphi(u, \Gamma_o[x], \zeta) = 0 \quad \text{if} \quad \zeta \in \Sigma_u$$

and

$$\varphi(u, \Gamma_o[x], \zeta) = f(u, \Gamma_o[x], \zeta) \quad \text{if} \quad \zeta \in \Sigma_u'.$$

For the functional

$$\Gamma_2[x|t] = \Gamma_o[x] + \int_{t_o}^t \varphi(u, \Gamma_1[x|u], x(u)) du$$

with the generating function $\varphi(u, \Gamma_1, \zeta)$, the relations

$$\Delta_\zeta \varphi = 0 \quad \text{if} \quad \zeta \in \Sigma_u,$$

$$\varphi(u, \Gamma_1, \zeta) = f(u, \Gamma_1, \zeta) \quad \text{if} \quad \zeta \in \Sigma_u'$$

hold, and we discover that Γ_2 meets all the conditions of Lemma 4.1.3. Hence

$$\Delta \Gamma_2 = 0 \quad \text{if} \quad x \in G$$

and

$$\Gamma_2\Big|_{G'} = Y_2 .$$

Continuing along the same lines, we obtain, together with the sequence Y_o, $Y_1[x|t]$, $Y_2[x|t]$,..., a sequence of functionals Γ_o, $\Gamma_1[x|t]$, $\Gamma_2[x|t]$, ... for which

$$\Gamma_{n+1}[x|t] = \Gamma_o[x] + \int_{t_o}^{t} \varphi(u, \Gamma_n[x|u], x(u))du ,$$

$$\Delta\Gamma_n = 0 \quad \text{if} \quad x \in G ; \quad \Gamma_n = Y_n \quad \text{if} \quad x \in G' .$$

The condition previously imposed on the set $\Sigma_t \cup \Sigma_t^{\prime}$ implies the boundedness of the set $\overline{G} = G \cup G'$: $G \subset \overline{V}_R$ with $\overline{V}_R$: $|x| \leq R$. Thus, taking into account conditions (i) and (ii) mentioned in the theorem and repeating the arguments of the proof of Theorem 9.1.1, we get

$$\Big| Y_{n+1}[x|t] - Y_n[x|t] \Big| \leq B\sqrt{\frac{(t-t_o)^n}{n!}} , \quad x \in \overline{G}, \quad B = \text{const} > 0 ,$$

i.e. $Y_n \rightrightarrows Y$ on the set $\overline{G}$, and $Y[x|t]$ is a Volterra functional. Consequently

$$\Big| \Gamma_{n+1}[x|t] - \Gamma_n[x|t] \Big| \leq B\sqrt{\frac{(t-t_o)^n}{n!}} .$$

This may be proved by writing down an explicit expression of the generating functions φ_o and φ_n related to Γ_o and Γ_n, respectively, by means of f_o and f, the generating functions of Y_o and Y_n.

(Remark. This statement also results from the fact that Γ_n is the mean value of Y_n $\forall$ n as will be proved below.)

Summarizing, $\Gamma_n[x|t]$ converges uniformly on the set $\overline{G}$ and, due to Lemma 4.1.2, the limit functional $\Gamma = \lim_n \Gamma_n[x|t]$ is also harmonic. In addition, $\Gamma = Y$ if $x \in G'$.

Finally, we construct the Picard functional

$$U[x] = \int_a^b \psi(t, \Gamma[x|t], x(t))dt ,$$

where

$$\Delta_\zeta \psi(t, \Gamma[x|t], \zeta) = 0 \quad \text{if} \quad \zeta \in \Sigma_t ;$$

$$\psi = g(t, \Gamma[x|t], \zeta) \quad \text{if} \quad \zeta \in \Sigma_t^{\prime} .$$

Following the same arguments we show that

$$\Delta U = 0, \quad x \in G ; \quad U = \Phi , \quad x \in G' ,$$

where Φ was defined at the beginning of the present section. This proves the first part of the theorem.

We now intend to show that the obtained functionals Γ and U are weakly harmonic. First of all, we remind the reader of two facts:

(i) The mean of the functional $F = \int_E g(x(t),t)dt^m$ over the sphere S_t: $|x-x_o| = \rho(t)$ is of the form

$$\underset{S_t}{M} F = \int_E dt_1 \ldots dt_m \frac{1}{\mu(t_1)\ldots\mu(t_m)} \int_{S_{t_1}} \ldots \int_{S_{t_m}} g(\underset{o}{x}(t_1)+\rho(t_1)\zeta_1, \ldots,$$

$$\underset{o}{x}(t_m)+\rho(t_m)\zeta_m; t_1,\ldots,t_m) d\sigma_{t_1} \ldots d\sigma_{t_m} , \qquad (3)$$

where $\mu(t_i)$ is the measure of the sphere S_{t_i} and $d\sigma_{t_i}$ the differential of this measure (E is some cube Q_m or a measurable subset of Q_m ; see (1) from Section 3.1).

(ii) If $h(\zeta_1,\ldots,\zeta_m;t_1,\ldots,t_m)$ is a harmonic function with respect to any vector ζ_i , then $H = \int_E h(x(t_1),\ldots,x(t_m);t_1,\ldots,t_m)dt^m$ is a harmonic functional both in the weak and the strong sense: $H \in \mathcal{H}(G)$, $H \in \mathcal{H}_o(G)$.

First of all, we discuss the case that the initial functional Y_o is a constant.

From (2) and (3) we have

$$\underset{S}{M} \Gamma_1[x|t] = \int_{t_o}^{t} \varphi(u,y_o,\underset{o}{x}(u))du + y_o = \Gamma_1[\underset{o}{x}|t] .$$

The proof of the analogous fact for Γ_2 is similar but slightly more complicated. The conditions imposed on the function f ensure that the function $\varphi(u,\Gamma_1,\zeta)$ is also continuous on the considered domain of the variables u, Γ_1, ζ. For $x \in \overline{G}$, the set of values of Γ_1 is obviously bounded and closed. Therefore $\varphi(u,\Gamma_1,\zeta)$ can be represented in the form $\lim_N p_N(u,\Gamma_1,\zeta)$, where p_N are polynomials in Γ_1 and the sequence p_N converges to φ uniformly with respect to all arguments. Moreover, it is not hard to understand that all coefficients of p_N may be assumed to be harmonic functions of ζ .

Thus the sequence of functionals

$$P_N[x|t] = \int_{t_o}^{t} p_N(u,\Gamma_1[x|u],x(u))du + y_o$$

converges uniformly to $\Gamma_2[x|t]$ on the set G . Furthermore, all the

P_N have the form

$$P_N[x|t] = \sum_0^N \int_{t_o}^{t} a_{N\nu}(u,x(u))\,\Gamma_1^{\nu}[x|u]\,du + y_o .$$

Replacing Γ_1 by its value, we can rewrite P_N as follows:

$$\sum_{\nu=0}^{N} \int_{t_o}^{t} \tilde{a}_{N\nu}(u,x(u))\left\{\prod_{i=1}^{\nu} \int_{t_o}^{u} \varphi(u_i,y_o,x(u_i))\,du_i\right\} du ,$$

where $\varphi(u_i,y,\xi)$ and $\tilde{a}_{N\nu}(u,\xi)$ (as well as p_N) are harmonic functions of ξ .

It follows from the remark (ii) just mentioned that $P_N \in \mathcal{H}_o(G)$. Consequently, since it is possible to pass to the limit under the sign of the operation $\underset{S}{M}$, we get $\underset{S}{M}\Gamma_2 = \Gamma_2[\underset{o}{x}|t]$, i.e. $\Gamma_2 \in \mathcal{H}_o(G)$.

If Y_o fails to be a constant, then for $\Gamma_o = \int_a^t \varphi_o(u,x(u))du$,

the relation $\underset{S_t}{M}\Gamma_o = \Gamma_o[\underset{o}{x}]$ holds. Furthermore, approximating the functional

$$\Gamma_1 = \Gamma_o + \int_{t_o}^{t} \varphi(u,\Gamma_o[x],x(u))du$$

by functionals of the form

$$\Gamma_o + \sum_1^N \Gamma_o^{\nu} \int_{t_o}^{t} b_{1\nu}(u,x(u))du ,$$

where $b_{1\nu}(u,\xi)$ are some harmonic functions with respect to ξ , we are able to prove that $\Gamma_1 \in \mathcal{H}_o(G)$.

In the same manner we can show that, for each n , $\Gamma_n \in \mathcal{H}_o(G)$ and $\Gamma \in \mathcal{H}_o(G)$.

At last, repeating the arguments just used, we succeed in verifying the inclusion $U[x] \in \mathcal{H}_o(G)$. The theorem is completely proved.

<u>9.2.2</u>. If $n \longrightarrow \infty$, we have

$$\Gamma[x|t] = \Gamma_o[x] + \int_a^t \varphi(t,\Gamma[x|t],x(t))dt$$

and, setting $\Gamma[x|t] = v(t)$,

$$\frac{dv}{dt} = \varphi(t,v(t),x(t)) , \quad v(t_o) = \Gamma_o[x] . \tag{4}$$

The obtained differential equation (4) defines a "harmonic control system" whose state function $v(t)$ coincides with the state function

$y(t)$ related to the input system on the boundary G' of the control domain. Unlike the values of $y(t)$, for those of $v(t)$ at each instant t the maximum principle holds: $v(t)$ cannot attain its extreme values in the interior of the domain G. This fact is a consequence of the representation of $\Gamma[x|t]$ (of the functional $U[x]$, respectively) in the form of the mean value of $Y[x|t]$ (of $\Phi[x]$) over the boundary G'.

9.2.3. Here we deal with the representation of a solution of the functional Dirichlet problem as the mean over the boundary G'. In order to obtain the mentioned representation, we need some generalization of the definition of a continual mean over a uniform domain stated in 3.1. We suppose that, for any $t \in [a,b]$, on the set Σ_t' the probability measure with density $p(\zeta, t)$ is defined.

Let $\langle f_n \rangle$ be the mean value of the function f_n (see Section 3.1) over the set $\Sigma_{t_1} \times \dots \times \Sigma_{t_m}$ corresponding to this distribution. If, under $n \longrightarrow \infty$ and $\max(t_i - t_{i-1}) \longrightarrow 0$, there exists the limit

$$M^p_G F = \lim_n \langle f_n \rangle ,$$

then it will be called the mean value of F over the domain G with respect to the measure p. In particular, if the distribution is uniform on G, we return to the definition from 3.1.

As in 3.1 it may be proved that for the Gâteaux functional (1) described in this section the mean M^p_G exists and has the form

$$M^p_G F = \int_{Q_m}\!\!\cdots\!\int dt_1 \dots dt_m \int_{\Sigma_{t_1}}\!\!\cdots\!\int_{\Sigma_{t_m}} g(\zeta_1, \dots, \zeta_m; t_1, \dots, t_m) \prod_{i=1}^{m} p(\zeta_i, t_i)\, dv_{t_i} \qquad (5)$$

provided that its generating function g is continuous on the set $(\Sigma_{t_1} \times \dots \times \Sigma_{t_m}) \times \overline{Q}_m$ (and, of course, under the assumption that the integral exists). Moreover, the mean M^p_G has all the properties indicated in 3.1.

Now we return to the Dirichlet problem for the domain $G(\Sigma_t, C_s[a,b])$. Let, for each $t \in [a,b]$, $w(\zeta, \eta, t)$ be the Green function of the domain Σ_t associated with the operator Δ_ζ, and let $\rho = \frac{dw_t}{dn_e}$ be its derivative in direction of the exterior normal to Σ_t'. It is well-known that $\rho > 0$ on Σ_t' and, clearly,

$$\int_{\Sigma_t'} \rho(\zeta, \eta, t)\, d_\eta \sigma_t = 1, \quad (t, \zeta) \in \Sigma_t, \quad \eta \in \Sigma_t' .$$

Hence ρ generates a family of probability measures with parameters t and ζ, and the solution φ of the interior Dirichlet problem for the domain Σ_t can be written in the form

$$\varphi(\zeta,t) = \int_{\Sigma_t'(\eta)} g(\eta,t)\,\rho(\eta,\zeta,t)\,d_\eta\sigma \quad .$$

Let G' be the boundary of the domain G and F be a functional defined on G'.

We construct the operator

$$E^{x_o(u)} F = M_{G_t'}^{\rho_{\underset{o}{x}(u)}} F ,$$

where the averaging on the right side is taken with respect to the distribution $p(\zeta,\underset{o}{x}(u),u)$, $\zeta \in \Sigma_u$, $\underset{o}{x}(u) \in G$.

Let the functions f_o and f in the differential equation (1) meet the conditions of Theorem 9.1.1, and let Y_o, Y_1, Y_2, ... be the sequence of iterations related to this equation.

Applying the operator $E^{\underset{o}{x}}$ to the functionals Y_n and utilizing formula (5) (where only Σ_t and G are to be substituted by their boundaries Σ_t' and G', respectively, we get

$$E^{\underset{o}{x}(u)} Y_n[x|t] = \Gamma_n[\underset{o}{x}|t]$$

and, passing to the limit,

$$E^{\underset{o}{x}(u)} Y[x|t] = \Gamma[\underset{o}{x}|t] \; .$$

By the same token, for the functional $U[x]$ we obtain

$$U[\underset{o}{x}] = E^{\underset{o}{x}} \Phi[x] \; .$$

Since the operator E^x refers only to the boundary values of the functionals Y and Φ, the desired representation is proved.

10. The Dirichlet problem in the space of summable functions and related topics

10.1. Functional elliptic operators of general type

Our results concerning the homogeneous and inhomogeneous equations $LF = 0$ and $LF = Q$ in function spaces (Sections 5-7) were related to the simplest case if L is the strong or the weak functional Laplace operator

$$L = \int_a^b F''_{x^2(t)}\, dt$$

and

$$L = 2 \lim_{\lambda \to 0} \frac{\mathfrak{M}\, F[x+\lambda y] - F[x]}{\lambda^2} ,$$

respectively. In accordance with this, the associated classical parabolic operator used in the diffusion method was of the form

$$\frac{\partial}{\partial \tau} - \sum_k \frac{\partial^2}{\partial \xi_k^2} .$$

In the present chapter we show that we succeed in extending the results obtained above to much more general equations.

10.1.1. First of all, we want to explain how general elliptic functional operators can be obtained, using the procedure of continual averaging. Let $x = (x_1,\dots,x_s)$ as well as $y = (y_1,\dots,y_s)$ be function vectors with components belonging, say, to the space $C_s[q]$, $q = [a,b]$, and let $\mathfrak{a}_1[x|t],\dots, \mathfrak{a}_\nu[x|t]$ be operators acting from $C_s[q]$ into $C[q]$: $\mathfrak{a}_i[x|t] \in \{C_s \longrightarrow C\}$.

To every $x \in C_s$ we assign the domain $D[y|x]$ of functions y having the distribution density $p(\xi_1,\dots,\xi_s;\ \mathfrak{a}_1[x|t],\dots, \mathfrak{a}_\nu[x|t])$ ($\mathfrak{a}$ are the parameters of this distribution; see Section 3.5). Let, furthermore, $a_1[x|t],\dots,a_s[x|t]$ be the vector of first moments of the distribution p (the "centre of the domain $D[y|x]$") and $b_{\alpha\beta}[x|t]$ be the matrix of its second moments (the existence of all a and b is supposed).

Consider a functional $F[x]$, $x \in C_s$, having the first and second variation:

$$F[x+\varepsilon y] = F[x] + \delta F + \tfrac{1}{2}\delta^2 F + o(\varepsilon^2) , \tag{1}$$

where

$$\delta F = \mathcal{E} \sum_{\alpha=1}^{s} \int_q U_\alpha[x|t] y_\alpha(t) dt \quad \text{with} \quad U_\alpha = F'_{x_\alpha(t)} , \tag{2}$$

$$\delta^2 F = \mathcal{E}^2 \sum_{\alpha,\beta} \iint_{Q_2} V_{\alpha,\beta}[x|t_1,t_2] y_\alpha(t_1) y_\beta(t_2) dt_1 dt_2$$

$$+ \mathcal{E}^2 \sum_{\alpha,\beta} \int_q W_{\alpha,\beta}[x|t] y_\alpha(t) y_\beta(t) dt \tag{3}$$

with

$$V_{\alpha,\beta} = F''_{x_\alpha(t_1) x_\beta(t_2)} , \quad W_{\alpha,\beta} = F''_{x_\alpha(t) x_\beta(t)} .$$

Let us define the operators L_1 and L_2 via the relations

$$L_1 F = \lim_{\mathcal{E}\to 0} \frac{\underset{D}{M} F[x+\mathcal{E}y] - F[x]}{\mathcal{E}} , \tag{4}$$

$$L_2 F = 2 \lim_{\mathcal{E}\to 0} \frac{\underset{D}{M} F[x+\mathcal{E}y] - F[x] - \delta F[x+\mathcal{E}y]}{\mathcal{E}^2} , \tag{5}$$

where, for every fixed x, the mean values $\underset{D}{M}\Phi[y]$ are calculated by the formula

$$\underset{D}{M}\Phi[y] = M \int_{Q_m} g(y,t) dt^m = \int_{Q_m} dt^m \int \cdots \int g(\zeta_1,\ldots,\zeta_m;t) \prod_{i=1}^{m} p(\zeta_i, t_i|x) d\zeta \tag{6}$$

$$\zeta_i = (\xi_{i1},\ldots,\xi_{is}), \quad d\zeta_i = d\xi_{i1}\ldots d\xi_{is}, \quad t = (t_1,\ldots,t_m)$$

($p(\zeta,t|x) = p(\xi_1,\ldots,\xi_s,t|x)$ is the distribution density of the domain $D[y|x]$). If, for any $x \in C_s$ mentioned above, U_α, $W_{\alpha,\beta}$ and $V_{\alpha,\beta}$ are continuous functions, i.e.

$$U_\alpha \in \{C_s \to C\}, \quad V_{\alpha,\beta} \in \{C_s \to C_2\}, \quad W_{\alpha,\beta} \in \{C_s \to C\} ,$$

and the estimate $o(\mathcal{E}^2)$ in (1) is uniform with respect to y, then we get

$$L_1 F = \sum_{1}^{s} \int_q U_\alpha[x|t] a_\alpha[x|t] dt , \tag{7}$$

$$L_2 F = \sum_{\alpha,\beta} \iint_{Q_2} V_{\alpha,\beta}[x|t_1,t_2] a_\alpha[x|t_1] a_\beta[x|t_2] dt_1 dt_2$$

$$+ \sum_{\alpha,\beta} \int_q W_{\alpha,\beta}[x|t] b_{\alpha\beta}[x|t] dt . \tag{8}$$

In this way, there results the general second-order operator

$$LF = L_1F + L_2F = \sum_{\alpha} \int_q F'_{x_\alpha(t)} a_\alpha[x|t]dt$$

$$+ \sum_{\alpha,\beta} \iint_{Q_2} F''_{x_\alpha(t_1)x_\beta(t_2)} b_\alpha[x|t_1] b_\beta[x|t_2]dt_1dt_2$$

$$+ \sum_{\alpha,\beta} \int_q F''_{x_\alpha(t)x_\beta(t)} b_{\alpha\beta}[x|t]dt .$$

(Remark. If the averaging in (4) and (5) is accomplished over different domains having different distribution laws, then the "drift coefficients" b_α differ from the quantities a_α occurring in the latter expression.)

In particular, if $\mathcal{O}\!\!\!\mathcal{l}[x|t]$ are superposition operators, i.e. $\mathcal{O}\!\!\!\mathcal{l}[x|t] = U(x(t),t)$, then $a_\alpha[x|t]$ and $b_{\alpha\beta}[x|t]$ in the formulae (7) and (8) take the form $a_\alpha = a_\alpha(x(t),t)$ and $b_{\alpha\beta} = b_{\alpha\beta}(x(t),t)$, respectively.

Below we restrict ourselves to the discussion of operators of the form

$$LF = \sum_{\alpha,\beta=1}^{s} \int_q a_{\alpha\beta}(x(t),t) F''_{x_\alpha(t)x_\beta(t)} dt$$

$$+ \sum_{\alpha=1}^{s} \int_q b_\alpha(x(t),t) F'_{x_\alpha(t)} dt + cF[x] , \tag{9}$$

where $a_{\alpha\beta}$ is a positively definite matrix and $c = \text{const} < 0$.

Remark. The investigation of a more general form of operators (4) and (5) is also possible if $\mathcal{E} = \mathcal{E}[x]$ is some continuous functional and $\mathcal{E} \to 0$ means that $\mathcal{E}$ tends to zero under one condition or another. An interesting case arises if a sequence of domains V_n centred at x and bounded by the surfaces S_n is given. Denoting $\mathcal{E}_n[x] = M_n(\rho^2_{nx}[y]/2)$, where $\rho_{nx}[y]$ has the sense indicated in 5.1, i.e. $M_n = M_{S_n}$, we get the operators

$$\tilde{L}_1F = \lim_{\mathcal{E}_n \to 0} \frac{M_nF[x+\mathcal{E}_ny] - F[x]}{\mathcal{E}_n} ,$$

$$\tilde{L}_2F = 2 \lim_{\mathcal{E}_n \to 0} \frac{M_n\{F[x+\mathcal{E}_ny]-F[x]-\delta F[x+\mathcal{E}_ny]\}}{\mathcal{E}_n^2} , \tag{10}$$

where $\mathcal{E}_n \to 0$ means that the sequence S_n is contracting to the point x .

There is some analogy between expression (10) and the characteristic operator in the theory of Markov processes, although the distribution according to which the averaging is carried out here need not necessarily be Markov.

The following considerations will be related to functional classes already met above, which are given in a constructive form, i.e. to a Gâteaux ring.

We shall discuss general functional boundary value problems from a somewhat different point of view. In doing so, the boundary values will be given as elements of commutative normed rings (B-algebras), and the solutions can be expressed as continual means over a certain regular measure constructed by the transition density of the diffusion process, especially, of the Brownian movement. The solution obtained is an additive and multiplicative operator on the rings under consideration, which permits us to use compact extensions of the domains of definition of their elements. The latter fact allows us to simplify the intermediate steps of the proof and to reconsider some results contained in the previous chapters from a new point of view.

10.1.2. Let the matrices

$$\Xi = \begin{Vmatrix} \xi_{11}, & \dots, & \xi_{1s} \\ \cdot & \cdots & \cdot \\ \xi_{m1}, & \dots, & \xi_{ms} \end{Vmatrix} = (\zeta_1, \dots, \zeta_m)$$

and

$$X(t) = \begin{Vmatrix} x_1(t_1), \dots, x_s(t_1) \\ \cdots \\ x_1(t_m), \dots, x_s(t_m) \end{Vmatrix} = (x(t_1), \dots, x(t_m))$$

be given, and let

$$F[x] = \int_{Q_m} g(X(t), t)\, dt^m \tag{11}$$

($x \in A_s(q)$, $q=(a,b)$, Q_m: $a < t_i < b$, $i=1,\dots,m$) be a Gâteaux functional constructed by the generating function $g(\Xi, t)$. For the sake of definiteness, as the space $A_s(q)$ we take the space $L_m{}^p(q)$ of vector functions $x(t)$ with co-ordinates summable on q to the p-th power, $p \geqslant 2$ (although all the following considerations may be formulated also in other spaces $A_s(q)$). Therefore, the function g is supposed to satisfy the following assumptions:

(i) the Carathéodory condition;

(ii) the estimate

$$|g(\Xi, t)| \leqslant a(t) + B \prod_{i=1}^{m} \|\zeta_i\|^p , \tag{12}$$

where

$$a(t) \in L_1(Q_m), \quad B = \text{const} > 0, \quad \|\zeta_i\| = \left(\sum_{\alpha=1}^{s} |\xi_{i\alpha}|^p\right)^{1/p} .$$

Under the conditions (i) and (ii), the functional (11) is continuous with respect to the metric $\|x\| = \left(\int_q \sum_1^s |x_i(t)|^p dt\right)^{1/p}$ of the space $L_s^p(q)$ and bounded on each ball $\overline{V}_R$: $\|x\| \leq R$ of this space:

$$\sup_{\overline{V}_R} |F| \leq K + BR^{mp}, \quad K = \int_{Q_m} a(t)dt^m .$$

Let V be a domain in $L_s^p(q)$ ("normal function domain") with the boundary V'. We suppose that, for some $R > 0$,

$$\overline{V} = V \cup V' \subset V_R .$$

By $R = R(\overline{V})$ we denote the ring of Gâteaux functionals (11) and introduce on it the norm

$$\|F\| = \sup_{\overline{V}} |F[x]| .$$

Finally, let $\overline{R} = \overline{R}(\overline{V})$ be the closure of $R(\overline{V})$ with respect to this norm.

10.2. Compact extensions of function domains. Compact restrictions

Before proceeding, we recall some topological notions and facts from the theory of normed rings (see LOOMIS [1], Chap. IV).

10.2.1. A topological Hausdorff space X is said to have a *compact extension* if there exists a compact space $[X] \supset X$ such that X is homeomorphic to some everywhere dense subset of $[X]$. A space X is called *completely regular* if, for every $x_0 \in X$ and every set $X_0 \subset X \setminus x_0$, one can indicate a functional $f(x)$ continuous on X such that $f(x_0) = 0$ and $f(x) \neq 0$ if $x \in X_0$.

It is common knowledge that every completely regular topological H-space admits a compact extension.

In 1940 I. GEL'FAND and G.E. SHILOV proposed a classification of compact extensions of spaces, using the theory of normed rings.

Let $C(X)$ be a ring of functions which are continuous and bounded on the completely regular space X, and suppose $[X]$ to be some compact extension of X. Furthermore, let $C([X])$ be the ring of bounded continuous functions on $[X]$. Since $f \in C([X])$ implies $f \in C(X)$, then $C([X])$ is a subring of the ring $C(X)$. The ring $C([X])$ is said to be generated by the compact extension $[X]$ of X. It goes without saying that $C(X)$ may also have subrings of other types (for instance, in concrete realizations of X and f, the subrings of functions that are smooth in the one sense or another). Rings of the type $C(X)$ are peculiar in having the following properties:

(i) if $C(X)$ consists of complex valued functions, then $f \in C(X)$ implies that the complex conjugate function f^* also belongs to $C(X)$ (symmetry);

(ii) for any $x_o \in X$ and $X_1 \subset X \setminus x_o$, there exists a continuous function f on X such that $f(x_o) = 0$, $f(x) \neq 0$, $x \in X_1$ (regularity).

These conditions taken together are sufficient for the existence of a compact extension $[X]$ and, consequently, for the existence of the ring $C([X])$.

It is also known that every ring R of functions bounded on X, in particular, the ring $C(X)$ admits an isometric and isomorphic mapping onto the ring of functions $x(\mathfrak{a})$ on the set $\mu(X)$ of maximal ideals of the ring R. The set of functions $x(\mathfrak{a})$ with $\mathfrak{a} \in \mu$ is additive and multiplicative:

$$x(\mathfrak{a}_1 + \mathfrak{a}_2) = x(\mathfrak{a}_1) + x(\mathfrak{a}_2), \quad x(\mathfrak{a}_1 \mathfrak{a}_2) = x(\mathfrak{a}_1) x(\mathfrak{a}_2) .$$

Moreover, $\mu(X)$ is compact in the weak topology. The mentioned isomorphic mapping $x(\mathfrak{a})$ induces on X a topology coinciding with the original topology of this space.

It follows from what was said above that every additive and multiplicative functional μ on the ring $C(X)$ can be represented in the form

$$\mu f = f(\theta) ,$$

where $\theta \in [X]$ and $\theta = \theta_\mu$ is one and the same for all functions $f \in C$.

It should be recalled that in Chapter 1 an analogous question was considered from an essentially different point of view. Namely, continual means $\underset{D}{M}F$ were examined on the class of Gâteaux functionals, where the operation $\underset{D}{M}$ was shown to be additive and multiplicative. Furthermore, the equation

$$\underset{D}{M}F = F[\theta]$$

was established, in which F belongs to the closure of the Gâteaux ring $\overline{R}(\overline{V})$ and θ is some generalized function being one and the same for all $F \in \overline{R}(\overline{V})$ (i.e., θ depends only on M and the domain D).

The indicated results from the theory of normed rings and the compact extension of a topological space (in our case, a function domain) will be used below in the investigation of boundary value problems for general elliptic functional operators.

10.2.2. We shall also employ the notion of a compact restriction of a functional domain. For each $x \in L_s^p(q)$ and $h > 0$, we define the Steklov function

$$^h x(t) = \frac{1}{2h} \int_{t-h}^{t+h} x(u)\,du \quad \text{if} \quad t \in q \;;$$

$$^h x(t) = 0 \quad \text{if} \quad t \overline{\in} q \;.$$

Let $^h L_s^p$ be the image of L_s^p under this mapping. It is well-known that:

(i) for every h, we have $\lim_{h \to 0} \| x - {}^h x \| = 0$;

(ii) for any fixed $h > 0$ and any closed ball $\overline{V}_R$ in L_s^p, the set $\overline{V}_R \cap {}^h L_s^p$ is compact in the strong topology of L_s^p.

Clearly, Steklov's function transforms every set E closed in L_s^p into a compact subset $^h E$ of L_s^p (compact restriction of E).

10.3. Averaging $M_{\eta,\tau} F$ of a functional $F \in \overline{R}$ with respect to a family of transition densities of diffusion processes

Let, for almost all $t \in q$, a family of diffusion processes in E_s uniform in time τ be given, and let $p(\tau, \zeta, \eta \mid t)$ be the transition density of this family.

We suppose that a.e. on q the coefficients $a_{\alpha\beta}$ and b_α of the infinitesimal operators

$$A(t) = \sum_1^s a_{\alpha\beta} \frac{\partial^2}{\partial \xi_\alpha \partial \xi_\beta} + \sum_1^s b_\alpha \frac{\partial}{\partial \xi_\alpha} + c \tag{1}$$

of these processes satisfy a Hölder condition with respect to ξ_α and are bounded on $E_s \times q$. Besides, c is supposed to be negative. In addition, we assume that in the well-known estimates of $p(t)$ applied below all "constants" can be regarded as independent of t (this property of p will be called the uniformity of the family under study).

As to $a_{\alpha\beta}$, we suppose that, for all ξ, almost all $t \in q$ and all λ,

$$\sum_{\alpha,\beta=1}^{s} a_{\alpha\beta}(\zeta,t)\lambda_\alpha\lambda_\beta \geqslant \gamma\sum_{1}^{s}\lambda_\alpha^2 \quad , \quad \gamma = \text{const} > 0 .$$

Thus we deal with a family of standard diffusion processes (see e.g. DYNKIN [1], Section 5.6). Henceforth τ plays the role of time, while t, the argument of the considered functions $x(t)$, is a parameter of the studied family of processes.

Let $F = \int_{Q_m} g(X(t),t)dt^m \in R$. We define the averaging operator

$$M_{\eta,\tau}F = \int_{Q_m} dt^m \int_{E_{ms}} g(\Xi,t)\prod_{i=1}^{m} p(\tau,\zeta_i,\eta_i|t_i)d\xi^{ms} . \qquad (2)$$

Under the conditions formulated above, the integral (2) exists and, for $x \in \overline{V}$, the operator $\mu F = M_{x,\tau}F$ is well-defined in $\overline{R}$.

If $F_n \in R$ and $F_n \rightrightarrows F$ on $\overline{R}$, then we set

$$M_{\eta,\tau}F = \lim_n M_{\eta,\tau}F_n .$$

The functional $H[x] \in \overline{R}(\overline{V})$ is called harmonic in V if, for every $x_0 \in V$, there exists a $\lambda = \lambda[x_0]$ such that, for $0 < \tau < \lambda[x_0]$,

$$M_{x_0,\tau}H = H[x_0] .$$

Let $\mathcal{H}(\overline{V})$ be the set of functionals harmonic on V. We formulate the following functional Dirichlet problem: Given $F \in \overline{R}(\overline{V})$ find a functional $H[x]$ such that: (i) $H \in \mathcal{H}(\overline{V})$, (ii) the conditions $x_n \in V$, $z \in V'$, $\|z-x_n\| \longrightarrow 0$ imply $\lim_n H[x_n] = F[z]$.

Theorem 10.3.1. Suppose $T[x]$ to be a functional on $\overline{V}$ fulfilling the conditions:

(i) $T[x] \in \overline{R}(\overline{V})$;

(ii) $T[x] > 0$ if $x \in V$;

(iii) $T[x] = 0$ if $x \in V'$;

(iv) $M_{x_0,\tau}T = T[x_0] - \tau$ if $x_0 \in V$.

Then the desired solution can be written in the form

$$H = M_{x,T[x]}F$$

and H is the unique solution in the class $\overline{R}(\overline{V})$.

Remark. The mentioned conditions (i)-(iv) are correct. In fact, below we shall establish the existence of domains for which (i)-(iv) are valid, moreover, explicit forms of T will be indicated.

Proof. 1°. Let us begin with two lemmas.

Lemma 10.3.1. For $F \in \overline{R}$ and $\tau > 0$, the inclusion $M_{x,\tau} F \in \overline{R}$ holds.

Proof. Obviously, it is sufficient to prove the lemma for $F \in R(\overline{V})$. The continuity of $g(\Xi, t)$ with respect to Ξ (a.e. on Q_m) implies the continuity of the function

$$h(\Lambda, \tau, t) = \int_{E_{ms}} g(\Xi, t) \prod_{i=1}^{m} p(\tau, \zeta_i, \eta_i | t_i) d\xi^{ms}$$

$(\Lambda = (\eta_1, \ldots, \eta_m) = \| \eta_{i\alpha} \|$, $i=1,\ldots,m$; $\alpha = 1,\ldots,s$) on the same set. Due to relation (12) from 10.1 and the known estimate

$$p(\tau, \xi, \eta | t) \leq \frac{K}{(\sqrt{\pi\tau})^s} \exp\left(-\frac{\lambda|\xi - \eta|^2}{\sqrt{\pi\tau}}\right), \tag{3}$$

where in view of the uniformity of the family p supposed above, all parameters may be assumed to be constants, we have

$$|h(\Lambda, \tau, t)| \leq \int_{E_{ms}} (a(t) + B\prod_{i=1}^{m} \|\zeta_i\|^p) \frac{K^m}{(\sqrt{\pi\tau})^s} \exp\left(-\frac{\lambda \sum_{i=1}^{m} |\zeta_i - \eta_i|^2}{\sqrt{\pi\tau}}\right) d\xi^{ms}. \tag{4}$$

If p is an integer, then the right-hand side of this inequality consists of integrals of the type

$$b \int |\xi|^{\nu} \exp\left(-\frac{\lambda|\xi - \eta|^2}{\sqrt{\pi\tau}}\right) d\xi, \quad b = \text{const},$$

being polynomials with respect to $|\eta|$ because here ν are integers. With regard to this fact, we obtain for h an estimate similar to (12) of Section 10.1. If p fails to be an integer, then we can replace the mentioned inequality (12) from 10.1 by the estimate

$$|g(\Xi, t)| \leq a(t) + B\prod_{i=1}^{m} \sum_{\alpha=1}^{s} |\xi_{i\alpha}|^{p_1}, \quad p_1 = [p] + 1,$$

which leads to the same conclusion.

In summary, since $h(\Lambda, \tau, t)$ is a continuous function of Λ and a measurable function of τ, we can write

$$\Phi[x] = \int_{Q_m} h(X(t), \tau, t) dt^m \in R(\overline{V}),$$

which proves the lemma.

Lemma 10.3.2. Let $F \in \overline{R}$ and $0 < \tau \leq \Phi[x] \leq \tau^1$ for $x \in \overline{V}$, where $\Phi \in \overline{R}$. Then $M_{x,\Phi[x]} F \in \overline{R}(\overline{V})$.

Proof. Obviously, it is again sufficient to verify the lemma for $F \in R(\overline{V})$. The continuity of the function $\varphi = g(\Xi, t) \prod_{i=1}^{m} p(\tau, \zeta_i, \eta_i | t_i)$ on the set $E_{2ms} \times [\tau', \tau'']$ (almost everywhere on Q_m) and the estimates (2) and (4) cause the existence of a sequence of functions $r_\nu(\Xi, \Lambda, \tau, t)$ which are polynomials of τ such that

$$\varphi = \lim_{\nu} r_\nu(\Xi, \Lambda, \tau, t)$$

almost everywhere on Q_m , where the coefficients of these polynomials are uniformly bounded on E_{2ms} a.e. on Q_m [1]. In addition, for $\tau \in [\tau', \tau'']$ and $\eta \in E_{ms}$, the function

$$\varphi_n(\Lambda, \tau, t) = \int_{E_{ms}} r_n(\Xi, \Lambda, \tau, t) d\xi^{ms}$$

admits an estimate of the form (12) of Section 10.1.

Since φ_n are polynomials in τ , then after replacing τ by $\Phi[x]$ and Ξ by X , we get a sequence of functionals

$$U_n[x] = \int_{Q_m} \varphi_n(X, \Phi[x], t) dt^m ,$$

which can be rewritten in the form

$$U_n = \sum_{\nu=0}^{n} \Phi^\nu[x] \, A_{n\nu}[x] ,$$

where owing to Lemma 10.3.1, $A_{n\nu} \in \overline{R}(\overline{V})$. Since $\Phi \in \overline{R}$, we also have $U_n \in \overline{R}$. But $\Psi = \lim_n U_n$ (uniformly on $\overline{V}$). Thus $\Psi \in \overline{R}$, which was to be proved.

From the lemma just proved as well as condition (ii) applied to the functional $T[x]$ it follows that, for every subdomain V_o with $\overline{V}_o \subset V$ the inclusion $M_{X, T[x]} F \in \overline{R}(\overline{V}_o)$ is valid. Moreover (see below 3°), $H[x] = F[x]$ for $x \in V'$. Hence

$$H = M_{X, T[x]} F \in \overline{R}(\overline{V}) .$$

---

[1] In the present case, the condition $\lim_{|\eta|, |\zeta| \to \infty} \varphi = 0$ holds true. Hence in view of the well-known theorem on the uniform approximation of continuous functions on $\overline{E}_N$, we conclude that r_ν may be expressed in the form $\sum_k \tau^k A_k(\Xi, \Lambda, t)$, where A_k are proper fractions of Ξ and Λ continuous on $\overline{E}_{2ms}$.

$\underline{2^o}$. Now we intend to show that $H \in \mathcal{H}(\overline{V})$. Let $x_o \in V$. Then

$$M_{x_o,\tau}H = M_{x_o,\tau} \int_{Q_m} dt^m \int_{E_{ms}} g(\Xi,t) \prod_{i=1}^{m} p(T[x],\ \zeta_i, x(t_i)|t_i) d\xi^{ms} .$$

Lemma 10.3.3. We have

$$M_{x_o,\tau}F = M_{x_o,\tau} \int_{Q_m} dt^m \int_{E_{ms}} g(\Xi,t) \prod_{i=1}^{m} p(M_{x_o,\tau}T[x],\ \zeta_i, x(t_i)|t_i) d\xi^{ms}. \quad (5)$$

Proof. In order to justify this equality, we show that the ring $\overline{R}(\overline{V})$ defines a compact extension of the set $\overline{V}$ (considered as a space in which the topology is induced by the norm $\|\cdot\|$ in L_s^p).

For each $x_o \in V$ we can find a closed subset E of V such that $\rho(x_o,E) = d > 0$. Let $0 < \mathcal{E} < d$.

We construct the functional

$$U[x] = \exp\left(-\frac{\mathcal{E}^p}{\mathcal{E}^p - \|x-x_o\|^p}\right) \quad \text{if } \|x-x_o\| \le \mathcal{E} \ ;$$

$$U[x] = 0 \quad \text{if } \|x-x_o\| > \mathcal{E} \ .$$

Since $U[x_o] > 0$ and $U[x] = 0$ for $x \in E$, this functional separates x_o from E . At the same time it belongs to $\overline{R}(\overline{V})$, because if $r_n(|\alpha|)$ is a sequence of polynomials converging uniformly to the function $u(|\alpha|)$ for $0 \le |\alpha| \le \mathcal{E}$, the sequence of functionals

$$U_n[x] = r_n(\|x-x_o\|^p) \quad \text{if} \quad 0 \le \|x-x_o\| \le \mathcal{E} \quad ,$$

$$U_n[x] = 0 \quad \text{if} \quad \|x-x_o\| > \mathcal{E}$$

converges uniformly to $U[x]$ on L_s^p . Since $U_n[x] \in \overline{R}(\overline{V})$, we have $U \in \overline{R}(\overline{V})$, too. This shows (see 10.2) the existence of a compact extension of the set $\overline{V}$ defined by the ring $\overline{R}(\overline{V})$. Let us denote this extension by $[\overline{V}]$.

Obviously, for $x_o \in V$, the operator $M_{x_o,\tau}F$ is an additive and multiplicative functional on $\overline{R}$. Therefore, for every $F \in \overline{R}$,

$$M_{x_o,\tau}F = F[\theta] \quad , \quad (6)$$

where $\theta = \theta_{x_o,\tau}$ is one and the same for all $F \in \overline{R}$.

Consequently

$$M_{x_o,\tau}H = \int_{Q_m} dt^m \int g(\Xi,t) \prod_{i=1}^{m} p(T[\theta],\ \zeta_i, \theta(t_i)|t_i) d\xi^{ms} . \quad (7)$$

On the other hand $T[\theta] = M_{x_o,\tau}T$. Thus, in view of condition (iv) concerning the functional T , we have $T[\theta] = T[x_o] - \tau$.

In this way

$$M_{x_o,\tau}H = \int_{Q_m} dt^m \int g(\Xi,t)\prod_{i=1}^{m} p(T[x_o]-\tau,\zeta_i,x_o(t_i)|t_i)d\xi^{ms} ,$$

From here, again using (6), we get

$$M_{x_o,\tau}H = M_{x_o,\tau}\int_{Q_m} dt^m \int g(\Xi,t)\prod_i p(T[x_o]-\tau,\zeta_i,x_o(t_i)|t_i)d\xi^{ms} ,$$

which proves the lemma.

From the very definition of the operator $M_{x,\tau}$ it follows now that

$$M_{x_o,\tau}H = \int_{Q_m} dt^m \int_{E_{2ms}} g(\Xi,t)\prod_i p(T[x_o]-\tau,\zeta_i,\eta_i|t_i)p(\tau,\eta_i,x_o(t_i)|t_i)d\eta^{ms}d\xi^{ms}.$$

Using the well-known Kolmogorov-Chapman relation

$$p(T-\tau,\xi,\eta)p(\tau,\eta,x)d\eta^s = p(T,\xi,x)$$

m times, we get

$$M_{x_o,\tau}H = \int_{Q_m} dt^m \int g(\Xi,t)\prod_i p(T[x],\zeta_i,x_o(t_i)|t_i)d\xi^{ms} = H[x_o] ,$$

i.e. $H \in \mathscr{H}(\overline{V})$.

3°. Let $x_n \in V$, $z \in V'$, $\|x_n - z\| \to 0$, $F \in R(\overline{V})$. Then, due to the continuity of the superposition operator (cf. KRASNOSELSKIĬ et al. [1], Chap. V), $g(x_n,t) \longrightarrow g(z,t)$ converges in measure on the set Q_m .

Since $T \in \overline{R}(\overline{V})$, the functional T is continuous on $\overline{R}$. Moreover $T[z] = 0$.

Taking into account the relation

$$\lim_{\tau\to+0} h(\Lambda,\tau,t) = \lim_{\tau\to+0} \int g(\Xi,t)\prod_i p(\tau,\zeta_i,\eta_i|t_i)d\xi^{ms} = g(\Lambda,t)$$

(a.e. on Q_m), we can write

$$\lim_n H[x_n] = \lim_n \int_{Q_m} dt^m \int g(\Xi,t)\prod_i p(T[x_n],\zeta_i,x_n(t_i)|t_i)d\xi^{ms}$$

$$= \int_{Q_m} g(z(t),t)dt^m = F[z]$$

(because of the uniform boundedness of all considered functionals the passage to the limit under the integral sign $\int_{Q_m}\ldots dt^m$ is possible here).

This concludes the first part of the theorem.

4°. The maximum principle and the unicity of the solution.

Suppose $\Phi[x] \in \overline{R}(\overline{V})$. Let us define the operator L at the point $x_o \in V$ via

$$L\Phi = \lim_{\tau \to 0} \frac{M_{x_o,\tau}\Phi - \Phi[x_o]}{\tau} . \tag{8}$$

Furthermore, by $\overline{R}_1(\overline{V})$ we denote the subset $\overline{R}_1 \in \overline{R}(\overline{V})$ of those functionals $F \in \overline{R}(\overline{V})$ for which LF exists on V. It is a straightforward matter to see that $\mathcal{H}_o(\overline{V}) \in \overline{R}_1(\overline{V})$ and that, for $H \in \mathcal{H}(\overline{V})$, $LH = 0$.

From the definition of the functional $T[x]$ (see the statement of the present theorem) it follows that $T \in \overline{R}_1(\overline{V})$ and $LT = -1$ if $x \in V$.

Lemma 10.3.4. Let $F = \int_{Q_m} g(X,t)dt^m \in R_1(\overline{V})$ and $g(\Xi,t) = g(\zeta_1,\dots,\zeta_m;t_1,\dots,t_m)$ be a function twice differentiable with respect to the arguments of each vector ζ_i. Suppose that for the function

$$\Psi(\Xi,t) = \sum_{i=1}^{m}\sum_{\alpha,\beta=1}^{s} a_{\alpha\beta}(\zeta_i,t_i)\frac{\partial^2 g}{\partial \xi_{i\alpha}\partial \xi_{i\beta}} + \sum_{i=1}^{m}\sum_{\alpha=1}^{s} b_\alpha(\zeta_i,t_i)\frac{\partial g}{\partial \xi_{i\alpha}} + cg = \mathfrak{A}_t(\Xi,t)g \tag{9}$$

the estimate (12) from 10.1 holds true with some $a(t)$ and B, where as above, a and b are the diffusion and drift coefficients of the operator $\mathfrak{A}_t$.

Then: (i) $F \in \overline{R}_1(\overline{V})$ and

$$LF = \int_{Q_m}\sum_i\Big[\sum_{\alpha,\beta} a_{\alpha\beta}(x_1(t_i),\dots,x_s(t_i),t_i)\frac{\partial^2 g}{\partial x_\alpha(t_i)\partial x_\beta(t_i)} + \sum_\alpha b_\alpha(x_1(t_i),\dots,x_s(t_i),t_i)\frac{\partial g}{\partial x_\alpha(t_i)}\Big]dt^m + mcF , \tag{10}$$

(ii) $$LF = \int_q \Big(\sum_{\alpha,\beta} a_{\alpha\beta}(x_1(t),\dots,x_s(t),t)\frac{\delta^2 F}{\delta x_\alpha(t)\delta x_\beta(t)} + \sum_\alpha b_\alpha(x_1(t),\dots,x_s(t),t)\frac{\delta F}{\delta x_\alpha(t)}\Big)dt + mcF .$$

Proof. We consider the space of elements of the matrix $\Xi = \|\xi_{i\alpha}\|$ as a product of the spaces of vectors $\zeta_1,\dots,\zeta_m$. For almost all $t \in Q_m$, the operator $\mathfrak{A}_t$ (cf. (9)) is the generating operator of a diffusion process in the space of variables Ξ.

The statement (i) results from (8) and the fact that the generating operator of a diffusion process proves to be the restriction of the characteristic operator of this process to the set of twice continuously differentiable functions (see DYNKIN [1], Chap. 5).

The postulated estimate (12) from Section 10.1 for the function $\Psi(\Xi, t)$ guarantees the existence of the integral (10) for all $x \in L_s^p(q)$ as well as the boundedness of the functional (10) on every ball of this space. Owing to the supposed symmetry of the function $g(\Xi, t)$ with respect to the pairs (ζ_i, t_i), $i=1,\dots,m$, from (10) and the definition of the variational (functional) derivatives $F'_{x_\alpha(t)}$, $F''_{x_\alpha(t)x_\beta(t)}$, we conclude the validity of (ii).

Lemma 10.3.5. Let $F \in \overline{R}_1(\overline{V})$ and

$$L_0F[x] = \int_q \Big\{ \sum_{\alpha,\beta} a_{\alpha\beta}(x(t),t)F''_{x_\alpha(t)x_\beta(t)} + \sum_\alpha b_\alpha(x(t),t)F''_{x_\alpha(t)} \Big\} dt .$$

If, for $x = y \in V$, the functional F attains on $\overline{V}$ its maximum, then

$$L_0F[y] \leq 0 .$$

Proof. Since F attains its extremum at the point $y \in V$, then $F'_{y_\alpha(t)} = 0$, $\alpha = 1,\dots,s$ (almost everywhere on q). Consequently

$$L_0F = \int_q \sum_{\alpha,\beta} a_{\alpha\beta}(y(t),t)\, F''_{y_\alpha(t)y_\beta(t)}\, dt . \tag{11}$$

We introduce the notations

$$\varphi_{\alpha\beta}(t) = a_{\alpha\beta}(y(t),t), \qquad \psi_{\alpha\beta}(t) = F''_{y_\alpha(t)y_\beta(t)} .$$

The matrices $\varphi_{\alpha\beta}(t)$ and $\psi_{\alpha\beta}(t)$ can be transformed to diagonal forms $\tilde{\varphi}_\alpha(t)$ and $\tilde{\psi}_\alpha(t)$, respectively, using some orthogonal matrix $\tau_{\alpha\beta}(t)$. After this, operator (11) will take the form

$$L_0F = \int_q \sum_\alpha \tilde{\varphi}_\alpha(t)\,\tilde{\psi}_\alpha(t)\,dt .$$

Since the matrix $\varphi_{\alpha\beta}$ is positively definite, one has $\tilde{\varphi}_\alpha(t) \geq 0$ and because F attains its maximum at the point y (both inequalities hold almost everywhere on q), we recognize that $\tilde{\psi}_\alpha(t) \leq 0$.

Therefore $L_0F[y] \leq 0$, and the lemma is proved.

Remark. The lemma remains valid and the proof does not change if we consider F and L_0F on a compact restriction ${}^h\overline{V}$ of the set V. Under the conditions of Lemma 10.3.5, if we replace x and y by ${}^hx$ and ${}^hy$, respectively, and if

$$\max_{{}^hV} F = F[{}^hy] \ , \qquad {}^hy \in {}^hV \ ,$$

then

$$L_oF[{}^hy] \leq 0 \ .$$

Lemma 10.3.6. Let

$$H[x] = M_{x,T[x]}F \quad \text{for} \quad F \in \overline{R}(\overline{V}) \ .$$

Then

$$\sup_{\overline{V}} H = \sup_{V'} H \quad \text{and} \quad \inf_{\overline{V}} H = \inf_{V'} H \ . \tag{12}$$

Proof. First of all, we show the validity of the lemma under the assumption that, for operator (1), $c=0$ (i.e., the process under study does not stop).
Let $h>0$ and ${}^h\overline{V}$ be a compact restriction of the set $\overline{V}$:

$$^h\overline{V} = \overline{V} \cap {}^hL_s{}^p \ , \qquad {}^hV' = V' \cap L_s{}^p \ .$$

Since $\overline{V}$ and V' are closed sets, then ${}^h\overline{V}$ and ${}^hV'$ are also compact (the compactness is everywhere understood relative to the metric induced by the strong topology of $L_s{}^p$). Furthermore, since $H[x]$ is a functional continuous on $\overline{V}$, it is continuous on ${}^h\overline{V}$, too. Therefore, it attains its extreme values on ${}^h\overline{V}$ and ${}^hV'$.

Set

$$M_h = \max_{{}^h\overline{V}} H \ , \qquad m_h = \max_{{}^hV'} H \ .$$

Evidently $M_h \geqslant m_h$. We show that the inequality $M_h > m_h$ is impossible. Let $\Phi[x] = \|T\| + 1 - T[x]$. We form the functional

$$\Psi[x] = H[x] + \frac{M_h - m_h}{2\|\Phi\|}\Phi[x]$$

and consider it on the set ${}^h\overline{V}$. In doing so, we have

$$\max_{{}^h\overline{V}} \Psi = M_h + \alpha \ , \qquad \alpha > 0 \ ,$$

$$\max_{{}^hV'} \Psi \leqslant m_h + \frac{M_h - m_h}{2} = \frac{m_h + M_h}{2} \leqslant M_h \ .$$

Since $LT = -1$ and $LH = 0$, from (12) the inequality

$$L\Psi = \frac{M_h - m_h}{2\|\Phi\|} > 0$$

results. In the case under study, if $c=0$, then $L = L_o$ and the obtained relations contradict Lemma 10.3.5. Thus $M_h = m_h$.

Having regard to the equations

$$\lim_{h\to 0} \max_{h_V} H[x] = \sup_{\overline{V}} H[x] , \qquad \lim_{h\to 0} \max_{h_{V'}} H[x] = \sup_{V'} H[x] ,$$

we get $\sup_{\overline{V}} H = \sup_{V'} H$ and, analogously, $\inf_{\overline{V}} H = \inf_{V'} H$, which proves the lemma.

From what was said above we deduce the unicity of the solution of the posed functional Dirichlet problem for a density related to the generating operator

$$\sum_{\alpha,\beta} a_{\alpha\beta}(\zeta,t) \frac{\partial^2}{\partial\xi_\alpha \partial\xi_\beta} + \sum_\alpha b_\alpha(\zeta,t) \frac{\partial}{\partial\xi_\alpha}$$

in the functional class $R(\overline{V})$. In the general case, if we study the operator (1) under the assumption $c \neq 0$, the above considerations are to be modified as follows.

Suppose that $L = L_0 + c$ and $H = 0$ on V' . Then, since $LH = 0$ on V , we discover that H cannot have on V neither a positive supremum nor a negative infimum. Thus $H = 0$ on the set V . Hence, in the class $R(\overline{V})$ the unicity theorem has been established.

$\underline{5^o}$. Above (see 3°) the relation

$$\lim_m H[x_m] = F[z] , \quad x_m \in V , \quad z \in V' \tag{13}$$

was derived for $F \in R(\overline{V})$. However, the same holds for any $F \in \overline{R}(\overline{V})$. Indeed, let $F_n \in R(\overline{V})$, $\| F-F_n \| \to 0$. Then, if H and H_n are two solutions of the Dirichlet problem associated with the boundary values F and F_n , respectively, from the inequality

$$\sup_{\overline{V}} |H_n - H_{n+p}| \leq \sup_{V'} |F_{n+p} - F_n|$$

it may be seen that the sequence H_n converges to H uniformly on $\overline{V}$. Furthermore

$$\left|F[z]-H[x_m]\right| \leq \left|F[z]-F_n[z]\right| + \left|F_n[z]-H_n[x_m]\right| + \left|H_n[x_m]-H[x_m]\right| .$$

Using the $\frac{\varepsilon}{3}$ - method, the latter inequality implies (13) for every $F \in \overline{R}$.

Since the convergence in $\overline{R}$ is uniform, it is a straightforward matter to prove the unicity of the solution in the whole class $\overline{R}(\overline{V})$.

The theorem is completely proved.

Now we focus once more our attention on the conditions (i)-(iv) concerning the functional $T[x]$ (see the statement of Theorem 10.3.1).

Let again the generating operator

$$A(t) = \sum_{\alpha,\beta} a_{\alpha\beta}(\zeta,t)\frac{\partial^2}{\partial\xi_\alpha\,\partial\xi_\beta} + \sum_\alpha b_\alpha(\zeta,t)\frac{\partial}{\partial\xi_\alpha} + c$$

considered for almost all $t \in q$ be given, which is related to the distribution density $p(t) = p(\tau, \zeta, \eta \mid t)$ of the diffusion process, and let $\varphi(\zeta,t)$ and $\psi(\zeta,t)$ be two functions satisfying on $E_s \times q$ the Carathéodory condition and, besides, for almost all $t \in q$, the following requirements:

1) $|\varphi(\zeta,t)| \le u_1(t) + c_1\|\zeta\|^p$, $|h(\zeta,t)| \le u_2(t) + c_2\|\zeta\|^p$, $u_1, u_2 \in L(q)$, $c_1, c_2 = \text{const} > 0$;

2) $\varphi > 0$, φ is twice continuously differentiable with respect to all ξ_α, and $\varphi < h$ in some domain $G \subset E_s$;

3) $\int p(\tau,\zeta,\eta\mid t)h(\zeta,t)d\xi^s = h(\eta,t)$ (in particular, as h we can take some positive constant).

Now we construct the functionals

$$Q[x] = \int_q \varphi(x(t),t)dt$$

and

$$\Gamma[x] = \int_q h(x(t),t)dt$$

and define the sets V and V' in the following way:

$$V:\ Q[x] < \Gamma[x], \qquad V':\ Q = \Gamma.$$

Setting

$$T[x] = \Gamma[x] - Q[x],$$

we obtain

$$M_{x_0,\tau}T = M_{x_0,\tau}\Gamma - \int_q dt \int \varphi(\zeta,t)p(\tau,\zeta,x_0(t)\mid t)d\xi^s$$

$$= \Gamma[x_0] - \int \varphi(x_0,t)dt - \tau = T[x_0] - \tau .$$

The constructed functional $T[x]$ is continuous on $\overline{V}$, and all the conditions (i)-(iv) mentioned in Theorem 10.3.1 hold true.

It is easy to see that the functional T can be taken as $\lambda[x]$ occurring in the definition of harmonicity (see the beginning of the present section). If $H_n \in \mathcal{H}(\overline{V})$, $\|H-H_n\| \to 0$, then $H \in \mathcal{H}(\overline{V})$. In addition, it is clear that $H', H'' \in \mathcal{H}(\overline{V})$ implies $H'H'' \in \mathcal{H}(\overline{V})$, i.e., $\mathcal{H}(\overline{V})$ is a subring of $\overline{R}(\overline{V})$. In particular, following the method from 5.2, the latter property permits us to construct different function domains for which the generalized functional Dirichlet problem discussed in that section can be effectively solved.

Under natural restrictions, we are able to prove the following results.

Let $\Gamma_o, \ldots, \Gamma_n \in \mathcal{H}(\bar{V})$ and Q be a functional for which: (i) $Q \in R_1(\bar{V})$, (ii) $Q > 0$, $LQ = 1$.

We suppose that the inequality

$$V_n: \ \Psi_n[x] = \sum_{k=1}^{n} Q^k \Gamma_k < 0$$

describes a domain in $L_s^p(q)$ having the boundary

$$V_n': \ \sum_{k=1}^{n} Q^k \Gamma_k = 0 .$$

If the multi-valued functional $\mu[x]$ defined by the equation

$$\sum_{k=0}^{n} \mu^k \Gamma_k = 0$$

has a real positive branch

$$\mu = f(\Gamma_1, \ldots, \Gamma_n) ,$$

then from the equation

$$\sum_{k=0}^{n} (Q+T)^k \Gamma_k = 0 ,$$

the functional

$$T_n[x] \equiv f(H_1, \ldots, H_n)$$

satisfying all the conditions (i)-(iv) can be defined.

The sequence T_n may also be used for approximating functionals of a more general kind and, in doing so, determining a domain $V: \ U < 0$ for which a functional T is defined that satisfies conditions (i)-(iv).

If the diffusion process considered is the Brownian movement, i.e.

$$A = \sum_{\alpha=1}^{s} \frac{\partial^2}{\partial \xi_k^{\,2}} , \qquad p = \frac{1}{(\sqrt{2\pi})^s} e^{-\frac{|\xi - \eta|^2}{\tau}} ,$$

then $M_{x_o, \tau}$ can be regarded as the mean over the Hilbert sphere $\|x-x_o\| = \sqrt{\tau}$. As was proved in 5.1 for $s=1$, $p=2$ and under more general conditions, in this case the solution H of the functional Dirichlet problem with boundary value F has the representation $\mathfrak{M} F[x+ \varrho[x,y] y]$.

The relation $M_{x_o,\tau} = F[\theta]$, $\theta \in [\bar{V}]$, used in the proof of Lemma 1o.3.3, which was based on the theory of normed rings, plays the same role as the equation $F = \mathfrak{M}F$ (a.e. on the sphere $\|y\| = 1$).

It is not hard to understand that both the approaches are equivalent. The method of compact extensions gives no information concerning "ideal elements" θ .

In 3.5 we have proved that the functions θ may be considered as certain generalized functions being points of concentration of a Dirac measure in a function space.

11. The generalized functional Poisson equation

The same method as that explained in Section 10 can be applied to solve the generalized boundary value problem for the Poisson functional equation if we make use of the compact extension of a given function domain V .

Let $M_{x,\tau}$ and L be the operations defined in Section 10. We study the Poisson equation

$$LU = F[x] , \quad x \in \bar{R}(\bar{V}) \tag{1}$$

and introduce the operator P :

$$PF = \int_0^{T[x]} M_{x,u}F\,du , \quad x \in \bar{V} , \tag{2}$$

where T was indicated in 10.3.

The following lemmas can be formulated (the proofs are omitted here).

Lemma 11.1. Let $\bar{R}_1(\bar{V})$ be the subset of the ring $\bar{R}(\bar{V})$ consisting of functionals F for which LF exists. Then:

(i) $\bar{R}_1(\bar{V})$ is a ring with respect to the usual multiplication operation and, in addition to the additivity, the relation

$$L(U_1U_2) = U_1LU_2 + U_2LU_1$$

is valid;

(ii) the ring $\bar{R}_1(\bar{V})$ is closed with respect to the norm

$$\|U\|_{\bar{R}_1} = \sup_{\bar{V}} |U| + \sup_{\bar{V}} |LU| .$$

__Lemma 11.2__. P is a linear operator on $\overline{R}(\overline{V})$, i.e.

$$P \in \left\{ \overline{R}(\overline{V}) \longrightarrow \overline{R}_1(\overline{V}) \right\} ,$$

and $\|P\| = \|T\|$.

The lemmas just mentioned yield directly the following

__Theorem 11.1__. The solution of equation (1) with the boundary condition $U\big|_{V'} = 0$ is given by equation (2). This solution is unique on the ring $\overline{R}_1(\overline{V})$.

COMMENTS

To the Introduction

The mean value and the Dirichlet problem for the sphere in a Hilbert space were first considered by R. GÂTEAUX in his remarkable papers published posthumously (GÂTEAUX [1], [2]). The further more general results on means and boundary value problems in a Hilbert space were obtained by P. LÉVY and presented in Part III of his book LÉVY [1]. This book contains interesting material about analysis in the Hilbert space, however, concerning boundary value problems LÉVY restricted himself to searching solutions. Questions of their existence, the problem of how the solutions might be effectively constructed, unicity theorems, applications of the theory and its interrelations with other branches are completely neglected.

As far as I know, during almost 35 years until the author's papers dealing with continual means and their applications (in particular, to boundary value problems), no new publication in the directions mentioned above appeared. (The second edition of LÉVY's book [1], the book LÉVY [2], refines some of the results of LÉVY [1], however, it does not contain any new theorems.)

To Section 1

Functionals $Y[x|t]$ generated by differential equations containing functional parameters x were introduced by VOLTERRA at the beginning of our century (see VOLTERRA [1]). VOLTERRA's considerations were related to the linear equation

$$y'' + x_1(t)y' + x_2(t)y = 0 .$$

He has obtained some interesting formulae for functional derivatives of the corresponding (nonlinear) functional $Y[x_1, x_2|t]$.

Some nonlinear equations involving functional parameters were studied by FANTAPPIE [1]. In particular, he considered the equations

$$R' + R^2 = x(t) , \qquad \frac{S'''}{S'} - \frac{3}{2}\left(\frac{S''}{S'}\right)^2 = x(t)$$

and called their integrals $R[x|t]$ and $S[x|t]$ the Riccati and Schwarz functionals, respectively.

In the paper POLISHCHUK [4] it was shown that, under some general conditions imposed on f_1 and f_2 , the equation

$$y^{(m)} = f_1(t,y,y',\dots,y^{(m-1)})x(t) + f_2(t,y,y',\dots,y^{(m-1)}) \qquad (1)$$

generates a harmonic functional $Y[x|t]$ in the sense of P. LÉVY. In POLISHCHUK [10] it was noted that this functional is closely connected with the harmonic functionals investigated by G. SHILOV [1,I].

Equation (1) as well as the Picard functional

$$F[x] = \int_a^b g(t,x(t),Y[x|t])dt$$

play an important role in the modern theory of control systems.

The term "Gâteaux functional" for the nonlinear functionals of integral type considered here was proposed by SHILOV.

To Sections 2 and 3

This notion as well as the classification of function domains (uniform, normal) were suggested by the author (see POLISHCHUK [11,I]).

General explicit formulae for continual means were derived by the author in POLISHCHUK [10]. They represent a far-reaching generalization of the Gâteaux formula (3) mentioned in Section 3.3. Another particular case (formula (2) from 3.3) was discussed in detail in the paper POLISHCHUK [1].

The notion of the law of distribution of a functional domain has been introduced by the author (see POLISHCHUK [10], where also the corresponding existence theorem for a general function domain can be found).

The notion of the centre of a function domain and its relation to the harmonicity of functionals was presented in the paper POLISHCHUK [10], which contains also a brief exposition of the Dirac measure in a function space based on the distribution law of a function domain.

The connection of the Lévy theorem quoted in 3.2 with the representation principle of statistical mechanics was pointed out in the introduction to the paper POLISHCHUK [9].

To Section 4

The Laplacians Δ, Δ_o, Δ^o were introduced by GÂTEAUX and LÉVY. The definition of Δ_{oo} and Δ^{oo} is due to the author. Section 4.1 is essentially the paper POLISHCHUK [11,I].

(Remark. Suppose $F = F[x]$, $x \in A(q)$, and let, as above, F possess the first two variations $\delta F[x,\eta]$ and $\delta^2 F[x,\eta]$ having the form

$$\delta F = \int_a^b F'_{x(t)}\, \eta(t)dt ,$$

$$\delta^2 F = \int_a^b\int_a^b F''_{x(t_1)x(t_2)}\, \eta(t_1)\,\eta(t_2)dt_1 dt_2 + \int_a^b F''_{x^2(t)}\, \eta^2(t)dt ,$$

or briefly

$$\delta^2 F = \int_q\int_q B_{12}(t_1,t_2)\,\eta(t_1)\,\eta(t_2)dt_1 dt_2 + \int_q B_{11}(t)\,\eta^2(t)dt . \quad (2)$$

V. VOLTERRA proposed the following definition of a functional Laplacian:

$$\Delta F = \int_q B_{12}(t,t)dt . \quad (3)$$

This definition was criticized by LÉVY [1],[2] on the strength of the fact that if $B_{12}(t_1,t_2)$ is a function summable over $q \times q$, then its value on the line $t_2 = t_1$ is not essential for (2) and, consequently, definition (3) does not correspond to $\delta^2 F$.

However, as was first emphasized by DALETSKIĬ [1], if we consider the restriction of $\delta^2 F$ to infinitely differentiable functions η with support q , then B_{11} can be considered as a generalized function concentrated at the line $t_2 = t_1$. This circumstance makes Volterra's definition quite reasonable.

Starting from these arguments, DALETSKIĬ suggested a new definition of an elliptic operator L in the Hilbert space:

$$LF = T_r\, F''[x] ,$$

where F'' is the second Fréchet derivative of the operator (especially, the functional) F , and T_r is the trace of the operator.

He considered the evolution equation involving this operator

$$\frac{\partial F}{\partial t} = LF$$

and expressed its solution as the continual integral over an appropriate measure (for related questions, see also DALETSKIĬ and FOMIN [1]).)

To Section 5

This section was written following the papers POLISHCHUK [2],[9].

In analogy with the idea of approximating given functionals of general type by polynomials

$$P_n[x] = X^n + H_1[x]\, X^{n-1} + \dots + H_n[x] \quad ,$$

where $X = \|x\|^2/2$ and H are harmonic functionals (the analogue to the classical Weierstrass theorem) employed in 5.2, in POLISHCHUK [3],[7] the author has developed the harmonic analysis of functionals for discrete and continuous spectra (see also POLISHCHUK [2]).

The Laplace and Poisson equations in a function space and their generalizations were also examined by M.N. FELLER [1]-[3], who used the integral over a Wiener measure instead of the Gâteaux formula (3) of Section 3.3. Another approach to the same problems in the Hilbert space was proposed by SHILOV [1,I] (see also DORFMAN [1], KALININ [1], NARODITSKIĬ [1], SIKIRYAVYĬ [1], SOKOLOVSKIĬ [1]).

Elliptic operators in general linear spaces were considered by FOMIN [1] (see also DALETSKIĬ and FOMIN [1]) from an interesting point of view by using the Fourier transforms of measures in these spaces. Different results on infinite-dimensional elliptic operators were obtained by BEREZANSKIĬ [1] and VISHIK [1]. In their papers DALETSKIĬ, FOMIN, BEREZANSKIĬ and VISHIK started from definitions essentially different from that considered in the present book. Naturally, their results provide developments in other directions.

Some connections between elliptic functional operators of various kind have been discussed in my paper POLISHCHUK [14].

To Section 6

Semigroups of continual means and their relations to boundary value problems in function spaces were examined by the author. The analogy of probabilistic solutions with classical boundary value problems was also emphasized by the author.

The conception of a regular measure used in 6.3 goes back to H. STEINHAUS and B. JESSEN. The application of these results to boundary value problems in a function space was performed by the author.

To Section 7

This section was written along the lines of the papers POLISHCHUK [5] and [8].

To Section 8

Boundary value problems for uniform function domains were not considered by other authors.

To Section 9

This section was entirely written on the basis of the papers POLISHCHUK [11,I] and [11,II].

To Sections 10 and 11

The brief explanation of Section 10 was formerly published in POLISHCHUK [12]. Some rings of spherical means and their maximal ideals were studied by SHILOV [1,II]. The opportunity to employ compact extensions in the theory of equations with functional derivatives was communicated to me by G. SHILOV in the summer of 1968.

The idea of applying Steklov's functions $^{h}x(t) = \int_{t-h}^{t+h} x(u)du$ to the unicity theorem for the considered equations is due to M. FELLER.

In the paper POLISHCHUK [13], on the basis of the employment of continual means, a construction of the continual Cauchy integral for different domains in complex linear spaces was described. Several results concerning the theory of infinite-dimensional elliptic operators of P. Lévy type (closure of operators, their self-adjointness, application of the Gauss measure in a Hilbert space) were obtained by FELLER [4-7], which, being related to the text of the present book, go beyond it.

I also want to indicate some connections of the theory of continual means presented in the present book (generalized Gâteaux formula, semigroups, functional elliptic operators) with probabilistic investigations of T. HIDA and his colleagues (HIDA [1,2], HASEGAVA [1]) (generalized white noise, functionals of Brownian motion, causal calculus). The analysis of these connections would be very desirable.

REFERENCES

Berezanskiĭ, Yu.M. (Березанский, Ю.М.)

[1] Самосопряженные операторы в пространствах функций бесконечного числа переменных, Наукова думка, Киев 1965.

Cramer, H.

[1] Mathematical methods of statistics, Princeton Univ. Press, Princeton, N.J., 1946.

Daletskiĭ, Yu.L. (Далецкий, Ю.Л.)

[1] Бесконечномерные эллиптические операторы, Успехи матем. наук 22 (136) (1967) 4, 3-54.

Daletskiĭ, Yu.L. and S.V. Fomin (Далецкий, Ю.Л. и С.В. Фомин)

[1] Меры и дифференциальные уравнения в бесконечномерных пространствах, Наука, Москва 1983.

Dorfman, I.Ya. (Дорфман, И.Я.)

[1] О средних и лапласиане функций на гильбертовом пространстве, Матем. сборник 81 (1970) 193-208.

Dynkin, E.B. (Дынкин, Е.Б.)

[1] Markov processes, Springer-Verlag, Berlin-Göttingen-Heidelberg 1963.

Fantappie, L.

[1] I funzionali analitici, Mem. Lincei, vol. 3, ser. 6^a, fasc. 11 (1930).

Feller, M.N. (Феллер, М.Н.)

[1] Об уравнении Лапласа в пространстве $L_2(C)$, Докл. АН УССР 4 (1966) 426-429.

[2] Об уравнении Пуассона в пространстве $L_2(C)$, Докл. АН УССР 12 (1965) 1558-1562.

[3] Об уравнении $\Delta U[x(t)] + P[x(t)]\,U[x(t)] = 0$ в функциональном пространстве, Докл. АН СССР 172 (1967) 6, 1282-1285.

[4] О бесконечномерных эллиптических операторах, Докл. АН СССР 205 (1972) 1, 36-39 (English transl.: Soviet Math. Dokl. 13 (1972) 890-894).

[5] О разрешимости бесконечномерных эллиптических уравнений с постоянными коэффициентами, Докл. АН СССР 214 (1974) 1, 59-62 (English transl.: Soviet Math. Dokl. 15 (1974) 61-66).

[6] О разрешимости бесконечномерных самосопряженных эллиптических уравнений, Докл. АН СССР 221 (1975) 5, 1046-1049 (English transl.: Soviet Math. Dokl. 16 (1975) 480-484).

[7] О разрешимости бесконечномерных эллиптических уравнений с переменными коэффициентами, Матем. заметки 25 (1979) 3, 419-424 (English transl.: Math. Notes 25 (1979) 221-224).

[8] Бесконечномерные эллиптические уравнения и операторы типа П. Леви, Успехи матем. наук 41 (250) (1986) 4, 97-140 (English transl.: Russ. Math. Surveys).

Fomin, S.V. (Фомин, С.В.)

[1] О некоторых новых проблемах и результатах нелинейного функционального анализа, Вестник МГУ, сер. мат., мех. 25 (1970) 2, 57-65 (English transl.: Moscow Univ. Math. Bull. 25 (1970) 1-2, 81-86).

Gâteaux, R.

[1] Sur la notion d'intégrale dans le domaine fonctionnel et sur la théorie du potentiel, Bull. Soc. Math. France 47 (1919) 47-70.

[2] Fonctions d'une infinité de variables indépendantes, Bull. Soc. Math. France 47 (1919) 70-96.

Hasegava, Y.

[1] Lévy's functional analysis in terms of an infinite dimensional Brownian motion I, II, Osaka J. Math. 19 (1982) 405-428, 549-570.

Hida, T.

[1] White noise and Lévy's functional analysis, Proc. Oberwolfach Conf. 1977 on Measure Theory Appl. Stoch. Anal., Lect. Notes Math. 695 (1978) 155-163.

[2] Brownian motion, Springer-Verlag, New York-Heidelberg-Berlin 1980 (Transl. from the Japanese).

Hille, E.

[1] Functional analysis and semigroups, Dover, New York 1949.

Hirschman, I.I. and D.V. Widder

[1] The convolution transform, Princeton Univ. Press, Princeton, N.J., 1955.

Jessen, B.

[1] The theory of integration in a space of infinite number of dimensions, Acta Math. 63 (1934) 249-323.

Kalinin, V.V. (Калинин, В.В.)

[1] Уравнения Лапласа и Пуассона в функциональных производных в гильбертовом пространстве, Известия вузов. Математика 3 (118) (1972) 20-22.

Kantorovich, L.V. and G.P. Akilov (Канторович, Л.В. и Г.П. Акилов)

[1] Functional analysis in normed spaces, Macmillan, New York 1964 (Transl. from the Russian).

Khinchin, A.Ya. (Хинчин, А.Я.)

[1] Mathematical foundations of statistical mechanics, Dover, New York 1949 (Transl. from the Russian).

Kolmogorov, A. (Колмогоров, А.Н.)

[1] Grundbegriffe der Wahrscheinlichkeitsrechnung, Springer-Verlag, Berlin 1933 (English transl.: Chelsea Publ. Co., New York 1950).

Krasnoselskiĭ, M.A., P.P. Zabreĭko, E.I. Pustylnik and P.E. Sobolevskiĭ (Красносельский, М.А., П.П. Забрейко, Е.И. Пустыльник и П.Е. Соболевский)

[1] Integral operators in spaces of summable functions, Noordhoff Int. Publ., Leiden 1976 (Transl. from the Russian).

Krzyżański, M.

[1] Partial differential equations of second order I, Warsaw 1971.

Lévy, P.

[1] Leçons d'analyse fonctionnelle, Gauthier-Villars, Paris 1922.

[2] Les problèmes concrets d'analyse fonctionnelle, Gauthier-Villars, Paris 1951.

Loomis, L.

[1] An introduction to abstract harmonic analysis, D. van Nostrand Co., Toronto - New York - London 1953.

Mikusinski, J. and R. Sicorski

[1] The elementary theory of distribution, Warsaw 1957.

Naroditskiĭ, V.A. (Народицкий, В.А.)

[1] Об операторах типа Лапласа-Леви, Укр. мат. ж. 29 (1977) 5, 671-676 (English transl.: Ukrain. Math. J. 29 (1977) 513-517).

Natanson, I.P. (Натансон, И.П.)

[1] Theory of functions of a real variable, Frederick Publ. Co., New York 1955 (Transl. from the Russian).

Nemirovskiĭ, A.S. and G.E. Shilov (Немировский, А.С. и Г.Е. Шилов)

[1] Об аксиоматическом описании операторов Лапласа для функций на гильбертовом пространстве, Функц. анализ и его прил. 3 (1969) 3, 79-85 (English transl.: Functional Anal. Appl. 3 (1969) 235-241 (1970)).

Polishchuk, E.M. (Полищук, Е.М.)

[1] Среднее значение и интеграл от функционала, Укр. матем. ж. 8 (1956) 1, 59-75.

[2] О разложении континуальных средних по степеням функционального лапласиана, Сиб. матем. ж. 3 (1962) 6, 852-869.

[3] Функционалы, ортогональные на сфере, Сиб. матем. ж. 4 (1963) 1, 187-205.

[4] О дифференциальных уравнениях с функциональными параметрами, Укр. матем. ж. 15 (1963) 1, 13-24.

[5] О функциональном лапласиане и уравнениях параболического типа, Успехи матем. наук 19 (116) (1964) 2, 155-162.

[6] Линейные уравнения в функциональных лапласианах, Успехи матем. наук 19 (116) (1964) 2, 163-170.

[7] Об интеграле Фурье-Гато, Сиб. матем. ж. 6 (1965) 2, 881-891.

[8] О функциональных аналогах уравнений теплопроводности, Сиб. матем. ж. 6 (1965) 6, 1322-1331.

[9] Об уравнении типа Лапласа и Пуассона в функциональном пространстве, Матем. сборник 72 (114) (1967) 2, 261-292 (English transl.: Math. USSR - Sbornik 1 (1967) 2, 233-262).

[10] Quelques théorèmes sur les valeures moyennes dans les domaines fonctionnelles, Bull. Sci. math. II. Sér. 93 (1969) 145-156 (1970).

[11] О некоторых новых связях управляемых систем с уравнениями математической физики, I: Дифференц. уравнения 8 (1972) 2, 333-348 (English transl.: Differential Equations 8 (1972) 252-264 (1974)); II: Дифференц. уравнения 8 (1972) 5, 857-870 (English transl.: Differential Equations 8 (1972) 651-661 (1974)).

[12] Эллиптические операторы на кольцах функционалов, Функц. анализ и его прил. 8 (1974) 1, 31-35 (English transl.: Functional Anal. Appl. 8 (1974) 26-30).

[13] Интегральные представления аналитических функционалов, Укр. матем. ж. 26 (I974) 4, 487- 495 (English transl.: Ukrain. Math. J. 26 (1974) 399-405 (1975)).

[14] Оператор $\sum_{1}^{\infty} \frac{\partial^2}{\partial z_k \partial \bar{z}_k}$ в пространстве с керн-функцией, Литовск. матем. ж. I6 (I976) 3, I23-I36 (English transl.: Lithuanian Math. J. 16 (1976) 399-410 (1977)).

Shilov, G.E. (Шилов, Г.Е.)

[1] О некоторых вопросах анализа в гильбертовом пространстве, I: Функц. анализ и его прил. I (I967) 2, 8I-90; II: Матем. исследования, Кишинев: Изд. АН МолдССР 2(I968) 4, I66-I85; III: Матем. сборник 74 (I967) I, I6I-I68.

Shilov, G.E. and Fan Dyk Tinh (Шилов, Г.Е. и Фан Дык Тинь)

[1] Интеграл, мера и производная на линейных пространствах, Наука, Москва I967.

Sikiryavyĭ, V.Ya. (Сикирявый, В.Я.)

[1] Оператор квазидифференцирования и связанные с ним краевые задачи, Труды Моск. матем. общества 27 (I972) I95-246 (English transl.: Trans. Moscow Math. Soc. 27 (1972) 201-253 (1975)).

Sokolovskiĭ, V.B. (Соколовский, В.Б.)

[1] Новые связи некоторых задач для уравнений с оператором Лапласа-Леви с задачами математической физики, Известия вузов. Математика II (222) (I980) 82-85 (English transl.: Soviet Math. (Iz. VUZ) 24 (1980) 11, 99-103).

Vishik, M.I. (Вишик, М.И.)

[1] Параметрикс эллиптических операторов с бесконечным числом независимых переменных, Успехи матем. наук 26 (I58) (I97I) 2, I55-I74 (English transl.: Russ. Math. Surveys 26 (1971) 2, 91-112 (1972)).

Volterra, V.

[1] Leçons sur les fonctions des lignes, Gauthier-Villars, Paris 1913.

SUBJECT INDEX